Principles of Management

Nirmal Kumar Gami
B.Sc. (Engg.), PGDPM, LLB
Formerly, Visiting Faculty SAIL College of Management, Ranchi,
Chief PM Bokaro Steel, DGM (Pers.) Hindustan Copper Ltd.,
Director (Admn.) Govt. of India, Visiting Faculty L.N. Mishra
Institute of Management and Social Changes, Patna

ATLANTIC
PUBLISHERS & DISTRIBUTORS (P) LTD

ATLANTIC
PUBLISHERS & DISTRIBUTORS (P) LTD
7/22, Ansari Road, Darya Ganj, New Delhi
Tel.: +91-11-4077 5252, 2327 3880
E-mail: orders@atlanticbooks.com
Web: www.atlanticbooks.com

Published by Atlantic Publishers & Distributors (P) Ltd 2024

Printed & bound in India by Atlantic Print Services

To

My Late Parents

Preface

The idea of writing a book on principles of management was developed during teaching this course to MBA students at different institutes. The book has been written with a view to present an in-depth insight into the principles and practices of management.

The business enterprises are working in an ever-changing dynamic, in an era of accelerating global competition. The need for effective managers has never been greater. Thus, given the increasing need for effective managers, the principles and practices of management are required to be followed while dealing with various aspects of business activities.

The book is intended for use as a textbook by engineering and management students, and as a reference book for practicing managers. It is designed to dwell upon five major managerial functions of planning, organizing, staffing, leading and controlling besides interweaving beautifully interconnected topics like organization structure, motivation, communication, etc. It is also imperative to understand the history of evolution of principles and practices of management, social responsibility and ethics of management. Interestingly, it includes productivity, total quality management and quality circle.

It has been tried to deal with the subject somewhat comprehensively while to be precise yet errors may have crept in inadvertently. Observations and suggestions from the readers to make the book more meaningful are welcome.

I would like to acknowledge with appreciation the support given by faculty of L.N. Mishra Institute of Management including the librarian in preparing the manuscript. I am indebted to my students for their insightful discussions and presentations.

This book is the product of the ideas and experiences of persons through which I have worked over the years as practicing manager, administrator and faculty member. Though I am unable to mention all of them individually, my debt of gratitude to them is no less.

Further, I would like to express my appreciation for my wife and children for their unstinting support and help in all my endeavours.

Nirmal Kumar Gami

Contents

Chapter 1
Management: Concept and Nature

1.1 INTRODUCTION

The people in order to accomplish specific goals form the organization. They provide resources like men, material, money, and machine. In order to make proper use of these resources, it requires methods for making decisions, ways of coordinating its activities, ways of communicating information and ideas, and ways of evaluating its success. These aspects of management act as a creative force in organization for getting the objectives fulfilled through people. Thus, management emerged as a separate field of study where business organizations serve the purpose of the people. The organization may be a manufacturing firm, a business concern, a governmental agency, a hospital, a university or a social organization or a religious trust. Each organization, whether business or non-business, has a goal and need of effective use of Principles of Management. In fact, there are evidences of practicing management principles by kings and ministers in olden days in their administration. The battle of *Mahabharat* and construction of pyramids are a few examples of fine management. However, during the last two decades, management as a discipline has attracted the attention of academicians and practitioners to a very great extent. The basic reason behind this phenomenon is the growing importance of management in survival of business in the fast-changing business environment.

1.2 CONCEPT OF MANAGEMENT

Management is a very popular term and has been used extensively for all small or large organizations working towards achieving some common goals. Managers are the people within the organizations who organize different kinds of resources like men, material, money, machine, and technology in the process of performing activities. In order to utilize these resources effectively and efficiently, managers perform functions of planning, organizing, staffing, directing and controlling. Effectiveness means doing the right task, completing activities and achieving objectives. In other words, it is concerned with the end result. Efficiency means doing the task correctly and with minimum cost. If by using less resources (i.e., the inputs) more benefits are derived (i.e., the outputs) then efficiency is said to be more. Efficiency is also increased when for the same benefit or outputs, fewer resources are used and less costs are incurred. Naturally, management is concerned with the efficient use of resources, because they reduce costs and ultimately lead to higher profits. Usually, high efficiency is associated with high effectiveness which is the aim of all managers.

1.3 MEANING OF MANAGEMENT

Management is the art and science of getting things done by a group of people with the effective utilization of available resources. The resources like men, material, machine, and money are directed towards achievement of the organizational goals, whether profit or service, through the various functions of management, i.e., planning, organizing, staffing, directing, and controlling.

1.4 DEFINITION OF MANAGEMENT

Mary Parker Follett says, "Management is the art of getting things done through people." The important point underlying in this definition is that manager is meant for getting the things happened through the efforts of others—not by performing the task himself. She has also mentioned that management is an art whereas it is also a science.

Koontz and Weihrich: "Management is the process of designing and maintaining an environment in which individuals, working together in groups, efficiently accomplish selected aims."

Stanley Vance: "In essence, management is simply the process of decision making and control over the action of human beings for the express purpose of attaining pre-determined goals."

Ordway Tead: "Management is the process and agency which direct and guides the operations of an organization in the realising of established aims."

Robert L. Trewelly and M. Gene Newport: "Management is defined as the process of planning, organizing, actuating and controlling an organization's operations in order to achieve coordination of the human and material resources essential in the effective and efficient attainment of objectives."

Kreitner: "Management is the process of working with and through others to effectively achieve organizational objectives by efficiently using limited resources in the changing environment."

Although different views have been given on what is management, the basic of management is that managers apply techniques of planning, organizing, staffing, directing and controlling of resources like men, material, money, methods, etc. to achieve the objectives of an organization. Organization may be profit oriented such as a business venture or a non-profit organization like university, hospital or a club where proper service is required.

Some of the managers that made their enterprises excellent are Steve Jobs at Apple Computers, Bill Gates of Microsoft, Ratan Tata of Tata Sons and Indra Nooyi of Pepsico.

1.5 CHARACTERISTICS OF MANAGEMENT

After going through some of definitions of management, we find the following features that may be called the basic characteristics of management:

1. Management is a group activity: It is a group activity of getting things done through people in an organization. An organization is a group of people working together to fulfill the common organizational goal. The organizations may be business unit like Tata Steel or Infosys or social organizations like a hospital or a church. They work in a structured framework of superior and subordinate relationship where work is assigned to each individual and their authority responsibility relationships are established.

2. Management is a continuous process: Management is a distinct process performed to determine and accomplish stated objectives of an organization. Managers use resources effectively and efficiently by applying functions as planning, organizing, staffing, directing and controlling. The day-to-day task of manager consists of an on-going series of these functions.

3. Management is required at all organizational levels: Management is required at all the levels—top, middle, and lower levels of the organization, though degree of functions of management is varied with different levels.

4. Management is goal-oriented: An organization has a set of basic goals which are basic reason for its existence. Different organizations have different goals. For example, the goal of a business unit may be to generate surplus but the goal of the hospital is to provide better healthcare to the society. Management unites the efforts of different individuals in the organization towards the establishment and achievement of these goals.

5. Management is universal: Wherever there is some human activity, there is management. The basic Principles of Management is universal and thus is applicable to all organizations: business, social, religious, cultural, sports, educational, politics or military.

6. Management is all-pervasive: The activities involved in managing an enterprise are common to all organizations whether business, social or political. A retail shop needs to be managed as much as a hospital or a college. What managers do in India, the USA, France or Japan is the same. How they do it may be quite different. This difference is due to the differences in culture, tradition, and history.

7. Management is multidimensional: Management is a complex activity that has three main dimensions. These are:

(a) *Management of work:* All organizations exist for a set of goals. All individuals are assigned the jobs so that total work is managed to achieve the goals.

(b) *Management of people:* Management gets the work done through people. Getting work done through people is a major task for the manager. Managing people has two dimensions: (i) it implies dealing with employees as individuals with diverse needs and behaviour and (ii) it also means dealing with individuals as a group of people. The skill of management is to direct people's work towards achieving the organization's goals.

(c) *Management of operations:* As we know an organization is to produce products or services. The operation transforms the input resources like men, material, money, and technology into the desired outputs of products or services at a profitable way. This requires efficient and effective management of work and the management of people.

8. Management is dynamic: Management is an ever-changing discipline and has to change itself to the changing environment. The new knowledge in science and art as well as innovations, research and development in the business sector necessitate change in management. Moreover, an organization interacts with its external environment like social, economic and political factors which also necessitates change in the roles of management. In order to be successful, an organization must change itself and its goals according to the situations at that time.

9. Management is an intangible force: Management is an intangible force that cannot be seen but its presence can be felt in the form of results. For example, when the organization is not able to produce the desired quantity, quality and employees are not happy, we say it is the result of poor management.

1.6 OBJECTIVES OF MANAGEMENT

Organization is formed for certain objectives—profit or service. Management helps it to achieve its objectives effectively through improvement in the following management's basic objectives:

1. **Organizational objectives:** Management is responsible for setting and achieving objectives for the organization. It has to achieve a variety of objectives to meet the interest of shareholders, employees, customers and the government. Management enables to use resources to achieve outputs at minimum cost.
2. **Personal objectives:** The performance of an organization mainly depends upon the human resource as such development of ability of managers is an important objective of management. Management provides scope to modify the personalities, and improve technical, human and innovative skills of human being. Management has to reconcile personal goals with organizational objectives to maximize prosperity for employers and employees.
3. **Effectiveness of objective:** Organization has to choose the most appropriate organizational objectives out of so many objectives. After choosing the objectives, manager is to do the right things in a right way in order to obtain maximum output with minimum resources and efforts.
4. **Human welfare:** Employees want to satisfy their various needs such as physiological (food, clothing, shelter), social and security needs. Management helps in knowing these needs and satisfies them through suitable remuneration, incentive and rewards.
5. **Social welfare:** Organizations operate in a larger social system. The operation of business largely affects the welfare of the society and the country at large. Management develops rules and provisions to suit the society at the same time driving benefits to the organization.

1.7 NATURE OF MANAGEMENT

1.7.1 Management—Science or Art: Management as Science

What is science? Science is an exact and systematized body of knowledge pertaining to an area of study and contains some general truth explaining past events and phenomena. It evolves through continuous testing and experiments of hypotheses which give rise to principles and later on theory and laws. Following are the essential features of science:

1. It is systematized body of knowledge.
2. It uses scientific methods for observation and experiment.
3. Scientific principles are exact and have universal applicability without any limitation.
4. Scientific principles establish a cause-and-effect relationship between various factors.
5. The validity of scientific principles can be verified and therefore, they provide a reliable basis for predicting future events.

Applying above features of science, one may try to analyze whether management is science or not.

1. **Systematized body of knowledge.** Management is an organized body of knowledge developed by management practitioners, thinkers and philosophers over a period of years. Management science provides a body of principles of laws for guidance in the solution of specific management problems and in the objective evaluation of results.
2. **Use of scientific methods.** The process of management makes use of scientific methods for observation. F.W. Taylor, the Father of Scientific Management applied scientific techniques to studies of planning, organizing, staffing, motivating, etc.
3. **Universal application.** In the words of Taylor, "The fundamental Principles of Management are applicable to all human activities from our simplest individual

acts to the working of our great corporations". The principles of 'Esprit de Corps'—unity is strength is applied in almost every organization and every situation. The knowledge of management has been accumulated and accepted with general truths which can be universally applied.

4. **Cause and effect relationship.** Scientific principles establish cause and effect relationship among facts. The Principles of Management establish cause and effect relationship, e.g., it is said that effect of poor planning causes low productivity.
5. **Validation of scientific principles.** The Principles of Management can also be verified for their validity. These are put to severe tests before accepting as Principles of Management. For example, the principles of unity of command states that a subordinate put under one boss will show better results than the subordinate who has to report two or more bosses. This principle is verified for time and again for future use.
6. **Limitations of management as a science.** On the basis of above discussion, management can be called science. But unlike Physics and Chemistry, it is not an exact science. Its principles cannot be considered as fundamental truths. At times, they may not bring desired results and may not have universal application. The science of management deals with human beings whose behaviour cannot be predicted with precision. Thus, it may be designated as 'inexact or soft science' or 'social science' like sociology.

1.7.2 Management as an Art

What is an Art? Art is understanding how a particular activity can be done? It is know-how to achieve a desired result. After knowing a particular art, practice is needed to reach the level of perfection. For example, art of music is learnt through knowledge of some principles, inherent skills, creativity, and constant practice.

Features of Art are:

(i) Personal skill, (ii) Practical knowledge, (iii) Result-oriented approach, (iv) Regular practice, and (v) Creativity. Application of these features of art to management will show whether it qualifies as an art.

(i) **Personal skill.** Management is the art of getting things done through and with people. This requires a range of skills which are conceptual skills, human skills, and technical skills. It is an art of dealing with people to achieve the enterprise objectives. Every manager has his own way of doing the things. Hence, there are differences in the performance of different managers in spite of their possessing equal technical qualifications.

(ii) **Practical knowledge.** The Principles of Management cannot be implemented as learnt unless these can be applied through practice based on the real-life situations. This is like a person who knows the basics of music but unless he practices to play musical instruments, he cannot be called good musician.

(iii) **Result-oriented approach.** A painter has a result-oriented approach to produce a painting at minimum cost and time. Similarly, a manager approaches his objectives in such a way so that it can be achieved at stipulated cost and time.

(iv) **Regular practice.** As an artist, the manager regularly practices of Principles of Management to attain higher and higher results up to the level of perfection. An experienced manager through the art of decision-making and leadership drives his enterprise according to changed situations and also alters the environment itself.

(v) **Creativity.** Management is one of the most creative art as it is concerned with getting work done through others by motivating them to work and by coordinating their activities.

Management is both a Science and an Art: On the basis of above discussion, one may conclude that management has elements of both art and science. The science of management provides certain general principles whereas the art of management can give insight to the managers with the application of skills, perception, intuition, and combined personal experiences in a unique and creative manner in managing people in every situation in the effective manner. Management in this sense is more an art. According to the American Society of Mechanical Engineers, "Management is the art and science of preparing, organizing and directing human efforts to control the forces and utilize the material of nature for the benefit of men." Managers can work better by using organized knowledge of management. It is this knowledge constitutes a science. On the other hand, managing a practice is an art. The organized knowledge underlying practice may be referred to as a science. Thus, science and the art of management go together hand-in-hand and both are mutually interdependent and complimentary.

1.7.3 Management as Profession

Meaning of profession: Profession refers to any occupation requiring specialised knowledge that is applied in the service of some relevant segment of society (for example, medical profession). A 'profession' is much more than a 'career' which denotes merely the way of making a livelihood or course of progress adopted by a person in his personal life.

A profession is characterized by the following features:

1. The existence of a body of specialized knowledge or techniques.
2. Specialized knowledge is acquired after formal education, training and experience such as doctors lawyers, etc.
3. Rendering services of specialized nature provide a person the status of a professional. Professionals acquire power through their expert advice and nothing else.
4. The formation of ethical codes for the conduct of professionals.
5. Though professionals practice their profession for making financial gains, yet they give due regards for

the priority of service over the desire for financial reward.

6. Every profession is guided by the professional association or council. For example, a doctor is registered under the Medical Council of India.

On the basis of above features, let us analyze whether management is a profession or not.

1. **Specialized knowledge:** Management is an organized body of knowledge built up by management practitioners, thinkers, and philosophers over a period of years. Of late it became a discipline. In this sense, modern management is certainly a profession.
2. **Specialized knowledge through formal education, training and experience:** A large number of formal institutes in the various countries, including India impart management education and training. Several concepts have been drawn from industrial psychology, business law, statistics, and sociology, etc. The managers who possess such specialized qualification (BBA and MBA) and experience serve better in their area of operation.
3. **Expert advice in management:** It is fundamental for gaining a universal acceptance of the practice of the profession. Honesty and personal integrity have an added advantage to this profession.
4. **Code of conduct:** Members of a profession have to abide by a code of conduct which provides statement of policies, principles, or rules, as well as norms of honesty, integrity, and professional morality. There exists a standard code of conduct in the traditional professions such as medicine and law. But there exists neither uniform code of conduct nor teeth in the sphere of management in the sense that they cannot punish guilty managers. There are no restrictions or licensing on the entry of management profession. On this point, management cannot be regarded as a profession.

5. **Priority of service over financial reward:** Although there exists no code of conduct in management in stricter term, yet an increasing emphasis is today being put on the social responsibilities of managers. Managers practice management principles and theories with dedication and commitment. They aim at providing maximum efficiency and effectiveness towards the attainment of organizational goals. Management is, thus, termed as profession on this basis.
6. **Professional association:** In India, there is an All-India Management Association. The main function of the association is not only to manage and coordinate the research work in various areas of management but also guide the conduct of managers. However, it does not have statutory power to regulate entry into management profession and also it does not impose any punitive action on the manager who violate the code of conduct unlike medical profession which is governed by its Medical Council of India. On this count, management cannot be completely termed as a profession.

From the above foregoing, it may be concluded that while in some respect management qualifies as a profession but it cannot truly be termed as profession on certain other features. There are many managers who have not acquired formal degree in the management courses but still prove to be successful managers. This is because of insight, experience and art of managing over a period of time by virtue of their holding various managerial positions. No formal code of ethics is, therefore, developed and followed by all successful managers. Peter F. Drucker is of the view, "No greater damage could be done to our economy or to our society than to attempt to professionalize management by licensing managers or by limiting access to management to people with a special academic degree." However, in the present world scenario and with the complexity of situation, it is prudent that managers possess some formal management education and training. In this regard, management is fast moving towards professional status.

1.7.4 Professionalisation of Management

With the advent of 20th century, professionalization of management became more prominent in India due to following reasons:

1. Size of business becomes large and complex.
2. Managers operate in a pluralistic society, in which many organized groups represent various interests.
3. The third wave economy is the knowledge age that encompasses data, culture, ideology, values, and information.
4. In the era of globalization, changes have taken place in external environment in terms of technology, management principles, and competition. The world today is single market and management cannot be confined within the national boundaries of the country. Management is gradually becoming a multinational discipline.
5. Corporate social responsibility and business ethics mean that the responsibility of business goes beyond profit maximization.

In the light of the above, management is independent of ownership, rank or power. Gradually, family management is being replaced by mixed management, i.e., family management and professional management. Availability of management education offered by many institutions as well as advocating of benefits of professional management in management conferences and seminars, many owners have sent their siblings to acquire formal management education. This has helped them to keep the element of decision-making in their hand, though they hire professional managers to play only the secondary role in managing the large industries. Therefore, only appointment of managers with management degree does not amount to professionalization of management unless they are given authorities including the process of corporate decision-making.

A number of Indian organizations in private sector are highly professionalized. They have inducted management trainees at entry level and also appoint proven managers at higher levels and are given adequate authority through their professional Board of Directors so that they can in a position to set the objectives conducive to the organization and also benefit to the society. Some examples of such companies are Hindustan Lever Limited, Infosys, Tata Iron and Steel Company Ltd. The situation in public sector undertakings in India is not much better. Most of these organizations are headed by civil servants who have the traits of bureaucracy, even though they have the facade of professionalization. Hence, professionalization cannot be expected at lower levels because they have no liberty in managing the affairs of the organization in professional way.

However, India is moving fast towards professionalization of management due to following reasons:

1. **International impact on the Indian management:** With the globalization of business and entry of multinational companies, it forces the Indian management becomes professional.
2. **Professionalization due to compulsion:** Civil servants failed as managements in some of the public undertakings. Hence, to professionalize the management, the government inducted professional managers in the undertaking. This action of government has given the positive result. Similarly, in the private sector, when the owner managers could not manage the company due to increase in size and complexity of business and also of competition they have to resort to professionalization in management.
3. **Availability of trained and educated professional managers:** After the Second Five-Year Plan, a number of institutions were started to impart training in management to young people in India. Government of India started four Indian Institutes of Management at Ahmedabad, Calcutta, Bangalore, and Lucknow which impart full time management education. Subsequently, various universities have offered full time management courses. Besides, there are many institutions and organizations which have started BBA and MBA courses for undergraduates and graduates. Further, some

specialized institutions like Administrative Staff College of India, Indian Institute of Management, National Institute of Bank Management, National Institute for Training in Industrial Engineering (NITIE), All India Management Association, etc. started imparting management training and development for college graduates and managers. In addition, many business organizations have started their own management institutes to impart training in management to their managers. Thus, these measures have paved the way of professionalization of management in Indian industries and non-business organizations.

1.8 ADMINISTRATION AND MANAGEMENT

In general, there is no fundamental difference between administration and management, whatever difference between the two terminologies exists, it exists only in terms of their usages in different walks of life. However, at the initial level of development of management thought, various views expressed in this regard have led to the emergence of three approaches:

1. Administration is above management,
2. Administration is a part of management, and
3. Management and administration are the same.

Administration is above management: According to many classical thinkers, prominent among them are Oliver Sheldon, William Spriegal, Milward, Ordway Tead, etc. that administration relates to decision-making/policy formulation and management relates to policy execution and these two functions are not the same. Administration is a top-level function which centers around the determination of plans, policies and objectives of a business enterprise. On the other hand, management involves "doing". It is lower-level function which is concerned with the execution and direction of policies and operations. As such, management is subordinate to administration.

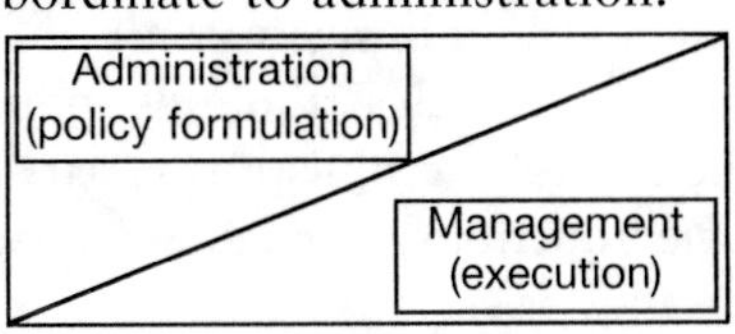

Based on the views of these authors, difference between administration and management are shown below:

Basis of difference	*Administration*	*Management*
Level in organization	Top level	Middle and lower levels
Major focus	Policy formulation and objective determination	Policy execution for objective achievement
Nature of functions	Determinative	Executive
Scope of functions	Broad and conceptual	Narrow and operational
Factors affecting decisions	Mostly external	Mostly internal
Employer-employee relations	Entrepreneurs and owners	Employees
Quality required	Administration	Technical
Generally, term used in	Govt. bureaucratic set-ups	Industry
Illustrations	Collector, Vice-chancellor, Administrator	Director, General Manager

Administration is a part of management: There is another school of thought which suggests management as more comprehensive function which includes administration also. For example, EFL Brech has viewed management and administration in the following way: "Management is a comprehensive generic name for the total process of executive control in industry or commerce. It is a social process entailing responsibility for the effective and economical planning and regulation of the operation of an enterprise, in the fulfillment of a given purpose or task. Administration is that part of management which is concerned with the installation and carrying out of procedures by which it is laid down and communicated and the process of activities regulated and checked against plans."

From this point of view, administration is concerned with day-to-day function and is a part of management. According to this view, the previous view that administration is above management stands reversed.

Management and administration are the same: According to the third approach which is the most popular and practical one, management and administration are the same. Both involve the same functions, principles, and objectives. Fayol has observed, "all undertakings require planning, organization, command, coordination, and control, and in order to perform properly, all must follow the same general principles. We are no longer confronted with several administrative sciences but with one which can be applied equally well to public and private affairs." Thus, there is no difference between management and administration. McFarland, at later date, revised his stand and viewed that it is difficult to make distinction between management and administration; both are similar to each other.

The difference between the two terms lies mostly in their usage. In the bureaucratic structure, the government often uses the word administrator, instead of manager, to formulate policy and also to execute the same. On the other hand, management is normally used in business sphere. In fact, even this distinction is also disappearing. For example, many authors have written books under the title "Business Administration" meant for managing the business of the companies. Similarly, many institutions offering management courses as M.B.A. degree for their management graduates while others offer M.B.M. degree for the similar types of students.

Some calls the formulation of policy is administration as it is performed by top people in the hierarchy whereas execution part is handled by lower-level people/managers. It means two sets of people are required to manage of entire gamut of business affairs which is not possible. The underlying concept may be that the content of policy formulation is more at higher level people and execution is high at lower level.

According to Peter F. Drucker, the basic difference between management and administration lies in the use of these words in different fields. The governance of non-business institutions (such as government, army, church) is generally called administration while the governance of business enterprises is called management.

1.9 UNIVERSALITY OF MANAGEMENT

Management is a universal process applicable all types of organizations and to all locations breaking the boundaries of the countries. Its fundamentals, i.e., planning, organizing, staffing, directing and controlling are universal, whereas, to some extent, variations in its application is limited to a particular culture or situation and also due to the people who practice such functions.

Some researchers observed that management fundamentals are applicable and adaptable in various cultures. Sometimes, it is observed that Japanese management is more efficient compared to some underdeveloped countries. This notion is due to the fact that the appropriate Principles of Management are applied in the right way in the particular situation. Haire, Ghiselli and Porter observe on the basis of their study of behaviour of over 3000 business executives spread over fourteen developed and underdeveloped countries that there is a high degree of similarity in managerial behaviour patterns, and variations are due to distinct inter-cultural differences. Richman found that managers of business enterprises in the Soviet Union perform the same managerial functions as their counterparts in the Western countries, viz. planning, organizing, staffing, directing, coordinating and controlling. Socio-cultural, economic, and political environmental dimensions affect the way in which management processes are effectuated and, this intern, affects managerial effectiveness. According to them, cultural and other environmental variables may materially influence the way in which a manager performs his functions but the fundamentals of management remain unchanged. As pointed out by Peter F. Drucker, "the rapid development of Brazil, Hong Kong, Singapore and Taiwan; are all traceable to the impact of management. This shows that management knowledge and skills are universal in nature and therefore transferable at a faster speed—a third wave effect."

1.10 MANAGERIAL SKILLS

Robert L. Katz identified three essential skills that are needed by a manager. They are technical, human and conceptual skills. The relative importance of these skills may differ at various levels in the organization hierarchy. The figure below shows the use of various management skills at different hierarchical levels:

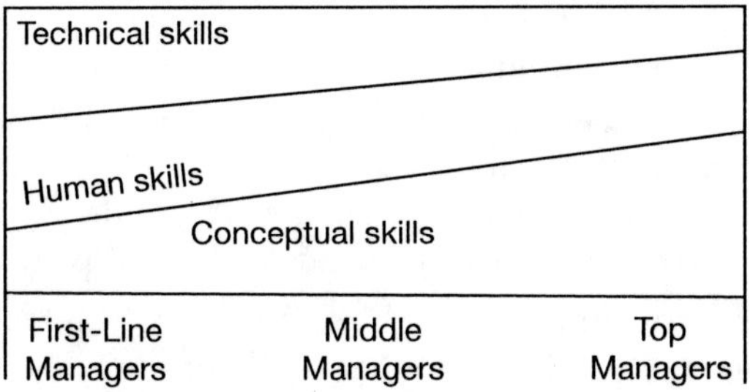

(i) **Technical skills:** These skills require specialized knowledge to use methods, processes and procedures to accomplish a task in the area of engineering, accounts, manufacturing or computers, etc. First-line managers require higher degree of technical skills to perform various jobs and supervise the daily activities of technical and professional employees who are not managers. Human skills are also helpful in the frequent interactions with subordinates. Conceptual skills, on the other hand, are usually not critical for lower-level supervisors.

(ii) **Human skills:** Management is the art of getting things done through people. This can be achieved when one is sensitive to others—a human skill. Managers at all levels are required to possess human skills to deal with people as individuals, group or team. These skills help employees to communicate, motivate, lead and inspire their subordinates, superiors, and peers in an organization.

(iii) **Conceptual skills:** These skills refer to mental ability of managers to conceptualize abstract and complex situations. Generally, conceptual skills are most important at the top management level. Top managers have the greatest need to see the organization as a whole, understand how its various parts relate to one another, and coordinate and integrate the organization's internal environment with its external environment. At the top management level, besides conceptual abilities, human skills are valuable, but there is relatively little need for technical abilities. Technical skills though in small amount must be available with top managers. Otherwise, they will have difficulty harnessing the technical abilities of their subordinates, fostering innovation, allocating resources efficiently, or devising strategies to stay ahead of the competition.

A fourth skill, namely **Design skills** was added later which are generally needed at higher levels of management.

1.11 MANAGERIAL ROLES

Managerial roles are specific behaviours associated with the task of management. Managers adopt these roles to accomplish the basic functions of management just discussed—planning and strategizing, organizing, controlling, and leading and developing employees. One of the earliest and most enduring descriptions of managerial roles comes from Henry Mintzberg who shadowed managers observing what they did during the day. According to this, ten managerial roles were identified and grouped into:

(a) Interpersonal roles, (b) Informational roles, and (c) Decision roles.

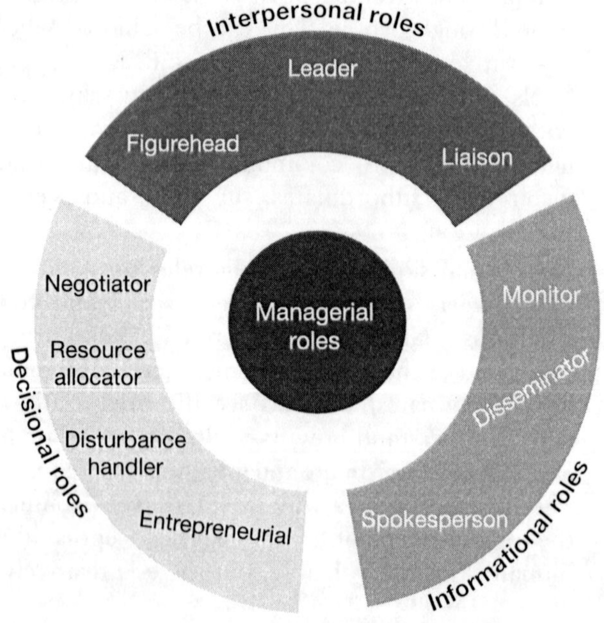

A brief description of the ten managerial roles identified by Mintzberg is given below:

(a) **Interpersonal roles**

1. Figurehead role (performing ceremonial and social duties such as receiving dignitaries, attending the wedding of employee, etc. as an organization's representative).
2. Leader role (motivating the subordinates).
3. Liaison role (communicating with outsiders).

(b) **Informational roles**

1. Recipient/Monitor role (receiving operational information).
2. Disseminator role (giving information to subordinates).
3. Spokesperson role (giving information to external parties).

(c) **Decision roles**

1. Entrepreneurial role (designing a change within the organization through innovation).
2. Disturbance handler role (taking action in the hour of crises such as strike, conflicts, etc.).
3. Resource allocator role (allotting all types of resources as per work distribution among people).
4. Negotiator role (negotiating with union leaders and various groups of persons).

The sample of five top executives used in Mintzberg's research is far too small in support to sweeping a conclusion. The roles of managers appear to be incomplete. For example, activities as structuring an organization, selecting and appraising managers, and determining the major strategies do not find place here.

1.12 MANAGEMENT FUNCTIONS

The main functions performed by all managers can be classified as follow:

1. Planning, 2. Organizing, 3. Staffing, 4. Directing, 5. Controlling

They are performed by managers at all levels in all organizations—business and non-profit organizations. They are thus called universal basic functions of management.

All these five managerial functions are blended into each other and even go on simultaneously in an organization.

REVIEW QUESTIONS

Long Answer Questions

1. "Management is concerned with ideas, things, and people". Comment.
2. How do you explain that management is important for all organizations?
3. "Management is the coordination of all resources through the five functions of management in order to achieve stated objectives of an organization". Elucidate.
4. Describe briefly the functions of management. If one or more of the functions are lacking, what are the implications?
5. "Management is getting things done through and with people." Elucidate.
6. Is management a science or an art or both? Comment.
7. Distinguish between management and administration. How far this distinction is justified or is it only for name's sake? Offer your views.
8. What are the attributes of a profession? Discuss in the light of management as a profession.
9. Describe how managerial skills differ according to hierarchical level. What are the implications for managers?
10. Explain the three general types of roles and the ten specific roles identified by Mintzberg that managers play. Assume that you have seven employees under your command. How might you use the ten roles in managing your organization?

Short Answer Questions

1. Describe three essential skills with their quantum that are needed by managers at their different hierarchical levels.

2. Describe management as defined by professionals.
3. Describe salient characteristics of management.

Match the following:

(A)	(B)
(a) Management is the art of getting things done through people	(i) Henry Mintzberg
(b) Roles of managers	(ii) Stoner and Freeman
(c) Planning is the process of establishing goals and suitable action for achieving these goals	(iii) Robert L. Katz
(d) Conceptual, Human, Technical skills	(iv) Mary Parker Follett

Answers

(a) (iv) (b) (i) (c) (ii) (d) (iii)

CASE STUDY

Indra Krishnamurthy Nooyi (born 28 October 1955) is an Indian-American business executive and the former Chairperson and Chief Executive Officer of PepsiCo, the second largest food and beverage business in the world by net revenue.

Nooyi received a Bachelor's degree in Physics, Chemistry, and Mathematics from Madras Christian College in 1974 and a Post Graduate Diploma in Management (MBA) from Indian Institute of Management Calcutta in 1976. Beginning her career in India, Nooyi held product manager positions at Johnson & Johnson and textile firm Mettur Beardsell. She was admitted to Yale School of Management in 1978 and earned a Master's degree in Public and Private Management. Nooyi joined the Boston Consulting Group (BCG), and then held strategy positions at Motorola and Asea Brown Boveri.

Indra Krishnamurthy Nooyi

Nooyi joined PepsiCo in 1994 and was named president and CFO in 2001. Nooyi has directed the company's global strategy for more than a decade and led PepsiCo's restructuring, including the 1997 divestiture of its restaurant chains Pizza Hut, KFC and Taco Bell in 1997 and engineered its unloading of its bottling operations. Nooyi also took the lead in the acquisition of Tropicana in 1998, and merger with Quaker Oats in 2001. The changes Nooyi made at Pepsico transformed the company. In 2006, she became the fifth CEO in PepsiCo's 44-year history. Her vision is performance with purpose—what is good for business with what is good for the world. Nooyi was named on *Wall Street Journal*'s list of 50 women to watch in 2007 and 2008, and was listed among *Time*'s 100 Most Influential People in the World in 2007 and 2008. *Forbes* named her the #3 most powerful woman in 2008. *Fortune* ranked her the #1 most powerful woman in business in 2009 and 2010. While CEO of PepsiCo in 2011, Nooyi earned a total compensation of $17 million.

Nooyi has been named 2009 CEO of the Year by Global Supply Chain Leaders Group. In 2010, she was named #1 on *Fortune*'s list of the "50 Most Powerful Women" and #6 on *Forbes'* list of the "World's 100 Most Powerful Women". After five years on top, PepsiCo's Indian American chairman and CEO Indra Nooyi has been pushed to the second spot as most powerful woman in US business by Kraft's CEO, Irene Rosenfeld.

Indra Nooyi was honoured with Padma Bhushan in the year 2011 by the President of India.

Questions

1. Analyse the case in terms of success due to managerial abilities.
2. What managerial roles she played to transform her company the second largest food and beverage business in the world?
3. State the massage given with this case study.

MAXWELL FOOTWARES PVT. LTD. A CASE STUDY

Maxwell footwares produced plastic footwares for middleclass target population. The GM of the company was an autocrat who believed in strict compliance to his orders. He stayed away from his workers hence communication did not flow from bottom to top even useful suggestions. Quality of products deteriorated and demand for company's products went down and company was at the verse of closure. At this juncture, Mr. K. Manohar was appointed as new GM of the company. He studied the working of the company, took a round in each and every department, met every worker personally to feel the culture of the company. He used Principles of Management in dealing with all aspects of organization. He formed the planning and quality committee consisting of top to bottom members of the organization. It decided the target of production, quality, and sales strategy for a year. Based on this he provided resources to execute the programme. He monitored all aspects of final products with executives and even with key workers and solicited their suggestions to improve efficiency and effectiveness of the organization. He was smart enough to scan the external environment including his competitors. Accordingly, he changed his strategy in terms of quality, design and introduction of newer technology. In a few months' time, production and productivity improved and profit started rising.

Questions

1. Compare the styles of both GMs and whose style is conducive for the company and why?
2. Did Mr. Manohar believe in the principle—"Management is the art of getting things done through and with people"?
3. If you were the head of the organization, would you adopt Mr. Manohar's strategy or refine over his? State the changes in the light of Mintzberg's managerial roles.

Chapter 2
Development of Management Thought

2.1 INTRODUCTION

Although examples of management practice go back several thousand years, the development of management as a field of knowledge is much more recent. Much of the impetus for evolution of management began with the industrial revolution which occurred in the early 1800s. With the advent of the factory system during this period, machines were designed to increase productivity and remove many of the laborious tasks from productive activities. This resulted into vast physical changes in the world economy and several economists during this period highlighted for the first time the importance of management discipline.

2.2.1 Pre-classical Era

During the period, following the industrial revolution, certain pioneers began to challenge the traditional character of management based on tradition or intuition by introducing innovative ways to run factories more efficiently. This group, known as the pre-classical contributors to management focused largely on particular techniques that might be applied to solve specific problems. This laid the groundwork for subsequent, broader principles and theories or approaches of management: classical, behavioural, quantitative, and contemporary. Among the principal pre-classical contributors are Robert Owen, Charles Babbage, and Henry R. Towne.

ROBERT OWEN (1771-1858) was a successful cotton mill entrepreneur in Scotland. He was the first person to recognize the importance of human resources and is known as the father of Personnel Management. He became particularly interested in improving the working and living conditions of his employees. Owen argued that improving working conditions would not only improve the workers' quality of life but would also lead to increase in productivity. He stated that men should not be treated as secondary and inferior to machines. At that time, his ideas were considered to be radical but later his views were widely accepted. His ideas laid the groundwork for the human relations movement found in Hawthorne experiment.

CHARLES BABBAGE (1792-1871) was English mathematician. He is widely known as "the father of modern computing." He was the forerunner of Scientific Management. His work was closely related to that of Adam Smith. He studied the working conditions of factories in England and France and observed that most of the factories used to work on the basis of estimates and guesswork. He emphasized the use of science and mathematics. He advocated the principles of division of work based on work specialization to increase human efficiency. His findings are also reflected in Taylor's scientific management. He introduced methods to improve industrial productivity and perceived this could be done through work measurement, cost determination, bonus plans, and profit sharing.

HENRY R. TOWNE (1844-1924) was President of the famous lock manufacturing company USA and a mechanical engineer. He focused on the development of management as a separate field of study. He suggested that the new discipline of management would be augmented by combining knowledge of engineers and economists. He outlined these views in a landmark paper titled *The Engineer as an Economist*, which was delivered in 1886 to the American Society of Mechanical Engineers in Chicago. One of the people who attended Towne's presentation, Frederick Taylor, was subsequently instrumental in building the management field.

Evaluating the pre-classical contributors. Pioneers of management thought were primarily related to their organizational set ups. They were largely oriented toward developing specific techniques, often to solve specific organizational problems in specific ways. There was no standard management theory which could be applied to all organizations at all times, hence their impact on the industry as a whole was meagre.

However, the development of management thought as a systematic study is a phenomenon of the twentieth century. Koontz was the first academician to have attempted to classify the various approaches into the schools of management theory.

The management thought in subsequent years has been classified into the following four categories:

1. **The classical theory of management** (1903-40). It is called "classical" because it encompasses early works and related contributions that formed the main roots of the field of management. It comprises three different approaches: Scientific Management, Administrative Management, and Bureaucratic Management.
2. **The neo-classical theory of management** (1927-60). The classical theory concentrated too much on one the best way from technical viewpoint and thereby forgotten man who was behind the machine.

   Neo-classical thought pushed the pendulum in the opposite direction and emphasized the importance of human side of organization. It comprises two approaches: Behavioural Science Viewpoint and, Human Relations Movement.
3. **The contemporary theory of management** (1950-90). With increasing complexities of organizations, modern management theories made further refinement, extension and synthesis of the classical and neo-classical approaches to management. These approaches are (1) quantitative approach to management, (2) systems approach to management, and (3) contingency approach to management.
4. **Emerging views** (1950 onward). With the passage of time business becomes complex and so is management. New approaches are constantly needed to improve the performance of management. Some recent perspective

that have gained attention are theory of Peter F. Drucker, theory of Michael Porter, theory of Tom Peters, theory of C.K. Prahlad, theory of Rensis Likert and McKinsey's 7-S Approach.

2.2.2 Classical Theory of Management

Scientific Management

Scientific management is an approach that emphasizes that scientific study of work methods in order to improve worker efficiency. Major contributors of this approach include Frederick Winslow Taylor, Frank and Lillian Gilbreth, and Henry Gantt. Main features of scientific management are:

(i) Separation of planning from doing. It means worker should do his job purely in a mechanical fashion, jobs being repetitive in nature while managers should accept the responsibility for planning and organizing thereby better division of work would result.

(ii) Standardization of tools, period of work, working conditions and cost of production.

(iii) Time and motion study is a process in which the work is divided into several motions and unnecessary motions are eliminated.

(iv) Financial incentive is considered to motivate workmen to maximize their full potentials. This may benefit to both workmen and the organization.

Frederick Winslow Taylor (1856-1915) is known as "the father of scientific management."

He started his career in 1871 in USA as an apprentice machinist for a local firm before moving on to Midvale Steel. At Midvale, his meteoric rise from a foreman to chief engineer in six years gave him an opportunity to tackle much disorder and wastage of human and other resources at workplaces. Meanwhile, he obtained graduation in Physics and Mathematics from Harvard University. Later he obtained the Master Degree in Engineering from the Stevens Institute of Technology. Then he joined Simonds Rolling Machine and Bethlehem Steel Company where he served from 1898 to 1901. After his retirement he devoted his time in writing and developing scientific management. He emphasized that there was a science of doing things and of getting things done. To prove his point, Taylor conducted time and motion study. He conducted experiments at workplace to determine right methods, measurement of time to do the various components of work with the standard tools.

His major publication *The Principles of Scientific Management* came out in 1911.

During his career spanning a period of 26 years, he conducted a series of experiments in the above three companies. His theory was based on the following principles popularly known as Taylorism:

1. Replace rule of thumb methods with methods based on a scientific study of the tasks.
2. Scientific select, train, and develop each worker rather than passively leaving them to train themselves.
3. Cooperate with the workers to ensure that the scientifically developed methods are being followed.
4. Divide work nearly equally between managers and workers, so that the managers apply scientific management principles to planning the work and the workers actually perform the tasks.
5. Greater productivity and worker efficiency through time and motion study.
6. Introduction of wage incentive plan to motivate worker to increase production. From such an approach, both workmen and the management would be benefitted.

Contributions

1. Scientific management principles were widely accepted. Most important, productivity and efficiency in manufacturing improved dramatically. One of the most famous examples of the

application of scientific management is the factory, Henry Ford built with assembly line facilities for mass production.

2. It introduced techniques of time and motion study to increase workers' contribution. This type of study involves breaking down the work task into its various elements, or motions, eliminating unnecessary motions, determining the best way to do the job, and then timing each motion through stopwatch to determine the amount of production per day (with allowances for delays and rest periods).

3. Taylor suggested scientific selection, education, and development of workers. These measures help workers in performing the jobs in right way.

4. He identified planning and execution of plans as two distinct jobs.

5. He introduced piece-rate system which gained wide acceptance because it is more closely aligned effort and reward.

6. With his effort, the concept of a management specialist gained prominence.

7. Taylor also emphasized the need for cooperation between management and workers.

Drawbacks and Limitations

1. While scientific management principles improved productivity, they also increased the monotony of work.

2. While in many cases the new ways working were accepted by the workers, in some cases they were not. The use of stopwatches often was a protested issue and led to unrest where "Taylorism" was being tested.

3. Taylorism was dehumanizing ignoring many job-related social and psychological factors by emphasizing only money as worker incentive.

4. Taylorism is infamous for meaningless work because employees are simply treated as machines that led to boredom, apathy and quality control problems.

5. Unions strongly opposed scientific management techniques because they believed management might abuse their power to

set the standards and the piece rates, thus exploiting workers and diminishing their importance.

In spite of the above criticism, Taylor's techniques were perfected by Henry L. Gantt, and husband and wife team of Frank and Lillian Gilbreth.

Administrative Management

It suggested that management is a profession and should be taught. A broad framework for administrative management emerged in 1916 when Henri Fayol, a French mining engineer turned a leading industrialist and successful manager, published a book titled *General and Industrial Management* summerised his experiences. He was referred to as the "father of modern management theory".

He divided industrial activities into six groups: technical, commercial, financial, security, accounting and managerial. Fayol recognized the importance of the managerial skills which had so far been the most neglected aspect of business operations. He defined five functions of management: planning, organizing, commanding, coordinating, and controlling. Fayol also outlined 14 Principles of Management as general guidelines—useful in running a large organization.

1. DIVISION OF WORK: Work should be divided among individuals and groups to ensure that efforts are focused on special portions of the task. Fayol presented work specialization as the best way to use the human resources of the organization.

2. AUTHORITY: The concepts of authority and responsibility are closely related. Authority was defined by Fayol as the right to give orders and the power to exact obedience. Responsibility involves being accountable, and is therefore naturally associated with authority. Whoever assumes authority also assumes responsibility.

3. DISCIPLINE: A successful organization requires discipline in every sphere. This can be brought by effective leadership, good supervision, and fair agreement with employees. Rewards and penalties should be applied judiciously to ensure discipline.

4. UNITY OF COMMAND: An employee should receive orders from one superior only.

5. UNITY OF DIRECTION: The entire organization should be moving towards a common objective in a common direction.

6. SUBORDINATION OF INDIVIDUAL INTERESTS TO THE GENERAL INTERESTS: The interests of one employee or group should not prevail over the interests and goals of the organization as a whole.

7. REMUNERATION: Compensation should be fair to both the employee and the employer. Many variables, such as cost of living, supply of qualified personnel, general business conditions, success of the business, and profit should be considered in determining a worker's rate of pay.

8. CENTRALIZATION: Fayol defined centralization as lowering the importance of the subordinate role. Decentralization is increasing the importance. The degree to which centralization or decentralization should be adopted depends on the specific organization in which the manager is working.

9. SCALAR CHAIN: Managers in hierarchies are part of a chain like authority scale. Each manager, from the first-line supervisor to the president, possesses certain amounts of authority. The president possesses the most authority; the first-line supervisor the least. Lower-level managers should always keep upper-level managers informed of their work activities. The existence of a scalar chain and adherence to it are necessary if the organization is to be successful.

10. ORDER: For the sake of efficiency and coordination, all materials and people related to a specific kind of work should be treated as equally as possible.

11. EQUITY: All employees should be treated as equally as possible.

12. STABILITY OF TENURE OF PERSONNEL: Retaining productive employees should always be a high priority of management. Recruitment and selection costs, as well as increased product—reject rates are usually associated with hiring new workers.

13. INITIATIVE: Management should take steps to encourage worker initiative, which is defined as new or additional work activity undertaken through self-direction.

14. ESPIRIT DE CORPS: Management should encourage harmony and general good feelings among employees.

Bureaucratic Management

German sociologist Max Weber (1864-1920) studied a number of organizations and realized that there is a need for uniform approach to tackle the management problems and situations rather than relying on the arbitrary whims and fancy of owners and managers. He coined the approach bureaucracy (based on the German buro, meaning "office") to identify especially larger organization that need to be operated on rational basis. According to Weber, "a bureaucracy is a highly structured, formalized, and impersonal organization." He propagated the belief that an organization should have a defined hierarchical structure managed by clearly defined regulations and lines of authority. Waber has observed three types of power in organization: traditional, charismatic and bureaucratic. He has emphasized that bureaucratic type of power is the ideal one. He outlined the five characteristics of ideal bureaucracy as shown below:

Major Characteristics of Weber's Ideal Bureaucracy

Division of work	Work is divided and distributed on the basis of specialization and division of labour. Each section/ department has boundary of operation and does not cross its boundary to step into others.
Formal rules and procedures	Written rules and procedures are developed to ensure uniformity.
Impersonality	Without hatred or passion, rules and procedures are applied. The impersonal relationships are necessary in order for bureaucrats to make rational decisions.
Well-defined hierarchy	Officers follow the principles of hierarchy, that is each lower officer is under control and supervision of a higher one in the form of a pyramid. It serves a line of communication and delegation of powers.
Career advancement based on merit	Selection and promotion is based on the qualification and general competence.

According to him, these characteristics do not exist in pure form and could be used as the starting points in dealing with organizations. Bureaucracy is popularly associated with the administration of government's departments, public services and public sector organizations.

Bureaucracy is sometimes used in a pejorative sense to denote red tape and excessive rules. It is not flexible enough to suit the complex changes in the environment. People who need to take a decision due to excessive rules and procedures they may not perform their best.

Functional Aspect of Bureaucracy

Bureaucratic organizations need to operate on more rational basis. It means functions are performed through a set of rules and procedures and every member of organization has to follow these rules. This leads to a greater efficiency.

1. Managing organizations through hierarchical chain of command by superiors leads to optimum utilization of resources.
2. Useful for large scale organization which has to regulate band of specialized staff in order to delegate specific responsibilities and functions to them.
3. Weber's belief was that the ideal official should be dominated by a spirit of formalistic impersonality without hatred or passion, and hence without affection or enthusiasm. The impersonal relationships are necessary in order for bureaucrats make completely rational decisions.
4. This system of organization is bound by objective rules, laws, and regulations and has stressed the need for maintaining records and files for systematic interpretation of norms and enforcement of rules which cannot be maintained through oral communication. Thus, trained bureaucracy is superior in terms of precision, speed, unambiguity, knowledge of files, continuity, direction, unity, strict subordination, controlling the behaviour of officials thereby reducing friction among themselves and of material costs. There

are basically two reasons for efficiency in a bureaucratic organization—first, there is high degree of rationality in administrative behaviour and second, there is high degree of predictability in such behaviour. Both these factors lead to efficiency in the organization. Since bureaucratic officials are selected on the basis of there technical competence, the efficiency improves because they are disciplined and responsible lots and will put their maximum efforts for furthering their career in the organization.

The rationality can be shown along a continuum ranging from complete rationality in the case of economic man to complete irrationality in the case of social man. The irrationality increases if the functioning is based upon socio-psychological factor. In this form of organization, decisions are based upon rationality and emotional attachment, either to subordinates or to clients, is avoided.

Dysfunctional Aspect of Bureaucracy

Such dysfunctional aspect emerges because of overemphasis on rules rather misuse of rules, strict devotion to regulations, external control through organization hierarchy as opposed to internal control. In bureaucratic organizations, the responsibility can be avoided very easily by using techniques originally designed to produce efficiency. The buck-passer always finds a way for avoiding responsibility. Treating individuals as machines actually affects morale. This leads to inefficiency.

Bureaucratic organizations often face value conflict between bureaucrats and professionals. The basic reason for this conflict is the difference in orientation between bureaucrats and professionals. Professionals like to be controlled by specific style not conducive to bureaucrats leading to conflict and inefficiency in the organization. Goal displacement occurs when resources are being used for the other goals than for which the organization exists leading to organizational dysfunctional.

Unlike stable environment, bureaucratic organization faces challenges in dynamic situation. Thus, bureaucracy which works on machine model is not flexible enough to suit the complex changes in the environment should be replaced.

Gilberth's Laws of Motion Economy. Frank Gilberth applied motion principles and techniques for efficient use of body movements in performing of all types of work. From these studies with the extensive use of motion pictures of tasks being performed, he established the laws of motion economy. Lilian Gilberth worked tandem with her husband and is credited with the publication of *Psychology of Movement* (1914), the first book relating to the application psychology to the principles of scientific management.

2.2.3 Neo-classical Theory of Management having Social System Approach

A new movement known as **Organization Behaviour** emerged in which besides man-machine concept of scientific management, an element of human behaviour has visualized. Elton Mayo (1818-1949) was the father of this movement. Later more social scientists, namely Kurt Lewin, A. Maslow and more recently Douglas McGregor were identified with further input of human relations.

Behavioural Science Approach

Hawthorne Studies. The Hawthorne plant of Western Electric Company, Chicago was engaged in producing bells and other electrical equipments for telephone industry. The company employed about 30000 workers and was treated to be the most progressive organization with pension, sickness scheme and numerous recreational and other facilities. However, there was a great deal of discontentment and dissatisfaction among its employees. The management was worried about this state of affairs and thought there is some thing beyond scientific management aspect which is required to be studied and referred the matter to a group of professors of Harvard Business School, U.S.A., namely Elton Mayo (psychologist as leader), Roethlisberger, and Whitehead (sociologists) and the company representative William Dickson. They conducted following three experiments for ten years.

1. Illumination experiments 1924-27;
2. Relay assembly test room experiments 1927-32;
3. Bank wiring observation room experiments 1931-32;
4. Researchers also conducted personal interviews, counseling and psychological testing.

1. Effect of changes in illumination on productivity: In the illumination experiment, workers were divided into an experiment room with varied illumination and a control room with constant illumination. When the intensity of illumination was increased, output also increases in the experimental room, but quite contrary to the expectation, output also increased in the control room where illumination was not varied. The researchers proceeded to decrease the illumination, but output once again increased in the experimental room. Thus, illumination alone had no effect on productivity and something is there which affected the productivity. This something more provided a significant clue to investigate the complex human variables affecting productivity which formed the basis of second experiment.

2. Effect of changes in working hours and other working conditions on productivity: In the relay assembly test room experiment, each relay consists of a number of parts which girls assembled into finished products. During experiments, girls were consulted for variables like incentive, rest interval, and additional physical facilities such as serving in the morning coffee or soup along with sandwich and in the evening snack and the productivity increased. Changes in working were introduced at various times, such as cutting an hour off the end of the day and eliminating Saturday work. The girls were allowed to disperse at 4.30 p.m. instead of 5.00 p.m. and productivity increased. Later, they were allowed to disperse at 4.00 p.m. and the productivity remained the same.

As each change was introduced, absenteeism decreased, less supervision was required and morale increased. On the basis of these findings, researchers concluded that there was definite relationship between productivity and various factors being adjusted. At this point of time, they decided to return to everything to its original status, that is, 48 hour week, Saturday working-day, no rest period and no free snack or coffee, surprisingly, productivity took a jump with an average production of 3000 relays per week as compared to 2400 relays before the start of experiments. This marginal productivity increase was because of a change in the girls' attitudes towards work and their work group. They developed a feeling of stability and sense of belongingness. Since there was more freedom of work, they developed a sense of responsibility and self-discipline. The relationship between supervisor and workers became close and homely.

3. Group influences individual behaviour: Bank wiring observation room study was conducted with a view to analyse the functioning of a small group and its impact on individual behaviour. Fourteen workers were employed in the bank wiring room. The hypothesis was that to earn more, workers would produce more individually and help others to produce more to take advantage of group bonus. However, the result was different. The group themselves set the production norm, anybody attempting to produce more was disfavoured by others and group pressure was applied to restrict his production. Restricted output envisaged due to (i) fear of unemployment, (ii) fear of raising the standard and (iii) protection of slower workers. It was observed that deviation from the norm was not very positively viewed by other workers. The rate busters (turn out too much work) and rate chisellers (turn out too little work) were not favoured. This gave the clue that informal relationship was important and attempt should the made to see that interest of the management and workers were identical, and attempt should also be made to modify informal group behaviour to realize organizational objectives and serves it through such interpersonal skills as motivating, counseling and communicating.

4. Improvement in productivity was due to such social factors as morale, a sense of belongingness with the group and effective management. During the course of experiments, massive interviews were conducted to determine employees' attitudes towards the company, supervision, insurance plans, promotion and wages. It was also observed during interview that worker's behaviour was being influenced by group behaviour which was reflected in terms of restricted output set up by the group norm. However, such observations were not satisfactory and researchers decided to go further deep to undertake bank wiring observation room experiments.

Human Relations Movement

Further research by psychologists, sociologists, anthropologists and other social scientists has thrown additional light upon the forces which stimulate people to perform effectively at work.

Workers' participation. Participation means the sharing of decision making among the members of group/section. Kurt Lewin and his associates conducted several studies over four years to establish the effect of participation. Another study was conducted to assess the resistance to change among members of a group. This resistance to change was able to reduce by getting workers involved in the process of change.

Motivation at work: Maslow's needs hierarchy theory— Human needs tend to follow the pattern below presented in the sequence in which individuals usually become concerned with them:

- Physiological needs—for survival, food, water, clothing, shelter, rest to overcome fatigue and the like.
- Safety and security—for protection against danger and deprivation.
- Social needs—for association with other persons acceptance, belonging to be given love and affection.
- Esteem needs—egoistic needs, recognition and prestige, to achieve status.
- Self-actualisation—for self-fulfilment of potential finding expression for one's creative abilities.

Maslow suggests that the various needs are interdependent and overlapping, each higher-level need emerging before the lower-level need in the hierarchical need structure has been completely satisfied. Since one need does not disappear when another emerges, all needs tend to be partially satisfied in each area, when the peak of a need is passed, that need ceases to be a primary motivator.

Herzberg's Theory. According to Herzberg, motivation is a two-dimensional problem. On one end are factors which can cause dissatisfaction if present. He calls these Hygiene Factors, namely policies and administration, supervision, working conditions, interpersonal relations, money, status, and security. On the opposite end are factors which can lead to positive attitudes and motivations, if present and can result in negative attitudes if absent. These are Motivation Factors, namely achievement, recognition, challenging work, increased responsibility, growth and development.

Another conceptual framework of motivation is **Douglas McGregor's theory X and theory Y** explaining individual needs (relationships) and not the needs of the organization (task). He says that the managers who believe in theory X are of the view that:

- Most people just don't like to work.
- To make them work, most people must be coerced, controlled and threatened to the extent of achieving organizational goal.
- Most people have no imagination of their own and need constant guidance to work.

As against this viewpoint, managers who believe in theory Y are of the opinion that:

- People do not like or dislike work inherently but rather on the basis of their experience of it.
- Authoritarian methods may be all right for achieving immediate result but they do not pay in the long run.
- People seek reward, material or psychological pat and for achieving that reward, they can work as vigorously as under a supervisor's pressure, i.e., carrot and stick approach to motivate employees.

Under the right circumstances, people do not shun responsibility but seek it.

Quantitative Management Approach

This approach emerged during World War II. This approach focuses on the use of mathematics, statistics, optimization models, and computer simulations in managerial decision making. It consists of three main branches: management science, operations management, and management information systems. Herbert Simon and others pioneered in this field.

- Management science aids in effective decision making by applying modern mathematical and statistical models to managerial practices in the areas of planning and control. It is also referred to as operations research techniques like LP, queuing, probability, game, programme evaluation and review (PERT), etc.
- Operations management is the field of study relating to effective management of production and delivery of goods and services. Forecasting, inventory analysis, networking models are some of the tools used by operational managers.
- Management information systems aid in designing and implementing computer-based information systems for management applications. Data is collected, analyzed, and made available to managers where they need it.

It is a mechanistic approach devoid of reality where lot of data is required where mere assumptions are made. Managers do not rely on these methods. They use these techniques as a supplement to their experience, intuition and judgment.

2.2.4 Contemporary Theory of Management

The earlier approaches were criticized because they ignored (1) the relationship between the organization and its external environment and (2) usually stressed one aspect of the organization or its employees at the expense of other considerations. In response to these criticisms, management scholars during the 1950s developed two important theories, namely the systems theory and the contingency theory.

Systems Theory: The systems theory approach is based on the notion that organizations can be visualized as systems. A system is a set of interrelated parts that operate as a whole in pursuit of common goals. It has four major components:

1. **Inputs** are the various human, material, financial, equipment, and informational resources required to produce goods and services.
2. **Transformation processes** are the organization's managerial and technological abilities that are applied to covert inputs into outputs.
3. **Outputs** are the products, services and other outcomes produced by the organization.
4. **Feedback** is information about results and organizational status relative to the environment.

It depends on input from external environment as well as raw materials, human resource and capital. They transform these inputs into outputs as goods and services. The environment reacts to the output through a feedback loop. This feedback provides input for the next cycle of the system.

The systems approach has a number of advantages. First, the systems view provides a framework for assessing how well the various parts of an organization interact to achieve a common purpose. Second, it shows that parts are interrelated, i.e. a change in one part of the system may affect other parts. Third, it considers how an organization interacts with its external environment.

The system assumed that the whole is greater than the sum of its parts called **synergy.** This implies that departments (parts) within an organization which are interacting in synchronisation are more productive than they would be if they operated separately. Systems theory has been advocated by Chester Barnard, Herbert Simon, C.W. Churchman and others.

OPEN VERSUS CLOSED SYSTEMS: Systems can be open or closed. An **open system** is one that operates in continual interaction with its environment. Through such interaction, the system takes in new inputs and learns about how its outputs are received by various important outside elements. In contrast, a **closed system** does little or no interacting with its environment and receives little feedback. From a practical point of view, all organizations are open systems to some extent, since it is virtually impossible for an organization to operate for a significant period of time without some interaction with the environment. Each system has its own boundaries which separate it from other systems in the environment. In an open system, the boundaries are permeable whereas in a closed system they are rigid. Still, organizations can vary in degree along the open-closed continuum. For example, an advertising company is far more open system than the government department.

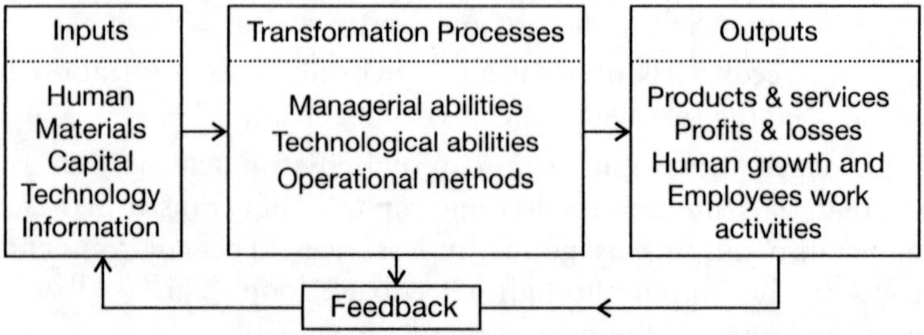

Fig. 2.1: A system view of organization

Because of the system approach, manager must consider all departments objective performance to get synergy as well as effect of environment such as trends in similar products, governmental guidelines and competitive technology.

2.2.5 Contingency Theory

The classical theorists, such as Taylor and Fayol, emphasized to identify "the one best principle" for managers to apply in every situation. Unfortunately, things were not to be that simple.

Contingency theory is a viewpoint that appropriate decisions by managers depend on (contingent upon) the characteristic of the situation. Situational characteristics are called contingencies. Understanding contingencies helps a manager know which sets of circumstances dictate which management actions. The essence of this approach is that manager should identify the situations, interpret them and apply managerial principles which suit the situation best. Contingency theory has been developed during the 1960s by Joan Woodward and others.

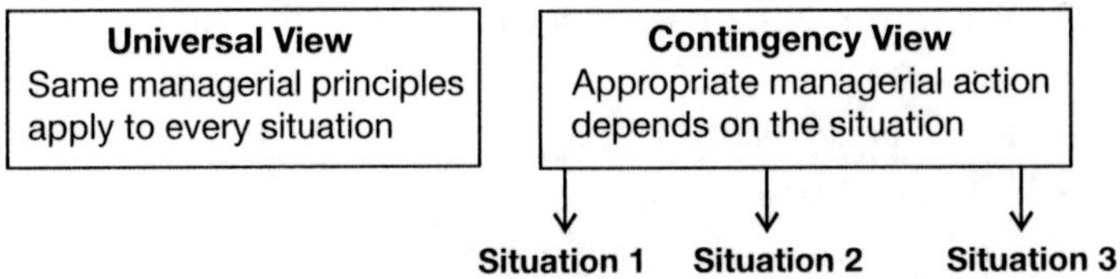

Contingency approach to various situations

Example: S.N. Singh is the production manager whose objective is to maintain the production line with a reasonable productivity. For which each person should report to only one boss (Fayol's principles of unity of command). It has to be followed by him. On the other hand, T. Raju marketing manager follow inter-relationship approach to take care of environmental situation, strategy, and organizational design.

2.2.6 Management Theories of Recent Origin

These theories represent a series of management thought developed by famous management thinkers. Some of the theories are discussed below:

Theory of Peter F. Drucker: His theories are of year 1954s.

Drucker is recognized as the founding father of modern management theory and practice. Contributions of Drucker are as follow:

1. Nature and role of management—management is a profession. It is important for all types of organizations.
2. (a) Manager's job—economic performance of organization is the main job of a manager.
   (b) Manager is to be made work productive.
   (c) Social responsibility is as important as profit.
3. Organization should spell out objectives in clear term.
4. Marketing and innovation are the most important functions of an entrepreneual organization.
5. Drucker introduced the concept of Management by Objectives (MBO).
6. Organization structure should be such that it delivers results—authority, responsibility decision-making and communication.

7. Whatever a manager does he does through making decisions.
8. Drucker stressed the need for management development for executives.

Manager keeps a searching eye of future activities with respect to technology, economic conditions, demographic change in worker.

Management by Objectives (MBO)

One technique used by organizations to facilitate the linkage of goals and plans is management by objectives (MBO). It is a process through which specific goals are set collaboratively for the organization as a whole and every department, unit and individual within it. Peter F. Drucker used the term MBO in 1954, one of the earliest management thinkers to do so.

Steps in MBO Process

MBO processes include the following six steps (figure below):

1. Develop overall organizational goals—At the first step, top management determine the mission and the strategic goals of organization. Goals should be based on targets to be achieved by the organization as a whole (e.g., a certain rate of return or specific increase in market share for a given period).
2. Establish specific goals (objectives) for various departments, units and individuals. In this steps, various departments, units and individuals (for their subordinates) set their goals in accordance with the overall goals of organization set in step 1. Goal setting is a joint and interactive process. At each level, goals are typically set in key result areas where results are critical and verifiable to the success of the organization.

   Although many organizations follow the top-bottom approach just described above, some use a bottom-up approach, in which goal setting begins at the lower levels. These levels propose their goals on the basis of what they believe they can achieve. Goals are then developed at the tactic levels that are based on the proposed goals provided by the operational level. The tactical goals are the proposed to strategic level. Even with a bottom-up approach, however, goal setting usually follows at least some general guidelines developed at the strategic level. In any event, with MBO, there is typically some give-and-take among levels before goals at various levels are finalized.

3. Formulate action plan—Once goals are set, action plans must be developed that focus on the methods or activities necessary to reach particular goals. Thus, action is a description of what is be done, how, when, where and by whom in order to achieve a goal. Action plans contribute to the feasibility of reaching goals, aid in identifying problem areas, assist in spelling out areas in which resources and assistance will be needed, and facilitate the search for more efficient ways to achieve objectives. For which there may be review of existing procedures, organization structure, job description, and even delegation of powers. Moreover, checkpoints should be established for evaluation of results in key result areas (KRAs). Such plans are usually developed by subordinates in conjunction with their supervisors.
4. Implement and maintain self-control—Once goals are set and action plans are prepared, individuals know what they are supposed to achieve and can gauge their progress against set goals giving considerable freedom to implement their plan. Therefore, it should not be necessary for the supervisor to become as involved in the individual's day-to-day activities as might be the case without MBO. The notion of self-control is particularly true with respect to managerial positions. Of course, supervisors still need to be kept informed about the progress and intern provides coaching and support if subordinates are having difficulties.
5. Review progress periodically if needed.
6. Appraise performance data.

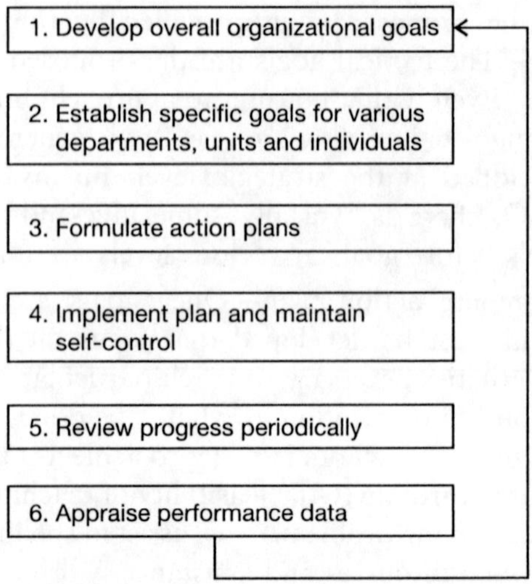

Fig. 2.2: Steps in the MBO process

Drucker's work will continue to guide managers, academicians, management thinkers, and students of management in the times to come. His contribution in the areas of MBO, concern for societal environment, role of management in improving the quality of life, role of marketing and innovation in improving organization's effectiveness are recognized even today.

Failure of MBO Programme

1. Inadequate top-management support.
2. Inadequate explanation of MBO programme to managers involved.
3. Poorly defined objectives.
4. Personality conflicts.
5. Insincere commitment by managers.
6. Inadequate reinforcement of MBO.
7. Over emphasis of paperwork.

Theory Z

On the basis of his research of both American and Japanese management approaches, management expert William Ouchy has offered **Theory Z** in the year 1981. Theory Z combines the best Japanese and American practices aimed at business paradigm shift from one of quantity to quality and second of a set of organizational and management style characteristics compatible with the norms and values of society and culture. The theory Z approach involves giving workers job security; including them in some decision making; emphasizing group responsibility; increasing quality; establishing gradual-advancement policies, more informal controls, and broader career paths; and showing greater concern for employees' well-being. A number of American companies, such as Ford Motor, Hewlett-Packard (HP), IBM, and Procter & Gamble have adopted aspects of Theory Z (Modified American).

Characteristics of Theory Z Management

American managerial practices	Japanese managerial practices	Theory Z (Modified American)-MA
Short-term employment	Lifetime employment, job security	Long-term employment
Individual decision-making	Consensual decision-making	Consensus decision-making
Individual responsibility	Collective responsibility	Individual responsibility (MA)
Rapid evaluation and promotion	Slow evaluation and promotion (MA)	Slow evaluation and promotion
Explicit, formalized control	Implicit, informal control	Implicit, informal control with explicit, formalized measures
Specialized career path	Non-specialized career path	Moderately specialized career-path
Segmented concern	Holistic concern	Concern including family

The practical implication of Theory Z is that managers need to adapt appropriate management styles from other cultures to local preferences.

McKinsey 7-S Approach

This approach was developed by McKinsey and Company, a very well-known management consultancy firm. It aimed to diagonised the causes of company problems and to formulate programs for improvement. Later, it became the basis for research for two famous books on management. One, *The Art of Japanese Management* and second, *In Search of Excellence*.

Thus, the model visualizes that there is a complex and interrelated relationship between the 7s—strategy, structure, systems, style, skills, staff and super ordinate goals. Any of the seven factors could be critical in changing a particular company at a certain point of time. As such managers are to tackle that variable first to maximize the result of change.

The 7s factors are:

1. *Strategy:* Plans that determine the allocation of an organization's resources and commit the organization to a specified course of action. In response to the market situation, strategy is to be changed from time to time.
2. *Structure:* The design of the organization structure depends upon the company strategy. While developing the structure care should be taken with respect to inter alia communication, decision-making and coordination among departments. The design also involves such issues as number of hierarchical levels, authority-responsibility relationships among positions to link the tasks of individuals and groups, delegation of authority, and matrix formation in achieving organizational goals or objectives.
3. *Systems:* "Systems" refer to all the rules, regulations, and procedures, both formal and informal that complement the organization structures. Systems are reviewed from time to time to suit the structure and the strategy.
4. *Staff:* Staffing is the process of acquiring right kind of people to suit the various positions then train and develop them so that they acquire the abilities and skills they would need to be effective in further assignments allotted to them.
5. *Style:* The style of a company becomes evident through the managerial behaviour of top management team over a period of time. Their actions are more likely to be noticed by people in the lower orders. Reporting relationships may also convey the style of the company.

"Style" also involves the culture of the company. Culture provides members a way to perceive, think, and feel in relation to their problems.

6. *Skills:* The term "skills" include those characteristics, which most people use to describe a company by its distinct abilities of the employees. For example, Hindustan Lever is known for its marketing skills whereas Larsen and Toubro is for its engineering skills.

   Companies may have strengths in a number of areas, but their key strengths or dominant skills are few. The dominant skills or the distinctive competence of a company are part of the company character. These are developed over a period of time.

7. *Super Ordinate Goals:* These refer to a set of values and aspirations often unwritten, which go beyond the conventional formal statement of corporate objectives. Super ordinate goals can provide a strong basis of stability to a company in a dynamic environment by providing a basic purpose to people working for the company. Example would include 3-M's dominating culture of "new venture": Hewlett-Packard's innovating people at all levels in the company.

REVIEW QUESTIONS

1. What would be the various dimensions of management?
2. Describe the two approaches of management indicating their common area.
3. As a manager, how do you apply these theories into practice consistent with the approach predominantly followed in your organization?
4. Define MBO. State the different approaches to MBO.
5. Explain the steps in management by objectives process, and assess the strengths and weaknesses of MBO.

Chapter 3
Corporate Social Responsibility and Ethics

3.1 INTRODUCTION

Traditionally, profit was the sole business objective, but this objective now no more holds good. If companies want to survive and maintain their profit and growth, they have to sacrifice a portion of their profits to look after the interests of society. Social responsibility of business refers to what the business does, over and above the statutory requirement, for the benefit of the society. The word social responsibility connotes that the business has some moral obligations to the society.

The corporate citizenship is also commonly used to refer to the moral obligations and compulsions of business to the society. This implies that, just as individuals, corporate is also integral part of the society and that their behaviour shall be guided by certain norms. Goyder conceptulises: "Industry in the twentieth century can no longer be regarded as a private arrangement for enriching shareholders, it has become a joint enterprise in which workers, management, consumers, the locality, Government and trade unions all play a part." He further elaborated that if the corporation has to function effectively, it has to be accountable to the public at large; and he sought to equate the suggestion of a responsible company with the trusteeship concept advocated by Gandhiji, the aim of which was to ensure that private property was used for the common good.

Corporate social responsibility (CSR) is now more prominent and evident than ever due to the emphasis laid on businesses regarding environment, social and ethical issues. This is because over the recent years, there have been social, political and economic pressure on corporate sector to pay attention on social and environmental consequences of corporate activities. Profit earning is the main goal of the organizations and they strive for it. But this era of globalization and cut-throat competition has changed the first concern of a company that is the happiness of the people connected to it. In today's world, companies believe in the philosophy that they are an indispensable part of the society.

3.2 MEANING

Corporate social responsibility is making socially responsible product engaging in socially responsible employee relations and making a commitment to the society around.

According to Keith Davis, the term "social responsibility" refers to two types of business obligations, viz. (a) the socio-economic obligation and (b) the socio-human obligation. The socio-economic obligation is to promote employment opportunities, to maintain competition, to curb inflation, etc. the socio-human obligation to nurture and develop human values such as moral, cooperation, motivation, and ethics.

Some define corporate social responsibility as a commitment of the business to contribute for sustainable economic development working with employees local community and business partners and to the society at large in order to improve their quality of work life.

Jamshedji Tata has very beautifully defined corporate social responsibility. The clear definition of CSR is that the community is not just another stakeholder in our business but the very purpose of our existence.

The World Business Council for Sustainable Development, in 1990 brings out the fact that CSR is "The continuing commitment by business to behave ethically and contribute to economic development while improving the quality of life of workforce and their families as well as of the local community and society at large."

H.S. Singhania classifies the nature of the CSR of business into two categories,

- The manner in which a business carries out its own business activity. It means business is not merely a profit-making occupation but a social function performed with ethics.
- The social welfare activity that it takes upon itself as an additional function.

3.3 HISTORICAL PERSPECTIVE

Classical perspective of social responsibility of business has only economic objectives and no other responsibility beyond that. Economist Milton Friedman's view which has roots traced back to eighteenth-century economist Adam Smith holding that the entire social responsibility of a corporation can be summed up as "*make profits and obey the law.*" According to this view, each corporation should actively attempt to increase profits through legal means. Friedman, further, argues that charitable activities by corporations are not socially responsible because, in making such contributions, the corporation prevents individual stockholders from making their own decisions about how to dispose of their funds.

The contemporary view of social responsibility of business is substantially broader and benevolent than the classical one. At the beginning of the twentieth century, there were few corporate acts of benevolence. At that time, two principles evolved providing the foundation for contemporary views on social responsibility. The first of these, the *principle of charity* suggests that those who have plenty should give to those who do not. Under the influence of this principle, corporate individuals decided to use some of their wealth for the social cause. For example, US steel baron Andrew Carnegie contributed his wealth in the field of education. Henry Ford adopted a health program available to company employees. Over a period, an increasing number of business leaders with a philanthropic attitude spread the idea that business has a responsibility to society beyond simply providing necessary goods and services.

A second principle that shaped corporate social responsibility is the *principle of stewardship*. This principle suggests that organizations have an obligation to see that the society's needs are served by vast corporate resources. In this way, managers and corporations become the stewards or trustees, for society.

The concept of Gandhi's *trusteeship* is on the same lines as the principle of stewardship. Gandhiji advocated that the owners of property would voluntarily manage their wealth on behalf of the people. He influenced various Indian companies to play active roles in nation building and promoting socio-economic development during the twentieth century.

The contemporary view of business is that business is integral part of the society to serve a social purpose. Proponents of this view like Davis and Blomstrom hold that business is a social institution, performing a social mission and having a broad influence on the way people live and work together. According to Steiner and Steiner, social responsibility is as follow:

1. Each business must take into account the situation in which it finds itself in meeting stakeholder expectations.
2. Business is an economic entity and cannot jeopardize its profitability meeting social needs.
3. Business should recognise in the long run, the general social good benefits everyone.
4. A business should tackle only those social problems for which it has social power and competence.
5. Business must assume its share of the social burden and be willing to absorb reasonable social costs.

B. Carrol has proposed a three-dimensional pyramidical model of corporate social responsibility. These responsibilities are economic, legal, ethical and discretionary. Since the firm being an economic entity, its primary responsibility is economic, hence economic responsibilities are at the base of the pyramid. Then it succeeded by legal responsibilities, ethical responsibilities and finally, discretionary responsibilities with a philanthropic attitude as shown below:

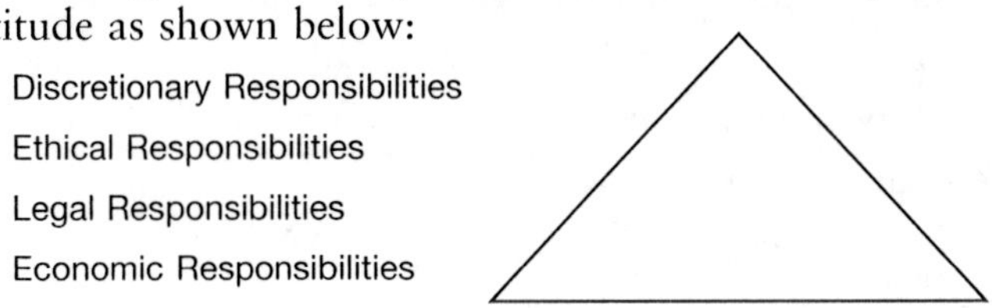

Social Stakeholders: There are six major, somewhat overlapping groups—shareholders, company employees, customers, the local community, general society (regional and national), and the international community. These groups are considered social stakeholders because they can be affected for better or worse by the business activities of corporation.

The most common form of an enterprise's responsibility is towards the groups that have a vested interest in its growth and profit, i.e., employees, shareholders, and consumers. Since the business functions within the social environment, there is a relationship between an organization and the society. And due to its ethical obligation towards society, social responsibility arises. Social responsibilities mean an intelligent and objective concern for the welfare of society that restrains individual and corporate behaviour from ultimately destructive activities, no matter how immediately profitable such activities are, and lead to a positive contribution for human betterment. Therefore, corporate social responsibility (CSR) is to contribute for sustainable economic development, working with employees, local community and business partners and to the society at large in order to improve their quality of work life. The concept of CSR has evolved from philanthropy to a more elaborate concept that encompassed the environment, employee relations, corporate governance and engaging with the community. Bill Gates, one of the richest businessmen in the world is doing one of the highest contributions in the area of social responsibility.

3.4 CORPORATE SOCIAL RESPONSIBILITY IN INDIA

There are number of drivers ranging from contributing for social causes to rural health care and education. But some of the leading drivers of CSR in India are as follows:

- To be a good corporate citizen
- Improved relationship with local community
- Stated philosophy of founding fathers
- Opportunity to enhance reputation/brand
- Enhanced shareholders value
- Improvement in employee relations

Indian ethos, based on the principle of 'Sarvejanaha Sukhino Bhavanthu' has approached the issues of managing people from a 'welfare' concept. Western philosophy of managing people stresses rewarding people based on their ability to contribute. When we are approaching the new market-driven and consumer-dominant business situations, there is a need to have an effective mix of 'welfare' and 'performance' philosophies, to ensure that the employees are looked after well and the organizations are also enabled to prosper. Now, the government under different statutes and business magnets have supported this concept. The modern large business enterprises are mainly conscious about profit however of late they have realized their obligation toward social environment. When people talk about social responsibility of business, they are thinking in terms of the problems that arise when a business enterprise casts its shadow on the social scene, and, of the ethical principle that ought to govern the relationship between business and society.

J.R.D. Tata, former Chairman of Tata Steel, once said, "To create good working conditions, to pay the best wages to its employees and provide decent housing to its workers were not enough for the industry. The aim of an industry should be to discharge its overall social responsibilities to the Community and the Society at large where the industry is located." Tata Steel is known for its exemplary standards of business ethics towards social responsibility and humanitarian cause of a very high order. Social and community development, for example, of Tata Steel is unsurpassed in India. Its multifarious Social Welfare, Rural and Community Development, Health and Family Initiatives, Sports and Adventures, Environmental Protection programmes are considered ideals by the social scientists all over the world.

The new Company Law is enacted in August 2013 having the provisions that every company with a net worth of at least ₹ 500 cr, or minimum turnover of ₹ 1000 cr, or profit of at least ₹ 5 cr in a year will have to have spent 2% of its average profits of three years on CSR. According to a study conducted by Social Research and Reform Foundation in middle of the year 2013, the CSR spending by top 100 listed firms in India is a mere

₹ 2300 crore, which is around 0.82% of their net profits. The study said that CSR investment is led by the Reliance Industries Ltd. that spent around ₹ 357 crore during 2012-13. Other leading firms with high CSR spend include Tata Steel (₹ 146 crore), SBI (₹ 123 crore) and ICICI (117 crore). CSR is no longer optional for business. Some major companies are tying its CSR efforts to its core mission. Company spent ₹ 36145 crore on CSR in 2019-21.

Amazon founder and the world's richest person Jeff Bezos said on 17.02.2020 that he plans to spend $10 billion of his own fortune to start giving grants to scientists, activists and non-profit organizations to protect Earth from the devastating impact of climate change.

Infosys, an IT company's social responsibilities include the following:

- Companies should be fair to the employees.
- There should be fair disclosure of accounts to investors to attract capital from them.
- Companies should be ethical to the government by paying taxes regularly.
- Its strategic plan includes social consciousness that helps managers in making decisions.
- It formed Infosys Foundation to assist health care, primary education, social rehabilitation, rural upliftment, art, and culture.

Infosys spends about ₹ 80 million on CSR. On the other hand, public sector companies are taking very less initiatives for CSR.

The companies are using natural resources of the country and polluting the environment in return they have to give something to the society. It is observed that companies with high revenue are taking more initiatives and small companies are not active in discharging their duties towards CSR. Views differ on the degree to which business should consider CSR in conducting its affairs.

Arguments for Social Responsibility

Justification for existence and growth: Business exists for providing goods and services to satisfy human needs. The prosperity and growth of business is possible only through continuous service to society. Thus, assumption of social responsibility by business provides justifications for its existence and growth.

1. *Long-term interest of the firm:* There are many firms that believe that CSR can prove to bring good business to them in the long-run. Some firms are strategic, as engaging in CSR activities will create competitive advantage for the firm and make it a differentiated company for reputation in public brings more revenues to the firm and thus it is a win-win situation for the company as well as for the community.

2. *Avoidance of government regulations:* From the point of view of a business, government regulations are undesirable because they limit freedom. Therefore, it is believed that business can avoid the problem of government regulations by voluntarily assuming social responsibility, which helps to reduce the need for new laws.

3. *Maintenance of society:* The argument here is that laws cannot be passed for all possible circumstances. People who feel that they are not getting their due from the business may resort to anti-social activities, not necessarily governed by law. This may harm the interest of business itself. Therefore, it is desirable that business enterprises assume social responsibilities.

4. *Availability of resources with business:* Business has a pool of management talent and capital resources, supported by years of experience in organizing the business. It can help society to tackle its problems better, given the huge financial and human resources at its disposal.

5. *Improvement of social balance:* Organizations have the social and moral responsibility to correct the social problems (such as air and water pollution) that organizations create.

Arguments against Social Responsibility

1. *Violation of profit maximization:* Economist Milton Friedman (1970) viewed that the firm is to make profit for the

shareholders. The firm has no right to spend a portion of profit for social purpose. There are government and philanthropists to carry out social activities.

2. ***Burden on consumers:*** It is argued that social responsibilities like pollution control and environmental protection are very costly and often require huge financial investments. In such circumstances, businessmen are likely to simply shift this burden of social responsibility by charging higher prices from the consumers instead of bearing it themselves. Therefore, it is unfair to tax the consumers in the name of social responsibility.

3. ***Lack of social skills:*** Skills of earning of profit and functions related to societal welfare are incompatible and may lead to the demise of business. Hence, it is advisable to avoid too much involvement in social activities.

3.5 SOCIAL AUDIT

One important issue related to social responsibility of business is how to evaluate the social performance of the firm. It is done through social audit. It involves:

1. Identify the firm's activities having potential social impact.
2. Assess and evaluate the social costs and social benefits of such activities.
3. Measure the social costs and benefits as far as possible in financial terms. It may be a social balance sheet with a "credit" side and "debit" side for inputs (costs) and outputs (benefits) in line with an ordinary commercial audit.
4. Reporting in a self-explanatory format.

The first comprehensive social audit in India was conducted by the Tata Steel in 1980. It was conducted by the Social Audit Committee appointed by the Board of Directors of the company, "to examine and report whether, and the extent to which, the company has fulfilled the objectives contained in Clause 3A of its Articles of Association regarding its social and moral responsibilities to the consumers, employees, shareholders, society and the local community." The report of the committee was a glowing tribute to the endeavours of the company in discharge of its social and moral obligations to the various segments of the society.

Companies, undoubtedly, are poised to play a critical role now, more than ever, in ensuring that India's Corporate Sector actively provides the economic strength to the nation besides joining the hands of government to fulfill the aspirations of common people lived around the environment. Information is necessary to assess welfare measures to society undertaken by the company. This information is although available in the company's annual reports, press releases, advertisements, etc., it lacks the essential social and environmental information. Though several reporting models were proposed, none of them were comprehensive enough. The social reporting model tries to overcome these deficiencies by including all costs and benefits in India.

Tata Steel has, for example, undertaken an excise of social audit of its social allocation. Later on, some companies like Cement Corporation of India, Infosys, RIL, BHEL, ONGC, etc. have been annexing social audit report in their Annual Reports.

3.6 ETHICS

The word 'ethics' has its origin in the Greek word 'ethos' meaning character; norms, ideals or morals prevailing in a group or society. Ethics is a set of standards and code of conduct that defines what is right, wrong, and just in human actions. Managers' decisions and actions affect the health, safety, moral, motivation, and behaviour of all organization members, as well as many stakeholders outside of the organization.

Raymond Baumhart has defined Ethics: It is conforming to principles of human conduct. According to common usage, the following terms are more or less synonymous with ethical—moral good, right, just, honest. In the words of Philip Wheelwright, "Ethics is that branch of philosophy which is the systemic study of selective choice, of the standards of right or wrong by which it may ultimately be directed." According to Peter F. Drucker, "there is only one ethics, one set of rules of morality, one code, that of individual behaviour in which the same rules apply to everyone alike." He further suggested that ethics deals with the right actions of individuals.

Ethical standards: principles or ideals of human conduct. In business, ethics refers to application of moral values, accepted character and behaviour to all business activities, dealings, offers, practices and such other issues. Business ethics influences various business activities as under:

- Business ethical policies and practices influence and shape the individual ethics, characters and behaviour. Ethics of any profession is unselfish service to mankind, not service to self. For example, HR professional can and should seek to achieve professionalisation through a higher standard of performance marked by better outlook, attitude, and practice.
- The ethical standards of the top management influence decisions at all levels. When any decision is in the knowledge of all concerned, no one gets any opportunity to do unethical act.
- The business ethics influences the functions of departments.
- Ethics and profit: Ethics and profit go together. A businessman who is inspired by ethical conduct may take profit as bye-product.

Ethical standards are often enacted into laws. But ethical behaviour is just and fair conduct which goes beyond observing laws and government regulations. Where law fails, ethics can succeed. Business ethics concerns itself with the relationship between business objectives, practices, and techniques and the good of society. Business ethics refer to the socially determined moral principles which should govern business activities. A few examples of business ethics are charging fair prices from customers, using fair weights for measurement of commodities, giving fair treatment to workers and earning reasonable profits. A businessperson behaves ethically when his actions are upright and serve the interest of society.

Elements of Business Ethics: Some of the basic elements of business ethics which can foster ethics in the employees are as under:

(i) **Top management commitment towards ethically upright behaviour:** They must give continuous leadership for development and upholding the ethical values of the organization.

(ii) **Publication of an ethics code:** Enterprises do define the principles of conduct for the whole organization in the form of written documents which is referred to as the "code". This generally develops on the basis of theological principles, such as, service, human welfare, sincerity, good behaviour, fundamental honesty and adherence to law; product safety and quality; health and safety in the workplace; conflicts of interest; employment practices; fairness in selling/marketing practices, financial reporting, etc.

(iii) **Establishment of compliance mechanisms:** In order to ensure that actual decisions and actions comply with the firm's ethical standards, suitable mechanisms should be established. Some examples of such mechanisms are: paying attention to values and ethics in recruiting and hiring; emphasizing corporate ethics in training; auditing performance regularly to analyse the degree of compliance; and instituting communication systems to help employees report incidents of unethical behaviour.

(iv) **Involving employees at all levels:** It is the employees at different levels who implement ethics policies to make ethical business a reality. Therefore, their involvement in ethics programmes becomes must. For example, an ethics committee can be formed to discuss the important ethics policies of firms and examine attitudes of employees towards these policies.

(v) **Measuring results through ethics audit:** Although it is difficult to accurately measure the end results of ethics programmes, the firms can certainly audit to monitor compliance with ethical standards. The top management team and other employees should then discuss the results for further course of action.

Until the recent past, the primary concern of the business enterprise was the profit ethics. Profits were considered to be the greatest incentive and a reasonable return on investment is essential to maintain and improve production. Wages linked to the net productive contribution of the workers are favoured by them, as an incentive for improved productivity and as a matter of simple justice. Businessmen also believe that increased production would lead to a higher standard of living and that the interests of both the labour and the capital must be in harmony. Therefore, the fundamental purpose of their efforts is to make profits. It is also a useful index to measure the efficiency of an enterprise. However, sole dependence on profit is now slowly changing on account of the changed value system and the changed role of government, social institutions and trade unions. With the changed situation, the objective of all economic activities is to contribute to human happiness and it is only an integrated, contented and socially cohesive society that could help to realize cherished-national objectives.

Profit is like health. We need it, and the more the better. But it's not why we exist. Of late, we found that companies whose only articulated goals are financial, they are not doing nearly as well financially as companies that have broader set of values. The benevolent culture and shared values are important in unifying the social dimensions of organizations. It is not just about the creation of wealth, it is about the creation of a better humanity, because business is, and always has been, about society and people who lived in it.

Trusteeship: Mahatma Gandhi sought to balance the economic interests of the organization with its social obligations by formulating the concept of trusteeship. According to the concept of trusteeship, those who had the possession of property were thus to consider themselves as trustees; but they were not to be its primary, let alone exclusive, beneficiaries. No one was to keep more to himself than he needed; everyone was to work according to his capacity and to receive according to his real need. This theory of trusteeship might seem a rationalization of the privileged position of the princes, landlords and business magnets. In fact, it was a radical theory which called for voluntary sacrifices from the 'haves' in the interest of 'have-nots'. It may be useful to classify an enterprise's responsibility on two facets—with the organization and the other with the society.

The Corporation and its Employees: Besides, welfare measures as deemed by legislations, the corporation has the social obligation to provide a number of welfare measures in the area where it is situated. The objective of the personnel function is to obtain individual employee satisfaction and harmonious industrial relations together with production/productivity. The personnel function offers many instances where improvements have been made in recent past in respect of wages, working conditions, welfare and job security reflecting, to some extent, the rising standards of ethics in business. Many now seem to see the desirable benefits to the corporation through formulating corporate policies and practices—if a corporation is concerned about obligations or social responsibilities to its employees. Social responsibility is concerned with the functions, programmes and policies of an enterprise, whereas the business ethics is related with the conduct and behaviour of businessmen. But, in practice, social responsibility of business and its policies are influenced by business ethics. The several areas are personnel selection, training and development, job design and wage and salary administration. The objective studies with professional ethics will certainly improve the productivity. These are shown below:

Personnel Selection: Selection is a process of searching of suitable personnel for the organization. It requires application of right kind of selection method, transparency at all stages and will have to select right type of personnel for right job at right time. We discuss the following ethical issues involved in personnel selection:

(a) Selecting the man to the job or job to the man: Selecting the man to the job is right approach and is expected. But, adjusting the job specification to suit a particular candidate's qualifications and experience due to some reasons is unethical practice.

(b) Selecting the unsuitable candidates due to recommendations and, or pressures. The selection of such unsuitable personnel due to pressure is not only increase the strength but also effecting efficiency of operation.

(c) Selecting the number of candidates more than that of required due to pressures: In this case, a greater number of candidates are appointed to accommodate their candidates. Besides pressures, probably money also plays a role in the selections.

A Relevant Case

ABC Foods India, a public sector company advertised for a post of Jt. GM (Personnel). For search and selection, the company hired M/S Desire Search India Ltd.—a recruiting agency. They shortlisted 10 applications including two internal applications from Mr. M.K. Johari and S. Deo, who are working as Asstt. GM (IR & Welfare) and Asstt. GM (HRD). Mr. Johari has been working in the same position since 2003 while Mr. Deo has been working since 2002. The management of the company is pressurized by the recognized trade union to select Mr. Johari while concern ministry has indicated that management should follow the seniority. Management, after protected deliberations, decided to create a new post in the same grade as Additional GM (HRD) and accordingly Mr. Johari and Mr. Deo both were promoted to higher grade. Following questions of ethics on the act of the management arise:

1. Was it necessary to hire a recruiting agency? Whether money has also played a role?
2. Whether it is a question of induction of fresh blood and experienced person from similar industries? If so, why no outside candidate was selected? Was the selection an eye wash? What happened to the image of management in the eyes of candidates applied for the post?

3. Was it not necessary to withstand the pressures of trade union and ministry as the post was at higher level and the merit should alone be the criteria for the selection?

A whistle-blower is an employee who reports that someone within the organization has engaged in an illegal, immoral, unethical, or illegitimate act to those who may be able to take appropriate action. When a whistle-blower goes to an outside person or organization, unfavourable publicity, legal investigations, and lawsuits often result. In order to persuade employees to blow the whistle inside an organization rather than to the press or to regulatory agencies, many organizations have set up systems to handle internal complaints. Some companies have an ombudsperson, whose job includes soliciting and dealing with whistle blowing in-house.

Types of Managerial Ethics

Managerial ethics are standards of conduct or moral judgment used by managers in carrying out their business. Such standards arise from the general norms and values of society; from an individual's experiences within family, religious, educational, and other types of institutions; and through the process of socialization. Therefore, managerial ethics may differ among individuals. An eminent researcher, B. Carrol, notes that there are three levels of moral, amoral and immoral behaviour of managers.

Immoral management is prevalent in managers pursuing unethical behaviour. This perspective is characterized by principal concern for company gains, emphasis on profits and company success at virtually any price, lack of concern about others' desire, and a view of laws as obstacles to be overcome.

Amoral management approach is neither immoral nor moral but, rather, ignore or is oblivious to ethical considerations. Amoral managers pursue profitability as a goal and pay little attention to the impact of their behaviour on others. They generally leave other managers free to behave as they wish unless their behaviour leads to outside notoriety or pressure.

Such managers think whether we make money with this decision or action within the letter of the law.

Moral management strives to follow ethical principles and the ideals of fairness, justice, and due process. Moral managers pursue business objectives that involve simultaneously making a profit and engaging in legal and ethical behaviours. They follow not only the letter but also the spirit of the law even at times well above the law. The central guiding principle of moral management is: "Is this action, decision, or behaviour fair to us and all parties involved?" Carroll believes that a moral management stance is more likely to be in the long-run best interests of organization.

Following are a few ethical guidelines for managers commonly used for ethical decision-making:

- Obey the law.
- Tell the truth.
- Show respect for people.
- Stick to the Golden Rule: "Do to others as you would have others do to you."
- Above all, do not harm. This principle—the rule of medical ethics—is considered to be bottom-line ethical consideration and one easily adaptable to business.
- Practice participation, not paternalism. This principle is aimed to elicit the views of all concerned before finalizing any plan of action.
- Always act when you have responsibility or capacity or resources to take action.

REVIEW QUESTIONS

Long Questions

1. What do you mean by corporate social responsibility? Why have they acquired added importance in India?
2. What are the basic social obligations of management? Do this conflict with the profit objective?

3. Explain the three major perspectives on social responsibility. Describe which one is more suitable in the context of Indian companies.
4. Build up arguments for and against social responsibilities of business.
5. Define management ethics. In what way ethics influences business activities?
6. "A tool available for assessing the firm's social responsiveness is social audit." Explain.

Short Questions

1. What do you understand by social responsibility of business? How is it different from legal responsibility?
2. What are the major areas of social responsibility of business?
3. Distinguish among the three major types of management ethics.
4. Describe some basic elements of business ethics which can foster ethics in employees.

Short Notes

1. B. Carroll model of corporate performance
2. Barriers to social responsibility
3. Whistle-blower
4. Ethics code
5. Social Audit

Chapter 4
Planning Function

4.1 INTRODUCTION

For any organization, planning function is first and primary function of management. Planning systematizes regarding what to do, when to do, where to do, who is to do and how to do. It precedes all managerial functions and control is an inseparable part of planning. Planning is an ongoing process of deciding in advance the activities to be performed. It bridges the gap between the organization's present existence and its future prospects. Proper planning minimizes risk and helps in effective and efficient utilization of resources.

4.2 MEANING AND DEFINITIONS OF PLANNING

Planning is the process by which managers in advance establish goals/objectives and specify how these goals are to be achieved. It deals with framing organizational objectives and deciding means to achieve them. It is done for all departments and sections of the organization. While top managers plan for the whole organization, middle-level managers plan for their respective departments and lower-level managers plan for their sections. Planning is a special kind of decision-making which involves forecasting, laying down objectives of the organization, thinking of different courses of action and deciding one of those to achieve the goals. Definitions of planning given by some eminent management thinkers are given below.

Peter Drucker defined planning as "a continuous process of making present entrepreneurial decision (risk taking) systematically and with best possible knowledge of their futurity, organizing systematically the efforts needed to carry out these decisions and measuring the result of those decisions against the expectations through an organized feedback."

According to Koontz and O'Donnel, "Planning is an intellectual process, conscious determination of courses of action, the basing of decisions on purpose, acts and considered estimates."

Terry and Franklin: "Planning is selecting information and making assumptions regarding the future to formulate activities necessary achieve organizational objectives."

Alford and Beatty: "Planning is thinking process, the organized foresight, the vision based on fact and experience that is required for intelligent action." Thus, major components of planning are mission, goals or objectives, and plans.

4.3 FEATURES OF PLANNING

1. Planning is primary function of management. For efficient functioning of organization, planning process must be tackled with utmost care and zeal. Other functions like organizing, staffing, leading and control would be sub-ordinate to planning.

2. Planning is a continuous process. It is looking into future so that whatever changes in environment in terms of economic policies, competitors' strength, value system of society, etc. is to be adopted for survival of the organization.

3. Planner first sets goal, i.e., future target or end result that an organization wishes to achieve.

4. Planning is all-pervasive function. It is carried out for all organizations—business and non-business, profit motive and non-profit motive, small and big.

5. Plan must be flexible so that it withstands the future jerk. As such plan must provide in-built contingencies for changes in technology, market finance and competitors. Planning discovers the most suitable alternative for the company out of available many alternatives. Thus, planning encourages innovation and creativity which are prerequisites to continuous growth and steady prosperity of business.

6. Planning is done for specific period.

7. Planning integrates various activities of organization where all the managers are involved.

8. Planning involves decision-making. Managers decide goals out of various goals and how to achieve them considering available resources under their command.

9. Control is part of planning. Control has an eye over its implementation of desired goals during a period through systematic feedback. Any deviation in terms of goals, resources, and timeliness is reported to all concerns for corrective action.

4.4 IMPORTANCE/OBJECTIVES OF PLANNING

1. **Reduce risk and uncertainty:** Planning is for later date. As such it is sensitized with environmental uncertainty. This includes uncertainty in financial, technology, social, competitors and prevailing laws even global situation. During planning, these factors are addressed carefully to minimize the effect of them during entire planning period so that stipulated goals are achieved with the minimum variation which can be tackled with ease. Planning does not deal with future decisions, but with the futurity of present decisions.

2. When business is planned and not random or adhoc, success is in more cases as compared to not planned.

3. In planning, managers set goals against which actual performance can be measured. Any deviation between goals and performance would be reported for timely corrections during planning period. This is called effective control of measures.

4. Planning is also an excellent means for training executives. They become involved in entire process of planning arising interest in owning the business.

4.5 PREREQUISITES FOR EFFECTIVE PLANNING

1. Establishing the right climate for planning like setting goals, proper information flow, remove obstacles/barriers, and effective implementation.

2. Having measurable specific objectives.

3. Planning premises, i.e., clear identification of internal and external environment with their assumptions with respect

to manpower, technology-based operation, sales volume, price, products, etc.

4. The top level taking the initiative. Managers of all levels—corporate, division, department and sectional level participating in the planning process.

5. Communicating the planning process to all the employees of the organization.

6. Integrating long-term and short-term plans.

7. Having an effective management information system including communication of essential information.

4.6 TYPES OF PLANS

Managers create many types of plans at organization level. These may be classified as hierarchical, frequency of use, time-frame and function levels.

Classification of Plans: Diagrammatic Representation

Types of Plans

Hierarchical	Frequency of use	Time-frame	Functional level
1. Strategic 2. Tactical 3. Operational	1. Single-use (a) Programmes (b) Budgets (c) Projects	1. Long-term 2. Medium-term 3. Short-term	1. Production 2. Marketing 3. Financial
	2. Standing (a) Policies (b) Procedures (c) Rules		

Strategic plans: Strategic plans are long-term plans meant for entire organization. They articulate the organization's mission and overall objectives and analyse various environmental factors that affect the organization. Strategic plans are developed by top management in consultation with the Board of Directors and with middle management.

Mission: Plans build on the mission. A mission statement is a broad outline of the basic, unique purpose and scope of operations that keeps the organization apart from others of its type. For example, the mission of a business organization is to provide products to consumers at a profit, in a manner consistent with corporate ethics and responsibilities. Mission statements may have the following eight components:

1. *Markets and customers* that the organization intends to serve.
2. *Products or services* provided by the organization.
3. *Technology* of the organization.
4. *Concern for survival*, i.e., organization's commitment to economic objectives.
5. *Philosophy* in terms of basic beliefs, core values, aspirations of the organization.
6. *Unique concept* in terms of major strengths and competitive advantages.
7. *Concern for public image.* What are organization's public responsibilities, and what image is desired?
8. *Concern for employees* in terms of compensation and overall attitude toward employees.

A mission statement should be prepared with the following guidelines:

1. Mission should be clear and easily understood by all employees, customers and public at large.
2. It should be challenging but achievable standards, neither too high nor too low.
3. It should be precise and attractive to read but covering major component of objectives.
4. The mission statement is stable over time and intent to win in the competitive environment. It means it contains two parts, i.e., one core values with core purpose which is stable for a long time, even if it were a disadvantage whereas second part is vivid objectives to win in the competitive environment.

Excerpt from McDonald's mission statement—it reads, "Be the best employer for our people in each community around the world and deliver operational excellence to our customers in each of our restaurants."

Tactical Plan: Middle-level managers develop tactical plans that support top-level strategic plans. In developing the tactical plans, managers consider a number of possibilities to develop the plans which are more specific and concrete than strategic plans.

Operational Plans: Lower-level managers in consultation with middle managers develop operational plans to support implementation of tactical plans and achievement of operational goals.

Single-use plans: Plans aimed at achieving a specific goal that, once reached, will most likely not recur in the future. There are two major types of single-use plans: programs and projects.

A **program** is a comprehensive plan that coordinates a complex set of activities related to a major non-recurring goal. Programs involve several different departments or units of the organization, are composed of several different projects, and may take more than one year to complete. Programs usually include six basic steps: (1) dividing what is to be done into major parts, or projects, (2) determining the relationships among the parts and developing a sequence, (3) deciding who will take responsibility for each part, (4) determining how each part will be completed and what resources will be necessary, (5) estimating the time required for completion of each part, and (6) developing a schedule for implementing each step. Programs frequently have their own budgets. A *budget* is a statement that outlines the financial resources needed to support the various activities included in the program.

A **project** is a plan that coordinates a set of limited scope activities that do not need to be divided into several major projects in order to reach an important non-recurring goal. Like program, projects often have their own budgets. A project may be one of several related to a particular program.

Standing Plans are plans that provide ongoing guidance for performing recurring activities. The three main types of standing plans are policies, procedures, and rules.

Policies: A policy is a general statement of understanding or intent. It guides decision making. It permits the exercise of some discretion. It guides behaviour (for example, no employee shall accept favour and/or entertainment from an outside organization). It specifies the broad parameters within which organization members are expected to operate in pursuit of organizational goal.

Principles of Policy Making

(i) A policy should be based on objectives. It includes procedures, rules, budgets, and programs.

(ii) A policy should be carefully developed which would be clear and definite and easily understandable.

(iii) A policy must prescribe the criteria for current and future action. It should provide general boundaries for action.

(iv) A policy should ensure uniformity of managerial decision-making in respect of various matters so that decision will be consistent every time it comes up.

(v) Policies should speed up decisions at various levels of management. These are guidelines to take further decisions to deal with the problem arises.

(vi) Policies should make it easier for the superior to delegate more and more authority to his subordinates because he knows that whatever decision the subordinates make it will be in accordance with policies.

(vii) Policies should be stable as well as flexible.

All policies should be communicated to the people who are to implement them and should be formulated in consultation with them.

Policies should be just, fair, and equitable without discriminating among employees on the basis of religion, sex, caste or creed.

Policies should be reviewed and revised periodically to keep them up-to-date.

Types of Policies: Policies may be classified on the basis of sources, functions or organizational levels.

(a) *Classification on the basis of sources/origin:*
(i) Originated policy—it is a policy formulated by

top management on their own initiative in order to guide decision-making at lower-level subordinates. These policies are part of policy manual. (ii) Applied policy—it is a policy formulation on the request or appeal made by lower-level managers to take decision with an issue not covered by originated policies. It is developed when existing policies are insufficient to solve the problem. They become precedents for taking decision in such cases in future. For example—give 2% discount if purchased in bulk say 1000 units. (iii) implied policies—these are generally oral understanding that can be inferred from the decisions of designated managers in specific situations. For example, if office cabin is repeatedly allotted to individual on the basis of seniority, this may become an implied policy of organization.

(b) *Classification on the basis of functions:* (i) Production—production/productivity policy, inspection and quality control policy. (ii) Marketing—pricing policy, advertising policy, discount policy. (iii) Finance—credit policy. (iv) Personnel—recruitment policy, promotion policy.

(c) *Classification on the basis of organizational levels:* Policies are formulated ranging from major company level policies through major departmental policies to unit level policies.

Procedure: Policies are carried out by means of more detailed guidelines called procedure. A procedure is a prescribed series of related steps of instructions in a chronological sequence involved in doing a certain organizational matter under certain recurring circumstances. For example, the procedure for applying for sick leave to the employees or issuing of items from stores. Well-established and formalized procedures are often called *standard operating procedures* (SOPs). Unlike policies, which tend to be fairly general, procedures provide detailed step by step instructions to be followed by one and all to accomplish a particular task recur in each and every time. Thus, they do not allow much flexibility or deviation.

Advantages of Procedures

(i) It provides a well-defined way of work without any confusion. Thus, it makes the work simple.

(ii) It results in work simplification and elimination of unnecessary and overlapping steps with a view to do the work fast. Thus, it improves organizational efficiency and employee satisfaction.

(iii) It relieves the top managers from rudimentary work thereby they may concentrate on more important activities.

(iv) Well-defined procedures provide consistency and uniformity of actions.

Limitations of Procedures

(i) They are inflexible. They cannot be easily changed.

(ii) As they are inflexible, they limit the initiative and creativity of employees.

(iii) By cutting across department lines and extending into various other departments they sometimes result into duplication, overlapping and conflict.

The above limitations can, however, be overcome if procedure should be implemented in the right earnest and reviewed periodically taking into the account of suggestions and situations in a constructive manner.

Rules: Rules are simplest type of plans that require specific, definite action. A rule is a statement that spells out specific actions to be taken or not taken in a given situation. Unlike procedures, rules do not normally specify a series of steps. Instead, they dictate exactly what must be or must not be done, leaving little flexibility or room for deviation. Rules must be in writing. They are not subject to managerial discretion and are, therefore, non-flexible. Rules may or may not form part of procedure. It is not a procedure because there is no time sequence to a particular action. It is mandatory on the part of employees to abide the rules. For example, employees have to follow the office timing as prescribed by rules.

4.7 PROCESS OF PLANNING

Planning process includes the following eight steps for formulating any major or derivative plan. However, it may be necessary at each step to look back at the earlier step and decide whatever it needs to be modified due to the prevailing contingency.

Step 1: Analysing opportunities: In the light of market, competition, their strengths and weaknesses, managers continuously keep up-to-date with changes in the external environment in order to investigate possible future opportunities, understand what problems they need to solve, and know what they expect to gain and accordingly decide the realistic objectives.

Step 2: Establishing objectives: For the organization and its divisions. Organization objectives provide direction to plans.

Objectives are to be set for the long-term as well as for the short-term. This is done for the entire organization including its divisions. Objectives form a network of strategies, tactical and operational objectives. Strategic objectives state what the organization would like to accomplish in terms of profits/assets, market share, growth, etc. while operational objectives are defined to control internal resources for example, cost control, output, employee turnover, etc. strategic objectives operate in an external environment having little control over it. While operational objectives, on the other hand, operate in an internal environment over which it can exercise considerable control.

Step 3: Determining one planning—premises. In what environment—internal or external—will our plans operate?

Premises are assumptions about the future environment in which the plan is to be carried out. Planning premises are classified as under:

- Internal and external premises.
- Tangible and intangible premises.

Internal and external premises. Premises may exist within and outside the company. Important internal premises include sales forecasts, policies and programs of the organization, capital investment in plant and machineries, and personnel forecasts. They are being managed by the company and thus can be controlled. The external premises are to be decided on the basis of studies of environmental forecasting regarding kind of market, demand of products, volume of sales, type of technologies, taxation, government policies, wages, etc. For this, managers should keep themselves abreast of various forecasting techniques for which information may be drawn from different sources, example, The *Economic Survey*, *Business Week*, *Business India*, *Wall Street Journal*, etc. These external premises are non-controllable because these lie beyond the control of a business enterprise. Managers analyse strengths and weaknesses of internal resources combined with environmental analysis of opportunities and threats of external factors. This technique is known as SWOT analysis.

Tangible and intangible premises: Some of the planning premises may be tangible while others may be intangible. Tangible premises are those which can be estimated in quantitative terms like production units, cost per unit, population growth, industry demand and resources invested, etc. On the other hand, intangible premises like goodwill of the firm, political and sociological factors, business and economic environment, employer-employee relationship, leadership, etc. cannot be quantified in exact form.

Step 4: Identifying alternatives. Explore many promising alternatives to achieve objectives.

Course of action determine how an organization will get from its current position to its desired future. Important is to search for alternative courses of action especially those not immediately apparent. There is seldom a plan for which reasonable alternatives do not exist, and quite often an alternative that is not obvious prove to be the best. The planner can use decision support systems to examine and reduce the number of trivial alternatives to a limited extent.

Step 5: Weighing alternatives. In the light of premises as well as objectives, decide alternatives which give optimum results.

Alternatives are weighed in the light of premises and goals. For example, an alternative may appear to be the most profitable but may suffer from the need for a large cash outlay; another may look less profitable in the short-term, but the returns may be cumulatively high in the long-run. Many variables in terms of risk and future objectives as well as limitations, both external and internal have to be studied. Though many methodologies and applications of operations research, mathematical and computing techniques are helpful, yet the uncertainty of environment, make the task of evaluation extremely difficult.

Step 6: Selecting the best alternative/plan. Deciding the most appropriate course of action/plan to execute.

The real point of decision-making is to select the most suitable alternative/plan which is to execute. Further, two or more supportive plans are formulated keeping in mind the unpredictability of the future.

Step 7: Implementing the best plan. Putting plan into operation.

At implementing stage, managers take a series of decisions in order to remove stumbling blocks.

Step 8: Reviewing the plan. Do course correction based on feedback to remove deviations.

Managers review and revise continuously based on feedback to bridge the gap between where it wants to go and its current position. Doing this is far easier than to correct inconsistencies.

Limitations of Planning

Though planning is beneficial and inevitable, it is not free from certain limitations:

1. Planning is costly and time consuming. In spite of that there is no guarantee of benefits as envisaged.
2. If information with respect to production, productivity, resources, futuristic indices, etc. provided to the planners is inaccurate or irrelevant, the quality of planning suffers.
3. Moreover, planning suffers from difficulty of formulating accurate premises. Since these premises

are the backbone for setting plans, they necessarily deal with the future. Since the future cannot be known with accuracy, premising must be subject to a margin of error.

4. Planning makes mindset in a specific direction curbing the initiatives of brilliant minds of middle managers. That is why it requires a high level of imagination, analytical ability, creativity and fortitude to choose and become committed.
5. Planning leads to probable results and not assured planned goals.
6. If planned goals are multiple to take care of large eventuality the scare resources then thinly distributed over them affecting achievement of goals.
7. When plans are made, management people think organization is secured for future uncertainty. But, this is not true. It gives a sense of false confidence in the minds of members of organization and slows down action. This may be harmful for the organization.
8. Planning does not give any benefits to an organization during emergency period. Spot decision dominates the planning. If planning is followed during the emergency period, there will be a possibility of delay in performing the work.
9. Tools of planning such as forecasting methods, statistical data supplied, political climate, technological changes, etc. if not done accurately then planning becomes limited.

REVIEW QUESTIONS

Long Questions

1. Discuss how a firm uses its planning process to position itself as global business.
2. Define planning. Discuss the limitations of planning. What steps can be taken to make planning effective?
3. Describe the universal steps involved in planning process.

Short Questions

1. Describe the types of plans mentioning special feature of single-use plan.
2. Define policies. Describe the principles of policy making.
3. Describe internal and external premises.

Short Notes

1. Procedures and rules, 2. Types of policies, 3. Kinds of single use plan

CASE STUDY

Hi-Protein Foods Ltd. is selling processed chicken products, i.e., pre-plated, ready to cook products. They propagated the concept of processed chicken products with the launch of 'heat and eat' meal-microwaving the items for two minutes before eating. The company launched three common varieties—butter chicken, chicken wings, and keema. The objective was outlined as catering to the officegoers, which had a time constraint, with high protein foods of the high quality and at reasonable price. The company analyzed the external environment to evaluate opportunities in the market.

The company then determined the premises, i.e., the market where the product would be launched first. The company's objective is to earn ROI @15%. In the meantime, the global outbreak of the covid-19 pandemic has caused disruption in restaurant sector. The company decided to change the market strategy. Instead of on the self-selling they have sold the items online selling through Zomato and Swiggy. In view of the situation, they have added vegetarian food like Paneer Dum Biryani and oats mushroom palaao with a slogan 'EAT HEALTHY'.

To work towards attaining the company's objective, the company test marketed the product before a full-scale launch. The company then determined the premises, i.e., the market where working couples reside, their population, general economic conditions, production costs and prices and probable competitive behaviour, the product would be launched first. After evaluating the response in the test market, the company implemented the plan by launching the product on a full scale. After reviewing the plan, the manager concluded that the company was showing a targeted growth of 10% and that it expected to grow at a much faster rate. Due to present scenario, the company has decided a plan of three-year period in this period, the company would also find alternative courses to have a better growth and ROI for the company.

Questions

1. Analyse the case in terms of its objectives.
2. What was the company's vision that helped the company turn into reality?
3. What are the internal and external premises on the basis of which the plan will be ultimately formulated?
4. How would the company has dealt with such a situation in the context of long-term planning?
4. Develop a mechanism for measuring and controlling the progress of plan.

Chapter 5
Objectives

5.1 INTRODUCTION

Defining objectives of the organization is an inherent part of effective managerial planning. Objectives are measurable organizational and individual activities organization sought to achieve. Objectives define organizational purpose, motivate accomplishment, and provide a yardstick against which actual performance can be measured.

Objectives are set and, in a way, they define what the organization has to achieve for its employees, shareholders, customers, etc. Objectives are defined keeping in mind with the internal strengths and weaknesses and external environment. Objectives are framed in line with the vision/mission of the organization. Objectives become the basis for strategic decision-making, as the strategies need to be formulated and implemented for achieving the objectives. Objectives are invariably quantitative. They provide clear measures and standards for performance. So they help in appraisal, to see if the organization is on the right track or not.

5.2 CHARACTERISTICS OF OBJECTIVES

In order that objectives be understood, so that the employees will be able to pursue them, objectives should have the following characteristics:

- Understandable
- Concrete and specific
- Measurable
- Challenging, not easily achievable
- Have a clearly defined time frame
- Actionable
- Controllable
- Correlate with different objectives

Targets on turnover, profit and market share form part of a firm's objectives. A company which had a ₹ 400 crores turnover, laid down the objectives of becoming a ₹ 550 crores company in the next three years with at least 10% growth each year and market share of over 25%.

Factors to be Considered

When setting objectives, the following factors need to be carefully evaluated:

1. Specific and Measurable: Objectives need to be specific and measurable so that employees clearly understood what is expected and know how the objective has been achieved. When possible, objectives should be stated in quantitative terms. Quantitative objectives encompass numerical standards that are relatively easy to verify. For example, production target of a shoe company would be 7000 pairs of shoes every month is a specific and measurable goal which can be verified. An objective of 'increase in sales' has no meaning unless it says increase in sales quantified by 10%. Qualitative objectives involve subjective judgment such as is to an idea for development of prototype of a new product that is useful, long lasting and inexpensive. This type of objective cannot be accurately measured. However, for some purposes, qualitative objectives are more appropriate. Further, the list of objectives should not be too long, yet it should cover the main features of the job.

2. Multiple Objectives and Hierarchy of Objectives: Objectives invariably are for different performance areas, hence they need to be multiplicity of objectives. A well-known management scholar, consultant, and writer, Drucker believes that to achieve organizational success, managers must try to achieve multiple goals simultaneously—namely market standing, innovation, productivity, profitability, physical and financial resources, manager performance and development, employee performance and attitude, and public responsibility. Sometimes departments within the organization may pursue goals that actually conflict with the goals of other departments. The marketing goal, for example, might conflict with the production department's goal of efficiency. Managers must strive to integrate the network of goals and resolve internal conflicts when they arise.

An organization sets organizational/corporate-level, divisional-level, departmental-level, sectional-level, and individual-related goals. These levels of goals form a means—ends chain where goals at lower-levels provide a means for attaining the ends (goals) at the higher level. This is called goal hierarchy and managers must make sure that lower-level goals combine to achieve higher-level goals. Interrelationship among objectives at different levels is shown below:

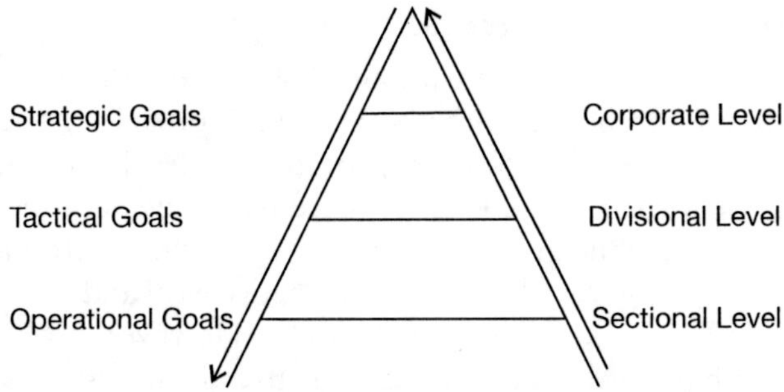

Periodicity—need to formulate different time frames, typically short-term, medium-term, and long-term and should linked and consistent.

Environments—are the objectives taking into account the environment. Also need to check whether they are fulfilling the needs of stakeholders in the business, like customers, shareholders, employees, suppliers, etc.

Reality—are the objectivity looking at the reality of the organization's resources and internal constraints, including policy and power relationships.

5.3 SETTING OF OBJECTIVES

Setting of objectives is important part of effective managerial planning. Setting of goals is specialized jobs for all managers. It requires intelligent guidance by superior and extensive practice by the subordinate. Organizational objectives are of multiple characters. Peter Drucker—a well-known management consultant—believes in multiple goals, namely market standing, innovation, productivity, profitability, physical and financial resources, manager performance and development, employee performance and attitude, and public responsibility. The list of objectives should not be too broad yet it should cover the main features of the job.

Managers at different levels in the organizational hierarchy are concerned with different kinds of objectives. Top managers are very much concerned with strategic level while divisional and department levels are involved in determining tactical level and operational levels have job-related objectives. In the process, managers must make sure that lower-level objectives combine to achieve higher-level objectives.

There are different views about whether an organization should use the top-down or the bottom-up approach in setting objectives. In the top-down approach, top-level managers determine the broad framework of objectives and subordinates follow the same, while in the bottom-up approach, subordinates initiate the setting of objectives for themselves and present them to their superiors for consideration. However, both the approaches have pros and cons. It is better to discuss it with planning specialist to decide a right course of action.

In view of the above, there are six main steps in setting objectives:

1. *Specify the goals to be accomplished.* Goals may be to increase productivity or increase sales.
2. *Specify how the performance will be measured.* Some performance can be measured more easily than others. Production, or profit is easy to be measured whereas boosting customer service is rather difficult to assess.
3. *Specify the standard or target to be reached.* This step spells out the degree of performance to be included in the goal.
4. *Specify time span involved.* In an operation situation, the goal may be in term of production per day. In a service situation, the goal may involve the time it takes to deliver the service.
5. *Prioritize the goals.* When multiple goals are present, as is with most jobs, they need to be prioritized so that effort and action can be directed in proportion to the

importance of each goal. Otherwise, individual effort can be gone hay way.

6. *Determine coordination effort.* It is necessary to know the effort required in cooperation and contributions of individuals positioned vertical and horizontal levels in the organizational hierarchy. Further, an extra effort is needed for coordination with boss whose valuable advice would help to excel in aiming your goals.

5.4 MANAGEMENT BY OBJECTIVES (MBO)

One technique used by organizations to facilitate the linkage of goals and plans is management by objectives (MBO). It is a process through which specific goals are set collaboratively for the organization as a whole and every department, unit and individual within it. Peter F. Drucker used the term MBO in 1954, one of the earliest management thinkers to do so. The detailed steps are described in Chapter 2.

REVIEW QUESTIONS

1. Elucidate—objectives are ends towards which all activities of an organization are directed.
2. Explain how to set objectives. List four objectives that you might set for yourself during the coming semester.
3. Explain the process and utility of MBO.

Chapter 6
Strategic Planning

6.1 INTRODUCTION

Strategic management involves the strategic planning, directing, organizing, and controlling of a company's strategy-related decisions and actions. Strategic planning analyses the current and future situation, determine the direction of the enterprise, and develop means for achieving the missionary objectives. Planning is done in an uncertain environment. The strategic planning process is extremely complex that demands a systematic approach for identifying and analyzing external environment as well as internal environment to evolve strategic goals to gain a competitive advantage over their competitors over a period of time.

6.2 ELEMENTS OF STRATEGY

Strategies. The globalization of industries and their markets and rapid and significant technological changes are the two primary factors for the firm to choose one or more strategies to remain competitive for years to come. Strategies are a stream of decisions and actions that help to achieve corporate objectives. On a very simple way, this process would have the following hierarchical critical tasks:

1. A plan/course of action/decision rules which are leading to particular direction to the company. According to **William Glueck,** "A unified, comprehensive and integrated plan designed to assure that the basic objectives of the enterprise are achieved."

2. It depends on vision, mission, goals and objectives of the company, where it would like to reach from its current position.

3. It deals with the future, which has uncertainties. Under such scenario, the firm analyzes its external and internal environments. Some key environment factors which need to be studies are political and legal, economic, competitive and social/cultural.

4. Management cuts across the narrow functional boundaries to determine their resources, capabilities, and define strengths/ weaknesses/core competencies.

5. Generate strategic alternatives.

6. Evaluate and select the corporate strategy. It is about making trade-offs between its different activities, and creating a fit among these activities.

7. Implement, feedback and control of the strategy.

As these tasks indicate, strategic management involves the planning, directing, organizing, and controlling of a company's strategy-related decisions and actions. Success of any company depends on how well the company has to choose the strategy out of various strategies. It increases when it is based on ethical intentions and behaviour, hard work, and honest analyses of situations.

6.3 LEVELS/TYPES OF STRATEGY

Organizations develop strategies at three different levels: corporate, business, and functional.

Corporate-level strategy is for the entire business and developed by top management. It would cover the various strategies and functions performed by different **strategic business units** (**SBU**). Thus, it would be for allocation of resources to each SBU and the broad-level functional strategies. Strategies at this level are most helpful by advising on new directions for growth, suggesting when major changes in strategy are needed, coordinating business of SBUs, and providing input on the timing of major investments.

Business-level strategy is at strategic business units and will be line to achieve the objectives, SBUs which are derived and in line with the corporate/company objectives. A strategic business unit is a distinct business, with its own set of competitors that can be managed relatively independently of other business within the organization. Business-level strategies while supporting the corporate-level strategy are aimed at deciding the type of competitive advantage to build, determining responses to changing environmental and competitive conditions, allocating resources within the business unit, and coordinating functional-level strategies. The heads of the respective business units develop business strategies, although such strategies are subject to the approval of top management. When an organization comprises only a single business, corporate-level and business-level strategies are essentially the same. Thus, the corporate-level and business-level distinction is only to organization with separate divisions that compete in different industries.

Functional-level strategy focuses on action plans for managing a particular functional area within a SBU in a way that supports the business-level strategy. Strategies at the functional level are for manufacturing or operations, marketing, finance, human resource management, accounting, research and development, and engineering. Functional-level strategies are important because they often reflect strong functional competencies that can be used to competitive advantage.

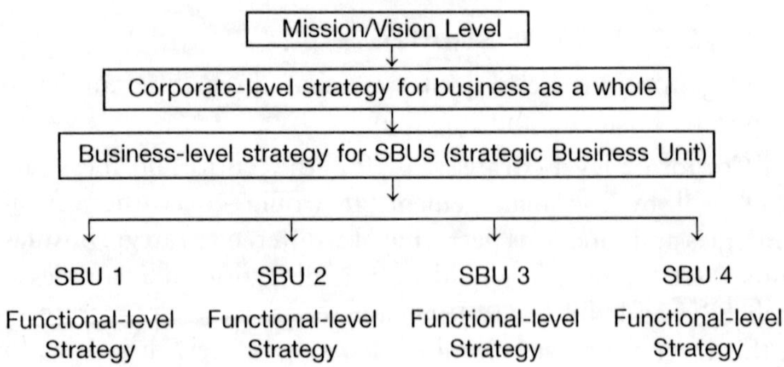

Levels of Strategy

These are the three levels at which strategic plans are made for most companies. In the dynamic environment and due to the complexities of business, strategies are needed to be set at lower level, i.e., at one step down the functional level, known as operational-level strategies. Typically, for example, marketing strategy could be further subdivided into sales strategies, even sales strategies for different segments and markets, pricing, distribution, product development advertising strategies. The strategies need to have synergies and contribute to the functional objectives of the marketing function. This would then be interlinked with other strategies at the functional level, like those of the finance, production, etc., functions.

6.4 COMPANY VISION AND MISSION

These are the initial tasks of strategic planning process. A vision statement articulates the ideal description of an organization's big picture and gives shape to its intended future. Vision is simple, positive, emotional, and relatively short, making it easily remembered. Example of vision statement is—*Our vision is to be the world's best quick service restaurant (McDonald's).*

The vision is the foundation for the firm's mission. The mission is the expression of the corporate intent. The mission defines the business. Together, vision and mission provide the firm's needs to choose and implement one or more strategies. Example of mission statement is—*Be the best employer for our people in each community around the world and deliver operational excellence to our customers in each of our restaurants (McDonald's).* The CEO and the other top-level managers develop the firm's vision and mission. Jerry Porras and James Collins in their book *Build to Last* have given a good framework for developing a vision and a mission. They divide this into two parts—core ideology and envisioned future.

Core ideology is the unchanging part of organization, its character. It would not change for the long time, even it were a disadvantage. Core ideology has two components, core values and core purpose. The core values are few values that are central to the firm. There are a few examples of values that some firms have chosen to be in their core: excellent customer service, pioneering technology, social responsibility. The core purpose is the reason that the firm exists. The purpose is to specify in the mission statement that how the firm will earn its profit since the "how" is what defines the firm.

Envisioned Future—is envision the future which also has two components of *audacious goals* and *a vivid description.* Most visionary goals fall into one of the following categories:

Target—quantitative or qualitative goals such as a sales target.

Common enemy—centered on overtaking a specific firm considered as firm's enemy.

Role model—to become like another firm in a different industry or market. For example, a cycle firm might strive to become "the Nike of the cycle industry."

Internal transformation—especially appropriate for large corporations. For example, GE set the goal of becoming number one or number two in every market it serves

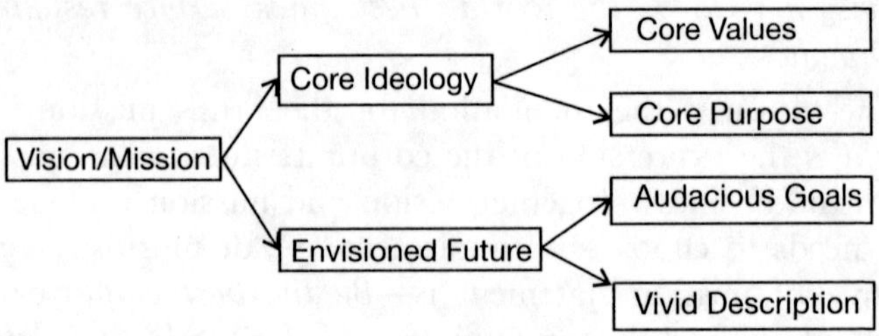

The vivid description is putting the goals into words that evoke a picture of what it would be like to achieve your audacious goals.

6.5 SWOT AND ENVIRONMENT APPRAISAL

Before managers can devise an effective strategy for edge over their competitors, they analyse organizational strengths (S) and weaknesses (W), as well as environmental opportunities (O) and threats (T). Identifying strengths and weaknesses requires assessing internal characteristics, while detecting opportunities and threats involves evaluating relevant environmental factors. Some potential issues to consider in SWOT Analysis are given below:

Internal strengths are distinctive competence, adequate financial resources, good competitive skill, super technology, cost advantages, product R&D, proven management, better manufacturing capability and others. These strengths are needs to be stabilised and improved further.

Internal weaknesses are no clear strategic direction, obsolete facilities, poor managerial depth and talent, less funding on R&D, hassled with internal operating problems, unfavourable product portfolio, poor marketing techniques, higher unit costs compared to competitors and others. These weaknesses are needed to be either reduced or eliminated.

External opportunities are availability additional customer groups as well as new markets, possibility of open up new product line, possibility of vertical integration, possibility of opening of foreign trade, faster market growth and others. These opportunities are to be harnessed for company's benefits. **External threats** are environmental challenges by way of entry of lower-cost in-land and foreign competitors, entry of substitutes, slow market growth, adverse trade policies of in-land and/or foreign governments, growing bargaining power of customers or suppliers, changing buyer needs and tastes, adverse demographic changes and others. These threats are to be watched and take necessary steps to turn these to company's advantages.

The impact of four variables (S, W, O and T) on strategy formulation in matrix form is shown below:

SWOT Matrix for Strategy Formulation

Internal factors External factors	Internal Strengths (S)	Internal Weaknesses (W)
Opportunities External (O)	SO Strategy Using organization's strengths to take advantage of opportunities	WO Strategy Organization minimizes weaknesses in order to take advantages of opportunities
Threats (T) External	ST Strategy Organization maximizes its strengths to minimize threats	WT Strategy Organization minimizes both its weaknesses and threats by way of retrenchment, liquidation or joint venture

SO strategy is the most desirable where organizations use their strengths to exploit opportunities and convert threats into opportunities.

Since the external and internal environments are dynamic, the strategy manager must prepare several SWOT matrices at different points in time of the past, present and in the future.

An integrated understanding of the external and internal environment is essential for firms to understand the present and predict the future.

The **external environment** is, by and large, beyond the control of a company. This is called Macro (General) environment such as the economic, socio-cultural, political/government and legal, demographic, global and technological. Some of the external factors have a direct and intimate impact on the firm. These factors are classified as micro environment, also known as task environment such as suppliers, financiers, publics, customers/ markets and competitors.

The **internal environment** would be of resources, capabilities and competencies.

There are tangible and intangible resources. Tangible resources can be quantified and are identifiable/visible—basically four types—financial resources, organizational resources, physical resources, and technological resources. Intangible resources are less visible—like human resources consist of a number of different factors, including structure, organizational processes, and people and their beliefs, that determine the climate of organization, innovation resources, reputation resources.

Capabilities are firm's capability to deploy resources that have been purposely integrated to achieve a desired end state. Capabilities enable the firm to create and exploit external opportunities.

Core competencies of a firm mean superiority over its rivals. Core competence is the collective learning of a firm, especially how to co-ordinate diverse production skills and integrate multiple steams of technologies and in organization of work and delivery of value. It is communication, deep involvement and commitment to work across organizational boundaries across all levels and functions.

Organizations interact dynamically with their external environment. Managers are sensitive and responsive to their environment thereby managing uncertainty of external environment.

External Environmental Analysis

Components of the External Environmental Analysis

Scanning	Identifying early signals of environmental changes and trends
Monitoring	Detecting meaning through ongoing observations of environmental changes and trends
Forecasting	Developing projections of anticipated outcomes based on monitored changes and trends
Assessing	Determining the timing and importance of environmental changes and trends for firm's strategies and their management

The various sources of information for collecting data for environmental analysis like publications, journals, books, annual reports of competitors, Internet, firm's internal documents, suppliers, customers and employees, academic research papers, etc.

Environmental Scanning

Techniques used for environment scanning are **scenario writing, simulation, game theory,** etc.

The external environment can be broken into the following categories for simplicity:

- The marketing environment would involve:
  - Customers' needs, preferences, perceptions, price, buying behaviour, etc.
  - Growth rate, demand v/s supply, differentiation, substitutes, etc.
  - Channels of distribution, intermediaries, logistic, etc.
  - Competition, nature of competition, entry and exit of competitors, etc.

  - Industry structure, integration of markets, globalization, etc.
- The financial environment would concern with the
  - Demand/supply of money, sources and cost of money, tenure of loans, securities asked for loans, etc.
  - Capital markets, intermediaries, interest rates, various financial instruments, and other factors in the financial sector, etc.
- The demographic environment would concern with the
  - Population's size, age, income groups and distribution
  - Family size and structure, geographic distribution, ethnic mix, etc.
- The economic environment would concern with the
  - Inflation rates, GDP, saving rate, etc.
  - Trade deficits, balance of payments, trade gap, trade cycles, etc.
  - Infrastructure like electricity/communication/roads/rail/air, etc.
  - Other such factors that affect the entire industry.
- **The political/legal environment** is concerned with
  - Govt. policies, stability, philosophy of government
  - Various laws, infrastructure for implementation of various laws/policies, etc.
  - Attitude towards labour, bilateral relations
  - Overall factors that may affect industry climate
- **The social/cultural environment** is concerned with
  - Attitudes about work/quality, concerns
  - Ethics, values, religion, corruption
  - Other such factors
- **The supplier and technological environment** is concerned with
  - The quality and number of suppliers, labour and people as suppliers, etc.
  - The logistics, raw material

- Trends and rate of change of technology, appropriate technology, cost/benefit of technology
- Other such factors

- **The international/global environment** is concerned with
  - Direction of globalization, trade blocs
  - Global trade and commerce, WTO, GATT, TRIPS, legal mechanisms, etc.
  - Global demographics
  - Technology and flow of technology and flow of technology
  - Standards and conventions
  - Other such factors.

6.6 FORECASTING

Scanning and monitoring are concerned with events and trends in the general environment at a point in time. Forecasting analysts develop feasible projections of what might happen, and how quickly, as a result of the changes and trends detected through scanning and monitoring.

The first step in environmental forecasting is identification of the environmental variables critical to the firm out of all variables that would have a significant impact on future planning.

The second step is the collection of the needed information.

The third step is choice of forecasting technique.

Types of Forecasting

Forecasts of the important business environments, viz. economic environment, social environment, political environment, etc. would be useful in formulating plans and strategies.

Forecasts are of three types: event outcome forecasts, event timing forecasts and time-series forecasts.

Event outcome forecasts are used when analysts to predict the outcome of highly probable future events. For example, what will be the sales in the first year of the new product? Information would be obtained through conducting a market survey.

Event timing forecast predicts whenever, given events will occur. For example, when will Maruti Suzuki launch its next model? Timing questions like these can be answered by going through its historical data.

Time-series forecasts rely on historical data. They are more suited to predict future projection for general economic prospects, employment levels, general sales levels, or cost trends. The figures may be based on past patterns that repeat over time.

Methods of Forecasting

Forecasting methods can be divided into two types: qualitative or technological and quantitative.

Technological, or qualitative forecasting is aimed primarily at predicting long-term trends in technology and other important aspects of the environment. This type of forecasting is used when past data are not available or reliable, e.g., sales forecasts of a new product and thus depends on such qualitative factors as expert knowledge, creativity, and judgement.

The Delphi Technique

This method is a structured approach to gaining the views of a number of experts separately on a specific issue relating to the future through the use of a series of anonymous written questionnaires and/or interview. It has the following steps:

1. A problem is identified.
2. Experts are identified and contracted.
3. A semi-structured questionnaire mailed to each expert anonymously for their evaluation and comments.
4. On receipt of evaluation and comments, these are analyzed and second questionnaire is prepared from the responses obtained to the first questionnaire and mailed back.
5. This process may be continued until a consensus view is arrived at.

Experts participating can come from inside or outside the organization. The Delphi technique is a lengthy, time-consuming method of forecasting. But this can be used to seek creative solutions to problems particularly predicting technological change.

Judgmental Forecasting

A type of forecasting that relies mainly on individual judgments or committee agreements regarding future conditions.

Quantitative techniques: The more reliable techniques for forecasting are quantitative methods.

Trend analysis: This involves the statistical technique of time-series analysis. This method involves predicting the future by projecting trends on the basis of past results. It is based on the underlying assumption that past and present tendencies will continue into the future.

Econometric methods: These are used in general economic forecasting, with particular emphasis on prediction of Gross National Product (GNP). Many organizations use the projected GNP figure to predict future sales based on past relationship between their sales and GNP. Many organizations use the projected GNP figure to predict future sales based on past relationship between their sales and GNP. These methods are also used to simulate the behaviour of markets.

6.7 INTERNAL ENVIRONMENTAL ANALYSIS

Resources, capabilities, and core competencies provide the foundation of competitive advantage. Resources are the source of a firm's capabilities. Capabilities in turn are the source of a firm's core competencies, which are the basis of competitive advantages. Resources cover a spectrum of individual, social, and organizational phenomena. Some of the firm's resources as inputs to the firm's production are tangible while others are intangible. **Tangible resources** are assets that can be seen and quantified. Production equipment, manufacturing plants, and formal organizational structures are examples of tangible resources. **Intangible resources** are less visible which include knowledge, trust between managers and employees, managerial capabilities, scientific capabilities, reputational resources are some of the examples of intangible resources. These are relatively difficult for competitors to analyse and imitate.

The four types of tangible resources are financial, organizational, physical, and technological. The three types of intangible resources are human, innovation, and reputational. Tangible resources which can have unique intangible attributes, such as quality control processes, unique manufacturing processes, and technology that develop over time create competitive advantage.

Capabilities exist when resources have been integrated to achieve a set of tasks often developed by the organization in specific functional areas such as manufacturing, R&D, and marketing. Capabilities often evolve and develop over time. Capabilities enable the firm to create and exploit external opportunities. The foundation of many capabilities lies in the unique skill and knowledge of a firm's employees and, often, their functional expertise leading to core competencies.

Core competencies are capabilities that serve as a source of competitive advantage for a firm over its rivals. Core competencies distinguish a firm competitively and add unique value to its goods or services over a long period of time. McKinsey & Co. recommends its clients to pursue three or four core competencies out of several capabilities for their strategic actions. Capabilities that are valuable, rare, costly to imitate, and non-substitutable are core competencies. Three tests can be used to identify core competencies—First it provides potential access to a wide variety of markets and diverse products. Second, it makes a significant contribution to the perceived benefits of the end product. Third, it is difficult for competitors to imitate. ITC's time-tested core competencies: unmatched distribution reach, superior brand-building capabilities, effective supply chain management and acknowledged service skills in hoteliering. **Outsourcing** is the purchase of a value-creating activity from an external supplier. By outsourcing activities in which it lacks competence, the firm can fully concentrate on those areas where the firm can achieve superiority and probably developing its core competencies as the source of its competitive advantages.

The strategic management process calls for **Merger and Acquisition strategy** to increase a firm's strategic competitiveness as well as its returns to shareholders.

A **merger** is a strategy through which two firms agree to integrate their operations on a relatively coequal basis because they have resources and capabilities that together may create stronger competitive advantages. In merger, generally, one party is dominant in regards to market share or firm size.

An **acquisition** is a strategy through which one firm buys a controlling, or 100 percent, interest in another firm with the intent of using a core-competence more effectively by making the acquired firm a subsidiary business within its portfolio. In this case, the management of the acquired firm reports to the management of the acquiring firm. Acquisitions, which are unfriendly, are termed as **takeovers.**

Porter's five competitive forces model: Strategy expert Michael E. Porter developed the **five competitive forces model** to analyse the nature and intensity of competition in a given industry in terms of five major forces. The forces are rivalry, bargaining power of customers, bargaining power of suppliers, threat of new entrants, and threat of substitute products and services. The collective strength of these forces directly affects the profit potential, or long-term return on investment.

Competitive forces	Reasons for lower profit
Rivalry	Various tactics like lower price, advertising battles, increased customer service or warranties.
Bargaining power of customers	Customers force price reductions or increase quality.
Bargaining power of suppliers	Suppliers force price increases or reduction of quality.
Threat of new entrants	New entrants bid prices down or cause incumbents to increase cost in order to maintain market position.
Threat of substitutes of goods	Availability of substitutes limits the prices that can be charged.

Grand Strategies

Corporate strategies comprise the overall strategy that an organization will follow. Its development generally involves selecting a grand strategy and using portfolio strategy approaches to determine the various business that will make up the organization. The three basic types of grand strategies are growth, stability and defensive. Growth strategies typically means increasing sales and earnings. Three growth strategies are concentration, vertical integration, and diversification.

Concentration focuses on growth of single product which takes place through market development, product development or horizontal integration usually by purchasing such businesses.

Vertical integration involves effecting growth through the production of input previously provided by suppliers. This process is known as backward integration. When organizational growth encompasses a role previously fulfilled by a customer, the process is known as forward integration.

Diversification entails effecting growth through the development of new areas.

All three growth strategies can be implemented through internal resources or through acquisition, merger, or joint venture.

Stability involves maintaining the status quo or growing in methodical, but, slow, manner. Organizations might choose a stability strategy if a company is doing reasonably well and there is no need to take risk for higher growth. Another reason for choosing stability strategy in an attempt to hold on to current market share.

Defencive Strategies focus on the desire or need to reduce organizational operations, usually through cost reductions and/or asset selling.

While grand strategies address an organization's overall direction, portfolio strategy approaches help managers determine the types of businesses in which the organization should be engaged. Thus, a **portfolio strategy approach** is a method of analyzing an organization's mix of businesses in terms of both individual and collective contributions to strategic goals. The most frequently used portfolio approach is the **BCG growth-share matrix.** This is the four-cell matrix developed by the Boston Consulting Group (BCG), shown below, compares various businesses in an organization's portfolio on the basis of relative market share and market growth rate. It becomes the standard approach to capital allocation in multi-sector, multi-segment companies. 'Stars,' 'Dogs', 'Cash Cows' and 'Question Marks' have become firmly embedded in the language of business. Relative market share is the ratio of a business's market share compared with the market share of its largest rival. Market growth rate is the growth in the market during the previous year relative to growth in the economy as a whole. In the BCG matrix shown in figure on next page, each business, represented by a circle, is plotted on the matrix according to its position along both dimensions. The size of the circle indicates the business's percent revenue relative to the revenues generated by other businesses in the portfolio. The resulting matrix divides the businesses into four quadrants. The vertical axis represents the market growth rate for a product in a specific market. The horizontal axis represents relative market share of a specific product in a specific market.

The *star* is a product or business unit has a high market share in rapidly growing market. Because of their high growth potential, star often initially require substantial investment capital beyond what they are able to earn themselves.

A *question mark* (also called *a problem child*) has a low market share in a rapidly growing market. Question marks present somewhat of a dilemma for their organizations. Like stars, they require substantial investment to take advantage of rapidly growing market, yet their low market share usually means that they have limited ability to generate large amounts of cash themselves also called "cash hogs". With question marks, managers must usually either provide substantial cash to fuel growth or divest the business.

The *cash cow* has a high market share in a slowly growing market. As a result, it tends to generate more cash than is necessary to maintain its market position. Cash cows, often former stars, can be valuable in a portfolio because they can be "milked" to provide cash for stars and question marks.

A *dog* has a low market share in an area of low growth. Thus, it is typically generates only modest cash flow.

The BCG matrix suggests using revenues from cash cows to fund the growth of stars, as well as to build the market share of the question marks with the best prospects. Dogs and the remaining are usually divested unless they provide sufficient positive cash flow to justify retaining them.

The matrix helps to develop a framework for allocating resources to some SBUs whereas divesting others.

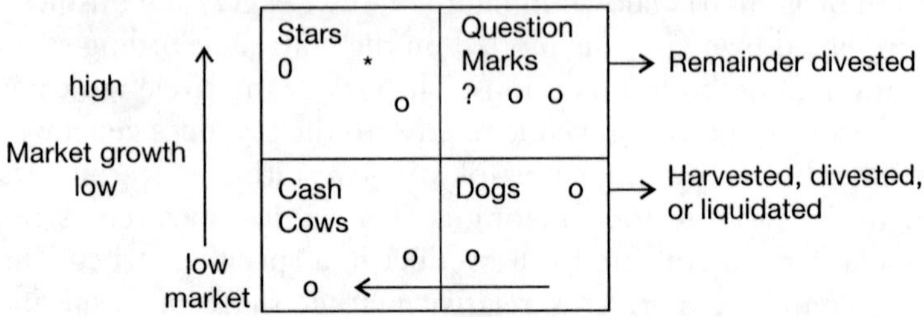

BCG Matrix

Based on the above, managers need to analyse the organization's competitive situation. This involves assessing both the environmental and the organizational factors that influence an organization's ability to compete effectively. Such an assessment can be made with SWOT analysis. S stands for organizational strengths, W for organizational weaknesses, as well as environmental opportunities O and for threats T.

Strength is an internal characteristic that has the potential of improving the organization's competitive situation. These are distinctive competence which outperforms the competitors and attain high level of performance, optimum utilisation of resources, proven management, innovative ability, profitable functional areas, efficient R&D, adequate financial resources, proprietary technology. In contrast, a *weakness* is an internal characteristic that leaves the organization potentially vulnerable to strategic moves by competitors. These are no clear strategic direction, obsolete facilities, low financial reserves, inadequate R&D facilities, plague with internal operating problems, weak distribution network, below-average marketing skill, etc.

An *opportunity* is an environmental condition that offers significant prospects for improving an organization's situation relative to competitors. These are boon in the economy, development of new technology, growing markets, liberal government policies, serve additional customer groups, etc.; whereas a threat is an environmental condition that offers significant prospects for undermining an organization's competitive situation. These threats are recession in the economy, changing consumer preferences, development of new technology by competitors, substitute products with high brand image or low cost, foreign competitors, political instability, slower market growth, vulnerability to recession and business cycle, etc.

6.8 STRATEGIC MANAGEMENT PROCESS

The basic steps followed in strategic management process are as follow:

Step 1: Goals Formulation

Strategies are goal-oriented. The overall purpose or mission of the organization must be clearly stated. Mission explains the reason why business is in existence. It identifies the scope of products/services, consumers, etc.; relationship between the organization's internal and external environment. Missions formulate objectives and that help to formulate strategies. Mission statement is stable over time and focuses on the essence of winning.

Creating goals is an inherent part of effective managerial planning. Goals define organizational purpose, motivate accomplishment, and provide a yardstick against which progress can be measured. Formulating goals demands from managers' necessary affirmation and verification of reasons or justification of the organization's existence, the definition of its mission or purpose, and establish strategic objectives. The beliefs, values, and expectations of the dominant coalition of stakeholders tend to shape any new mission statement and concomitant goals and strategies. Managers vary in their attitude and expectation. For example, some managers are found more concerned about delivering new goods and services and, hence, give more importance to research and development of goals.

Managers aspiring to dominate the market would like to design goals in terms of acquisitions of and merger with other companies.

Managers with social orientation and responsibility tend to set goals likely to produce favorable social effects along with profits.

In the case of large organizations, in particular, the process of goal development is complex, "Individuals and groups, both internal and external to an organization, engage in a process of bargaining and out of this exchange organizational goals emerge.

The relative power of these various stakeholders in the organization determines the nature and character of the bargaining process and the goals that ultimately emerge.

Peter Drucker offers the perspective that organizations to their success must simultaneously pursue multiple goals. Sometimes goals of one unit conflicts with the goals of other internal units. Such as the innovation goal of a research and development department might conflict with the production department's goals of efficiency. Managers must strive to resolve conflicts when they arise.

Step 2: Analyzing the External Environment

The step two is to look into the external environment which must be assessed in terms of threats and opportunities. Scanning or assessing the environment is the process of collecting information from the external environment about factors having the ability to exert influence on the organization.

The evaluation is done on the competitive situation as well as economic, social, political, legal, demographic, and geographic factors. In addition, the environment is scanned for technological developments, for products and services in the market and for other factors required to determine the competitive situation of the enterprise.

The main purpose of an environmental assessment is to identify opportunities and threats to the organization so that managers can develop a strategy to face them.

This step may be taken along with the step, i.e., step three, analyzing the internal environment or the organization's resources.

Step 3: Analyzing Internal Environment (or Own Organizational Resources)

The analysis of the internal environment or the organization's resources from within identifies its present strengths and weaknesses by examining its internal resources.

Audit and evaluation should be undertaken in matters of research and development, production operation, procurement, marketing, products, and services.

Other internal factors that are important for formulating a strategy as human resources and financial resources, the image of the company, the organization's culture and organization structure, climate, the planning and control system as well as relations with customers should be assessed.

The critical factor in an organizational analysis is a statement of what the organization does better or worse than its competitors. Thus, managers should assess their strengths and weaknesses compared with their competitors so far as internal resources are concerned.

Step 4: Identifying Strategic Opportunities and Threats

Now, they identify their opportunities to achieve their goals, on the one hand, and the threats that could hamper and halt them. Both of these factors must be considered for effective strategic planning.

In short, managers should use all the information provided by their scanning of both sides of the environment in the course of strategic planning that is likely to affect their organization in the future.

Step 5: Performing Gap Analysis

Gap analysis identifies the expected gaps between where managers want the organization to go and where it will go if they maintain the current strategy. Gap analysis helps to point out areas in which an organization is likely to succeed, but its real value lies in identifying the limitations of the present strategy and pointing out the areas requiring change.

Thus, gap analysis helps determine the causes of the gaps and, most importantly, makes managers concerned about the issues to be seriously addressed in designing a new strategy—the core issue of step six.

Step 6: Developing Alternative Strategies

At this step of the strategic planning process, managers are faced with the question of whether a new strategy is required and, if so, what kind of strategy it will be.

If no gap is found from the above analysis (step five), there is hardly any problem.

But gap analysis quite often tends to show that some changes in strategy are required. Hence, managers as a matter, of course, have to identify new alternatives, evaluate each of them, and choose a new or an alternative strategy.

The nature and extent of gaps exercise considerable influence on the complexity of the process. Sometimes only minor adjustments in existing goals and strategies are required. For example, an image problem of the company might be rectified by some simple measures such as a change in advertisement or modernization of equipment to expedite delivery of products or services.

At other times, important changes in matters of organizational strategy become necessary. For example, an organization may require entering into a new market, redesigning a product, or even merging with or acquiring another organization to face new and changing competition.

Finally, various alternatives have to be carefully considered and evaluated before the choice is made. Strategic choices must be examined in light of the **risks involved** in a particular situation.

Although some opportunities appear to be profitable, they might not be pursued for the risk of failure and consequent bankruptcy of the company.

Time is another critical factor in selecting a strategy. For example, even a very high-quality product may fail if it is introduced to the market at the wrong times.

Step 7: Implementing Strategy

However, good a strategic plan may be, it cannot fully utilize its potential unless it is implemented effectively at each business unit of the organization. Within each business unit, supportive functional strategies for the major organizational divisions, subdivisions and each major functional area must be developed.

Managers must also remember that a strategy must have the support of the employees at every level for its success. It is therefore important for the managers to give due consideration to the attitudes, values, and goals of organization members at the time of implementing a new strategy.

Step 8: Measuring and Controlling Progress

In the last step, managers must evaluate the effectiveness of the strategy being pursued.

Necessary check and balance should be done by management to see whether it conforms to the strategy that they designed in step six and is achieving the goals that they outlined in step one.

The results of the evaluation and control measures during this last step of the process inform managers about the actions required to enforce a strategy, which is not being followed or to revise or improve a strategy that is not working.

At this final stage, managers can employ several criteria to measure the success of a strategy. Some of them are:

- **External consistency:** How far is the strategy of helping the organization to cope with the demands of the external environment?
- **Internal consistency:** Is the strategy using organizational resources to achieve the objectives set by management?
- **Competitive advantage:** Does the strategy enable the organization to do things better than its competitors?

If the plan fulfills these above criteria at the final stage of the strategic planning process, managers might feel assured that the strategy is working well and according to their expectations.

REVIEW QUESTIONS

Long Questions

1. What are important aspects of strategic management and the notion of competitive advantage?
2. Explain the term strategy and various dimensions of strategic decisions.
3. What do you mean by environment in the context of strategy? Briefly explain the components of environment.
4. What is meant by 'merger' and explain various forms of mergers.
5. What is environmental forecasting?
6. Outline the major steps of strategic management process. Explain why engaging in strategic management is likely to be beneficial for an organization.
7. Describe Porter's competitive strategies for the business level. Assess the competitive strategy of an organization with which you are familiar, and explain its usefulness in dealing with Porter's five competitive forces.
8. Distinguish between internal and external environment.

Short Notes

1. Acquisition
2. BCG (Boston Consultancy Group)
3. SWOT analysis
4. Different kinds of business strategies

Chapter 7
Decision Making

7.1 DECISION MAKING—DEFINITION

Decision making is defined as the selection and the aim is to select the best alternative out of various alternatives available to solve a problem. Decision is judgment either consciously or sub-consciously in everyone's daily life. It is an integral part of planning which cannot be said to exist unless a decision is made. Managers' central job is decision making to choose what is to be done, who is to do it, and when, where, and how it will be done. Decision making is a purposive activity directed towards the achievement of goals and objectives.

Lopez has defined, "A decision represents a judgement; a final solution of conflict of needs, means, or goals; and a commitment to action made in face of uncertainty, complexity and even irrationality." Managers have to take decisions for solving problems, resolving crises and conflicts and for tackling various situations. It is important that managers possess good decision-making skills because their evaluation and rewards are dependent on the outcome of their decisions.

In decision making, three aspects of human behaviour are involved: (1) Cognition—activity of mind associated with knowledge (power of reasoning and perception), (2) Conation—the action/active part of mind implied by such words as effort/willing, desire, and aversion, and (3) affection—the aspect of associated with emotion, feeling and temperament.

Decisions may be major or minor, strategic or operational, long-term or short-term. They are made for each function at each level. Long-term, major and strategic decisions are taken by top level and relatively short-term. Minor, operational and routine nature of decisions are taken at lower levels. Decision making permeates every managerial function. Various authors/ thinkers have viewed decision making as follows:

1. A Danish Maxim, "Hear one person before you answer, several before you decide."
2. Peter F. Drucker, "He does through making decisions."
3. George R. Terry, "Decision-making is the selection based on some criteria from two or more possible alternatives."
4. H. Koontz, "Process leading to making a decision might be thought of as premising, identifying alternatives, evaluating alternatives in terms of the goal sought, and choosing an alternative, that is, making a decision."

Models of Decision Making: Two types of models have been developed to better understanding the way in which managers make decisions. The **rational model** suggests that managers are almost perfect information handlers and would always make optimal decisions that were in the best economic interests of their firms. In contrast to the rational view, several **non-rational models** of managerial decision making suggest that information-gathering and processing limitations make it difficult for managers to make optimal decision. Within the non-rational framework, there are three models of decision making: satisficing, incremental, and garbage-can. **Satisficing model** states that managers seek alternatives only until they find one that looks satisfactory, rather than seeking the optimal decision. **Incremental model** states that managers make smallest response possible that will reduce the problem to at least a tolerable level. **Garbage-can model** states that managers behave in virtually a random pattern making it difficult for them to make optimal decisions.

Significance/Merit and Limitations of Rational Decision Making

Rational decision making is significant in many ways:

(i) Managers who use rational decision making tend to provide better solutions to problems. They are effective managers.

(ii) Rational decision makers have a clear understanding of the alternative courses of action through which accomplish a goal under a given set of conditions and limitations.

(iii) Rational decision making helps the manager decide on the best solution by selecting the alternative that effectively facilitates goal achievement.

Example: Significance of Rational Decision Making

'Coca-cola' made a number of important decisions after 1981. The most difficult one was to extend the venerable Coke name to another product, namely 'Diet Coke'. Another decision that of changing the formula of Coke was also critical to the company's strategies. Market research showed a strong consumer preference for the new, sweeter-testing formula. However, people did not accept it under the original brand name 'Coke'. Therefore, within three months of the launch of the new formula, the company brought back the original product to retain its customer base. Coke's ability to recognize decision-making mistakes and take corrective measures is largely responsible for its growing strength.

However, rational decision-making has some limitations too:

(i) It is difficult to make completely rational decisions since the decisions are made predicting the future, which is itself uncertain.

(ii) It is sometimes difficult to determine the alternative courses of action to achieve a particular goal.

(iii) Rational decision-making is difficult in those areas which have not been venture into before.

(iv) It may become difficult to arrive at rational decisions because of limitations of information, time, and lack of certainty.

(v) Managers sometimes allow their tendency to avoid risks to disrupt rational decision-making process.

7.2 DECISION-MAKING PROCESS

Decision making is a systemic process through which managers should make decisions. The process basically involves following six steps:

Step 1: Identifying the Problem—The first step in the decision-making process is to know whether a problem exists which needs to be solved. Organizational problems are discrepancies between a current state or condition and what is desired. This step has three stages: scanning, categorization, and diagnosis.

> In the **scanning stage,** work environment is monitored for changing circumstances that may signal the emergence of a problem. For example, during the 1970s, Swiss watchmakers began to notice the appearance of relatively inexpensive watches being produced in Japan and Hong Kong.
>
> The **categorization stage** attempts to understand the performance gap between the expected and actual performance levels. For example, sales of the Swiss watches, which were relatively expensive, began to decline rather precipitously.
>
> The **diagnosis stage** involves gathering additional information and specify both the nature and the causes of the problem. For example, by 1983, Swiss firms manufacturing Omega, Rado, etc. observed that cheaper watches from Japan and Hong Kong posed a serious long-term threat to the Swiss watchmakers.
>
> Management expert Tom Peters notes that managers must learn to "thrive on chaos." Change must be relished with enthusiasm and energy. The high-achieving organizations will be those that develop the ability to scan their internal and external environments and identify and seize opportunities for change. At this juncture, managers must act to take decision.

Step 2: Generating Alternative Solutions—Alternative solutions fall into two categories: existing solutions and creative solutions. Existing solutions are alternatives that have been used by other decision makers in similar situations, also called programmed decisions. These programmed solutions are frequently adapted with or without modification.

Creative solutions lead to higher-quality solutions, particularly when the situation calls for creative and innovative ones. The development of alternatives can often be facilitated through **brainstorming**, a technique that encourages group members to generate as many ideas as possible on the topic without evaluating them. There are four principles involved:

1. *Don't criticize ideas while generating possible solutions*—Criticism inhibits thinking thereby only a few ideas are generated.
2. *Freewheeling*—Members may offer some wild and outrageous ideas including some usable ideas.
3. *Offer as many ideas as possible*—Pushing for a large number of ideas increases the probability that some of them will be effective solutions.
4. *Combine and improve on ideas that have been offered*—Often the best ideas come from combinations of the ideas of others.

Step 3: Evaluating Alternatives—Once managers develop a list of alternative solutions, the next step is to evaluate the advantages and disadvantages of each alternative based on research, experimentation, and drawing on experience. Managers estimate how well each alternative meet the organization's goals and objectives. In addition, it is important to evaluate alternatives on six general criteria: feasibility, quality, acceptability, costs, reversibility, and ethics.

Feasibility. Each alternative assesses its feasibility in terms of time, budgets, technology, and policies. Alternatives that do not meet the criterion of feasibility should be eliminated from further consideration.

Quality. Alternatives that do not meet the criterion of quality should be eliminated at this stage.

Acceptability. Acceptability has been recognized as an important criterion against which to judge decision. The criterion refers to the degree to which the decision makers and others who will be affected by the implementation of the alternative are willing to support it.

Costs. How much will each alternative cost, in terms of money, human resources, and also more intangible issues having undesirable side effects such as possible vigorous competitor retaliation.

Reversibility. This criterion refers to the extent to which the alternative can be reversed with ease if so needed in the long run.

Risks. What risks are associated with the alternative?

Ethics. The ethics refers to the extent to which an alternative is compatible with the legal, regulatory, social responsibilities, or ethical standards.

The decision-making process usually eliminates some alternatives because they are not satisfactory.

Step 4: Choosing an Alternative—After the evaluation process, the final stage in the decision process involves making judgments and choices.

Quantitative and qualitative tools often help managers select the most favoured alternative. Quantitative technique like *break-even analysis,* which identifies the sales revenue will equal the total cost of producing a product. Whereas qualitative technique like *Delphi* aids decision to choose the alternative.

Decision makers must ultimately decide what they want to accomplish. Three decision criteria are optimizing, maximizing, and satisficing. If decision makers hope to optimize, they search for the best possible decision. If the decision makers hope to maximize, the alternative should meet the maximum number of objectives. According to Herbert Simon, decision makers try to find the most satisfactory alternative.

Many organizational decisions are made by compromising and achieving consensus. If not done, decisions are governed by emotion based on personal experience and mainly rely on intuition even disagreements with a decision-making body.

Decision trees help managers find different opinion, as well as consider the potential impact of various alternative branches of the tree. The model begins on the left and answer each prescribed question (Fig. 7.1). Depending on your answer, a branch on the decision tree leads you to the next question, and the process is repeated until you arrive at the end of a branch. Next to the branch you will find a list of appropriate strategies for your situation. If more than one alternative appears at the end of a branch, use the one with the lowest costs or the one you prefer if cost is not an issue. As shown in figure, these decisions are answered in terms of "high/low" or "yes/no."

The model calls for "group decision making when the alternative A has the question of quality is low. When further goes to the branch it gives the cost at the low level. Alternative B is high in quality but no to cost in one branch whereas other branch support cost hence the alternative B is most suitable."

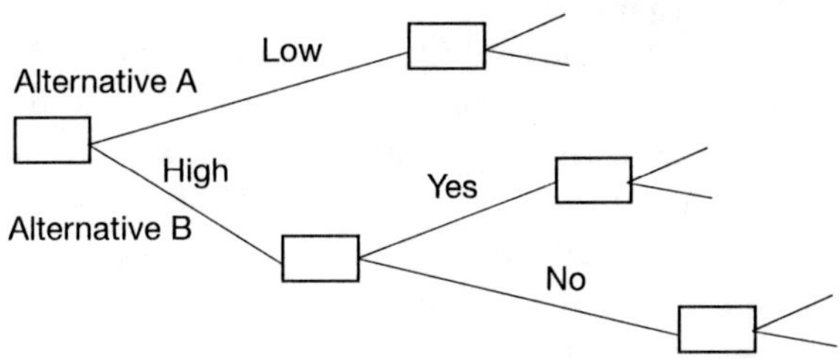

Fig. 7.1: Illustration of a decision tree model

Step 5: Implementing the Chosen Solution—Implementing the chosen solution depends on two main factors: careful planning and sensitivity to those involved in the implementation and/or affected by it. In regard to planning, minor changes in terms of organization, special funding, etc. would be required. In regard to persons involved, orientation and training would be required to implement the solution smoothly.

Step 6: Monitoring the Solution—Managers need to monitor things which are progressing as planned and problem that triggered in-between the decision-making process has been resolved. Appropriate follow-up mechanism is important to provide the feedback.

7.3 TYPES OF DECISIONS

There are different types of decisions which are taken by the managers. Generally, managerial decision situations fall into two categories: programmed and non-programmed.

Programmed decisions are those made in routine, repetitive, well-structured situations through the use of predetermined established policies, rules, and procedures meant for basic employee disciplinary problems. They are surely the easiest for managers make. They relate to the present. The primary purpose is to achieve as high a degree of efficiency as possible in the company's on-going activities. Usually, they are simple in nature requiring little discussion and money. They are taken by first-line managers and many of those made by middle managers. For example, determining salary payments to employees who are on leave, provision of car parking space according to level of officers, etc.

Although programmed decisions are applicable to routine, well-structured situations, they can be quite complex. Computers have enhanced the possibilities for making sophisticated programmed decisions, because they can collect and analyse vast amounts of information that can facilitate programmed managerial decision-making. When a person shops with a credit card, a programmed decision is made by computer regarding the authorization of the purchase.

Non-programmed decisions are novel, unique, ill-structured and non-repetitive in nature. If a problem has not arisen before or if there is no readymade solution, it is non-programmed decision. Because of their nature, non-programmed decisions usually involve considerable amounts of uncertainty. Decisions made under uncertainty involve risk, the possibility that a chosen action could lead to losses rather that the intended results. For better result, these decisions involve creativity, judgement and intuition. Thus, organizations make considerable effort through formal training programs and job experience to develop managers who can effectively handle non-programmed decision situations. Peter F. Drucker called non-programmed decisions as strategic decisions and regard them as truly managerial decisions. Strategic decisions include decisions on business objective, capital investment, product-mix, and social responsibility, etc. Top-level managers make non-programmed decision however a few programmed decisions are also undertaken by them as a special situation.

The proportion of non-programmed decisions that managers must make increases as they go up in the hierarchy. Because such decisions require effective decision-making skills and creativity, they provide the biggest decision-making challenges to managers.

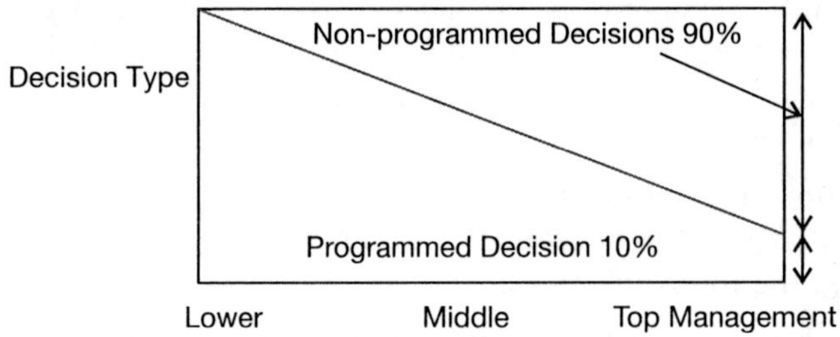

7.4 GROUP DECISIONS

Large and complex organizations practice group decision making instead of individual decision making. It facilitates pooling of knowledge, abilities, skills, information and judgements of managers which contribute to improve in the quality of decisions. It also acts as mechanism for integrating differing viewpoints. One of the major strengths of group decision making is that the decisions can be implemented with ease.

It also provides a sense of worth and importance and motivation to the group of managers. Finally, it acts as training ground for future managers.

One of its limitations is that it is costlier and more time consuming than individual decision making. Second, it often tends to reduce the chief executive to figure head. Third, committee decisions often have a dampening effect on aggressive and creative executives. Fourth, quality of group decisions may not be as good as that of individual decisions because of the levelling effect. Finally, it is not possible to pin down responsibility of group decisions on any individual manager.

Improving Group Decisions

Some of the techniques for improving group decisions are brainstorming, Delphi technique, and nominal group technique.

In **brainstorming,** the members of the group develop as many potential solutions as possible for this flexibility and cost efficiency. A number of alternatives have been generated and they are evaluated later. This technique is useful in generating creative solution to problems.

Delphi technique as discussed earlier is also a decision-making technique of obtaining expert opinions and thereby consensus is arrived by means of a series of anonymous written questionnaires.

Nominal group technique (NGT) represents an attempt to integrate a number of group decision techniques. The technique follows the following steps:

(i) *Listing*: Working individually, group members respond to the group task, which is usually to list ideas regarding a particular issue of problem.

(ii) *Recording*: Each group member represents one idea at a time to the facilitator, who records the ideas in full view of the group.

(iii) *Discussion*: When each member's response has been recorded on the master list, group members discuss, clarify and elaborate on the responses.

(iv) *Voting*: Each member votes on the best ideas generated. The results are tabulated and decisions are based on pooled results.

The technique is similar to the Delphi but has the advantage that it reduces the time and coordination problems associated with the Delphi. It allows for face-to-face discussion. Its success depends on the facilitator who should play a neutral role and control discussions when the groups go off-track.

REVIEW QUESTIONS

Long Answer Questions

1. Contrast the rational and non-rational models of decision making. Describe the merits and disadvantages of rational model of decision making.

2. Explain the difference between programmed and non-programmed decision situations. Identify two programmed and two non-programmed decision situations.
3. Describe each of the steps in an effective decision-making process.
4. Assess the advantages and disadvantages of group decision making. Give an example of a situation in which you felt the advantages outweighed the disadvantages.

Short Notes

1. Brainstorming
2. Nominal Group Technique (NGT)
3. Decision tree
4. Satisfying solution
5. Importance of decision making in management

CASE STUDY

You are the managing director (MD) of Hilton Tech Ltd. The company produces inverter as home appliances. For this, company buy micro-processor from a renowned brand. In the recent past, competition in the field of manufacturing of invertor becomes intense. This causes reduction of ROI. This is due to higher cost of manufacturing, higher inventory as well as stagnation in selling of invertor. In such situation, a brain-storming session with managerial heads is called. Outcome of meeting is a few alternative options such as development of their own micro processing, sold the unit to a competitor and go for similar electrical home appliances or make alliance with such unit which manufactures micro-processor.

The company also examine the financial outlay, recent government financial support, poaching experts in this field. In such scenario, the company is to solve the crisis.

Questions

1. Which model of decision making will be best matches the situation involving the company?
2. Explain the conditions under which the company is taking decision—certainty, uncertainty, risk and dealing with subsequent problems. What was the impact?

Chapter 8
Organizing

8.1 MEANING OF ORGANIZING

Organizing is one of the significant managerial functions. Organizing follows the planning stage. People working together must fulfill goals of the organization. Goals have number of activities. These activities are grouped into tasks/functions. Tasks are assigned to managers having responsibility to fulfill the tasks, managers are delegated the authorities. Accordingly, organization structure is developed so that managers communicate to higher authority vertically and coordinate horizontally to other departments. Organization is also referred to as an enterprise, as Steel Authority of India Ltd. (SAIL) or Department of Defence.

8.2 DEFINE ORGANIZING

According to L.A. Allen, "organizing is the process of identifying and grouping the work to be performed, defining and delegating responsibility and authority, and establishing relationships for the purpose of enabling people to work most effectively together in accomplishing objectives."

According to Amitai Etizoni, "an organization is a social unit or human grouping deliberately structured for the purpose of attaining specific goals."

Theo Haimann, "Organizing is the process of defining and grouping the activities of the enterprise and establishing the authority relationships among them. In performing the organizing function, manager defines, departmentalizes and assigns activities so that they can be most effectively executed."

8.3 PRINCIPLES OF ORGANIZATION

Certain basic principles of organization are enumerated below:

1. Objectives—clearly specified.
2. Specialization—the activities of enterprise should be divided according to functions and assigned to persons according to their specialization.
3. Span of management—a manager can supervise a limited number of his subordinates say six or eight persons under him.
4. Exception—only exceptionally complex problems be referred to the higher levels of management and routine matters be dealt with by executives at lower levels.
5. Scalar principles—every subordinate must know to whom he has to report for decision beyond his own authority.
6. Unity of command—each subordinate should have only one superior whose command he has to obey. Multiple subordination/reporting must be avoided. It causes uneasiness, disorder, indiscipline and undermining of authority.
7. Delegation—authority should be delegated commensurate with responsibility. Sufficient authority should be delegated to have freedom of work—a factor for innovation.
8. Simplicity—the organization structure should be as simple as possible. Hierarchical levels should, as far as possible, be minimum. A large number of levels create difficulty in communication and coordination.
9. Flexibility—the organization has inbuilt provision of revision in changed circumstances.
10. Balance—there should be a reasonable balance in the size of various departments, between centralization and decentralization and short span of control.

11. Personal ability—as people constitute an organization, there is need for proper selection, training and development of employees.
12. Facilitation of leadership—organization structure should be so devised that there is enough opportunity for the management to give effective leadership to enterprise.

8.4 CLOSED SYSTEM VS. OPEN SYSTEM

The various views on division and coordination of work activities and resource allocation can be divided into two theories: the classical closed system concept and the open system concept.

Closed system: The concept of closed system was developed by traditional theorists. In a closed system, organizations operate without any exchange with the external environment in which they exist. In reality, a totally closed system is only a theoretical concept as all organizations, to a relative degree, are dependent on the external environment.

Open system: The failure of the closed system led to the development of the open system by modern thinkers. The open system concept stressed on the need of flexibility and adaptability in organization structure, and the mutual interdependence between the organization and the external environment. The modern system model of organizing allow an organization to interact with its environment and evolve its organizational structure gradually over time.

8.5 PROCESS OF ORGANISING

Planning establishes enterprise objectives, policies, and plan. This is followed by organizing function. Functions of organizations include determination of activities, grouping of activities, allotment of duties to specific persons, delegation of authority, defining reporting relationships, and the coordination of various activities. Process of organizing consists of the following four steps.

Step 1: Identification and classification of required activities—Tasks/duties allotted to managers for achieving the goal.

Step 2: Grouping of activities into departments—This is to be done on the basis of homogeneity such as production, marketing, finance and account and personnel. Each department is further divided into different sections. Managers are placed under departments and sections in the form of organization structure. Organization structure is to determine the span of management specifying the number of subordinates who should report directly to each executive.

Step 3: Delegation of authority—Depending upon responsibilities, authority is delegated to managers. The Production Manager may be delegated with the authority to produce the goods and fixed with the responsibility of producing quality goods.

Step 4: Vertical reporting relationship and horizontal coordination—Communication from superior should be such that decisions are goes down fast and with ease to subordinates whereas feedback from subordinates should also go up smoothly. Moreover, managers should coordinate with managers for specialized activities on horizontal level with ease to achieve organization's goals and reduce inefficiency and conflicts.

Constant appraisal and re-organization of organization structure is an integral part of the organizing process.

8.6 FORMAL AND INFORMAL ORGANIZATION

Formal organization structures are created officially for a specific purpose. These people-to-people and people-to-work systems are designed to help people pool their time, energy, and talents to reach common objectives. Formal organization is a well-defined structure of authority and responsibility that defines delegation of authority and relationships among various organizational members. It works through predefined job descriptions, rules, policies, and operating procedures. It has clear division of work and relationships among people through effective system of communication in the entire organization. It results in optimum utilization of organizational resources. Formal organization hierarchy avoids overlapping of activities between two individuals or two departments. Two individuals are not assigned the same task.

These are two types of formal group: functional group and task group. A functional group consists of a manager and all the subordinates who report to that manager. Each subordinate forms a linking pin between a lower-level and higher-level manager. A linking pin is an individual who provides a means of coordination between functional groups at two different levels by fulfilling a supervisory role in the lower-level group and a subordinate role in the higher-level group. Thus, organization are made up of functional groups arranged in pyramidal fashion, with linking pins tying them together.

A **task group** is a formal group created for a specific purpose that supplements or replaces work normally done by functional groups. Task groups can be either permanent or temporary. A permanent task group, often called a **standing committee** handles recurring matters/subjects for a longer period. For example, a quality improvement committee. A temporary task group also called *adhoc committee* consisting of managers from different departments is to deal with specific issue within a specific time frame is a group that loosely formed by employees, rather than by the organization, to serve group members' interests or social needs. Informal groups reflect relationships that do not appear on the organization chart. Such groups might include the tea-break, lunch-break, and the Friday-evening bridge partners. Such groups whose existence is neither "for" nor "against" the goals of formal organization.

Informal organization—According to social psychologists, informal organizations can evolve in a natural and unplanned manner. They are an outgrowth of the social and personal needs of organizational members. These needs, when coupled with physical proximity and opportunity, give rise to interactions that, when repeated, become an informal organization.

Overtime, informal groups develop fairly stable memberships, their own communication networks, leaders, norms of acceptance and unacceptable behaviours, rewards, and sanctions. Virtually, all formal organizations have informal organizations. For example, when hospital nurses face problems with doctors and patients they evolve an informal group to provide solutions to problems to formal organization.

Managers need to recognize that both formal and informal organizations exist and, therefore, harness the benefit from them. Informal norms requiring ethical behaviour can be useful, as can be "grapevine" that keeps people abreast of happenings at all levels of the formal organization. There are two types of informal groups: interest and friendship.

An **interest group** is to pursue employees' pursuits of common concern. The types of interest can be wide-ranging, such as a radical new technology that may not be practical for the company at that time or alter some policy. Interest groups can benefit the organization, but they can also create difficulties for the formal organization.

A **friendship group** that evolves primarily to meet employee social needs. Such group stem from mutual attraction, often based on common characteristics, such as similar work, backgrounds, and/or values. Members of friendship group may eat lunch together frequently, attend plays or engage in other friendship-related social activities. Types of work groups are depicted at Fig. 8.6.

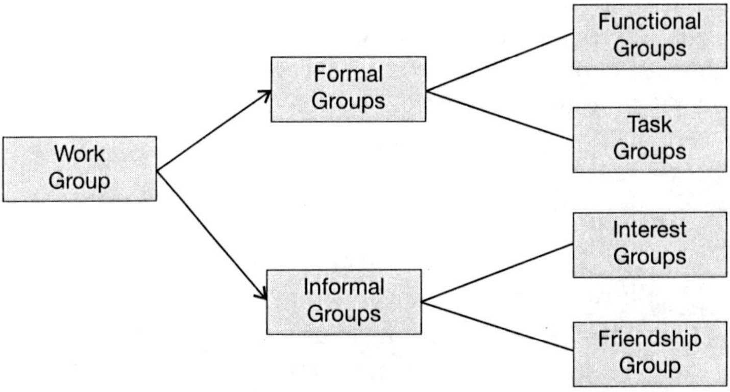

Fig. 8.6: Types of work groups

8.7 GROUP DYNAMICS

Group is defined as two or more persons who are interacting with one another in such a manner that each person influences and is influenced by each other to achieve a common objective. Groups are formal as well as informal.

Group dynamics refers to the 'forces operating in group members in a social situation'. Group dynamics deals with the nature and development of small groups, interactions among members, and group and intergroup behaviour. The basic assumptions underlying the study of group dynamics are: (i) groups are inevitable and ubiquitous, (ii) group mobilize powerful forces that produce effects of utmost importance to individuals, (iii) groups may produce good or bad consequences on the organization, and (iv) correct understanding of group dynamics permits the possibility that desirable consequences from groups can be deliberately enhanced. Managers believe that groups display synergy. **Synergy** a dynamic that occurs when group performance levels be greater than that achieved by employees working on their own. Expectations of increased productivity have prompted widespread experimentation with work groups and teams.

A **team** is a small group of people with different backgrounds, skills and knowledge, who are drawn from different functional areas of the organization, to work together on a specific and defined task. A team share responsibility for outcomes, who see themselves and are seen by others as an intact social entity embedded in one or more large social systems, and who manage their relationships across organizational boundaries.

There are several key components for establishing the self-managing autonomous work teams:

- Team should be responsible for identified task;
- Work assigned to the team should be designed so that it causes social and cooperative interaction;
- Members of the team should learn all of the jobs that are a part of the team's total responsibility;
- They should be self-contained—that is, it should have the power, information, skills and knowledge, materials, and equipment needed to perform the work assignment without having to turn to outside expertise; and
- The team should have the information necessary to evaluate their own performance.

8.8 COMMITTEE

A committee is a group often set up where new kinds of task and/or unfamiliar problems seem to involve decisions, responsibilities and powers beyond the capabilities, knowledge, information, abilities and interests of any one member or department.

Committees are of two types: advisory committee and executive committee. Whenever committee is vested with staff authority, it is known as advisory committee. Advisory committee has only offer recommendations for consideration by executive authority. Example—joint labour-management committees. Whenever committee is vested with line authority, it is called executive committee. Unlike advisory committee, executive committee decides the issue and implement the same. Example—Board of Directors of a company.

Committees may also be classified as *standing committees* and *adhoc committees*. Standing or permanent committees are formed to deal with recurring problems. Example—admission committee and promotion committee. Adhoc committees have a short duration. They are dissolved after the task is over, or the problem is solved.

Advantages: (i) pools information, abilities and interests for the formation of policies, plans, etc.; (ii) deals with complex problems; (iii) reduces bias and conflict; (iv) improves interpersonal relations; (v) democratizes the decision process; (vi) gains commitment to implement decisions; (vii) pools splintered authority; (viii) pools abilities, information and judgement; (ix) owns responsibility; and (x) acts as a coordinating mechanism.

Disadvantages: (i) its decisions are least denominators of its members—no body baby; (ii) it creates conflicts among members; (iii) causes diversions from main problems; (iv) acts as a device for shifting responsibility and postponing decisions; and (v) splits accountability committee members represent different departments, and their first and foremost obligation is to represent the interests of their department.

Conditions for Effective Functioning of Committees: These are: (i) number of members should ordinarily not exceed five; (ii) members should be conversant with its structure and processes; (iii) it should deal with specific problems; (iv) members should be committed to task accomplishment; (v) members should be trained in group processes and interpersonal skills; (vi) members should not be related in superior subordinate relationship, and should be homogeneous in personality characteristics; (vii) the committee chairman should possess leadership qualities of a very high order; (viii) the agenda for discussion should be communicated to members in advance; (ix) support should be forthcoming from executives who are responsible for implementing committee decisions; (x) members should take time to develop healthy interpersonal relationships; and (xi) committees for problem solving should be differentiated from committees used for developing managerial abilities.

8.9 GROUP DEVELOPMENT

New groups are always being formed in organizations. These groups go through developmental stages: forming, storming, norming, and performing. With appropriate care and direction, a team becomes fully mature team to perform.

Stage 1. Forming—a stage in which group member attempt to assess the ground rules that will apply to a task and to group interaction. At this stage, members require some time to get **acquainted/oriented** with the task and with each other to proceed in earnest with task responsibilities.

Stage 2. Storming—a stage in which group members frequently experience **conflict** with one another with respect to key issues like task, group leadership and interpersonal differences, etc. as they find and attempt to resolve these differences. Tension and hard feelings may arise. It is far better to accept the stage as a necessary part of team development and to concentrate to find out the ways and means to sort out the differences.

Stage 3. Norming—a stage in which group members begin to build group **cohesion,** as well as develop a consensus about norms and roles for performing a task and relating to one another. During norming stage, an informal leader may emerge.

Stage 4. Performing—is the period in which energy is channelled toward a task and in which norms support teamwork. The roles of group members, in this stage become clearer and more functional as the group works to achieve positive synergy and group goals.

Group Cohesiveness

Group cohesiveness as the interpersonal dynamic that includes: (i) attraction to the group and resistance to leaving it; (ii) morale, or the level of motivation displayed by members; and (iii) coordination of efforts of members. Cohesiveness reflects the strength of a group's esprit de corps. Members of highly cohesive teams accept the goals of the group, internalize its norms and adhere to them, and endeavour to satisfy the team's task-maintenance-oriented needs. If needs are threatened, as well as success, time spent together, attractiveness of being a team member, group size (large groups make cohesive less likely), and similarity in attitudes, and values play a significant role in developing group cohesiveness. At the same time, low absenteeism, low turnover, motivation for team goals, high involvement, and high productivity are some of the positive consequences associated with team cohesiveness. Cohesive groups tend to make decisions that meet group needs; if these needs are inconsistent with the organization's needs, their decisions can be detrimental to the organization.

8.10 SPAN OF MANAGEMENT

Span of management or span of control in organization structure indicates the number of subordinates who report directly to a manager because he can most likely effectively supervise them. With too many subordinates, managers can become overloaded, experience difficulty coordinating activities, and loose control of output. On the other hand, with too few subordinates, managers are underutilized and tend to engage in excessive supervision, leaving subordinates little freedom in doing their work.

While organizing the activities, organization structure is formed depending upon the hierarchical levels and span of control. A wide span of management is associated with few levels, a narrow span, with many levels. Relationships between the span of control and the hierarchical levels are shown in Fig. 8.10.

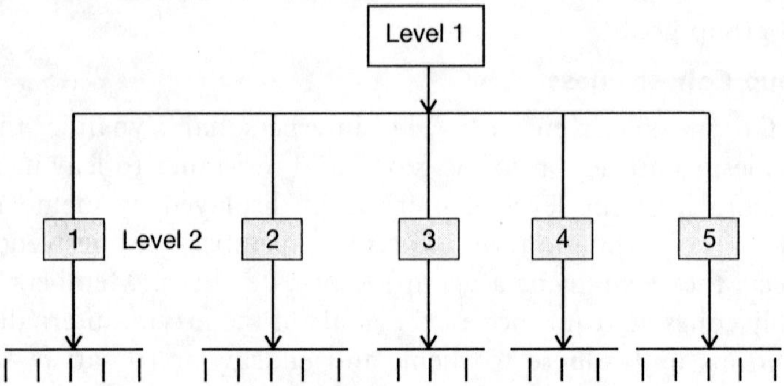

Fig. 8.10: Span of control

Five subordinates report Level-1. Subordinates 1 and 2 have their five subordinates. 3 and 4 have their three subordinates. Fifth manager have six subordinates. Span of control, i.e., supervising the subordinates depends upon factors mentioned below.

Factors Affecting Span of Management

1. *Competence of managers*: High job-related skills and abilities of managers and/or subordinates make it possible for managers to handle more subordinates. It means managers can have a wide span of management.

2. *Nature of work*: If employees perform similar and repetitive jobs where low interaction required here managers can supervise large number of subordinates thus, have a wide span of control. Non-repetitive and challenging work requires narrow span of control.

3. *Organizational level*: Top executives look after important and specialized activities and, therefore, the span is narrow at the top level but at lower levels the span can be wide, since supervisors are mainly concerned with routine jobs.

4. *Assistance to managers*: Managers can supervise more subordinates when they have considerable additional help, such as technical and secretarial support. Thus, span can be wide.

5. *Physical proximity*: When subordinates are located within close physical proximity of one another, managers can coordinate activities more easily thereby span can be wide.

6. *Few nonsupervisory duties of manager*: Managers can handle more subordinates when they have few nonsupervisory duties to perform, such as doing part of the subordinates' work themselves.

7. *Clearly defined authority*: If authority-responsibility structure is well defined and understood by everyone clearly, superior can supervise more number of subordinates.

8. *System of control*: Effective control mechanics can enable the manager to supervise more number of subordinates.

9. *Financial factors*: A narrow span requires additional managers at extra cost. Wide span on the other hand may result into organizational inefficiencies. Adequate span is to be maintained taking into consideration of costs and benefits of organization structure with such span of management.

Taking into the above conditions, companies can reduce the hierarchical levels of middle management thereby increasing the span of control. This process of shrinking the size of work force at the same time improving organizational efficiency and effectiveness is called **downsizing.**

A **tall** organization structure is one that has many hierarchical levels and narrow span of control whereas **flat** organization structure is one that has few hierarchical levels and wide span of control.

What is an Appropriate Span of Management?

For long, management consultants argued over, what will be the appropriate number of subordinates directly reporting to a specific manager? Some people felt it should be narrow, others felt that it should be wide. For example, Urwick suggests that no manager should supervise directly the work of more than five, or at the most six direct subordinates whose work interlocks.

According to J.C. Worth, consider that a manager can effectively manage the work of as many as 20 subordinates.

V.A. Graicunas, a French management consultant introduced a theory on span of management where he explained three kind of relationships that a superior can have with his subordinates.

1. Direct one-to-one relationships: These are relationships of the superior directly with his immediate subordinates. Thus, A with two subordinates B and C will have two direct one-to-one relationships, viz., A to B and A to C.

2. Cross-relationships: These relationships are created when subordinates consult amongst one another. Here two cross-relationships created are B with C and C with B. The formula for finding the number of these relationships in $n(n-1)$ where n stands for the number of subordinates.

3. Group relationships: Direct group relationships exist between the superior and each possible combination of subordinates. Here, A may talk to B with C in his presence or A may talk to C with B in his presence. Where the number of subordinates is large, the number of direct group relationships can be found out by the formula: $n\ (2^2/2-1)$.

The formula to calculate the total number of all the three kinds of relationships with and among subordinates is $n\ (2^n/2+n-1)$. When $n=2$ the no. of relationships will be 6 on the other hand when $n=4$, the total relationships go up to 44.

Graicunas' formula, however is not very practical use for the following two reasons:

1. It ignores the frequency of interaction of manager with its subordinates which takes the time of manager on daily basis or that each relationship is important for efficient managing a group of subordinates.
2. The actual span of management is determined by a number of factors affecting span of management which have not been taken into consideration while framing the formula.

Drucker suggested wide span to build the least number of management levels and forged the shortest possible chain of command. Van Fleet in 1983 described how the Lockheed Corporation assigned point values to the span of control factors. For example, in the case of job function, he assigned the rating of '1' to the job if all the functions were identical, a '2' if the functions were essentially similar; 'up to 5' if the functions were fundamentally distinct. Similarly, other span factors like complexity of functions, coordination and planning time required were assigned values on a 5-point scale the higher the number of points, the narrow the span. Recent studies suggest that the appropriate span of control must be determined by the contingent upon specific situation and value judgement.

REVIEW QUESTIONS

Long Answer Questions

1. Define the term 'Organization'. Explain the mechanism involved in organizing.
2. Describe the principles of good organization.
3. What is the importance of organizing? Describe the various steps involved in the process of organizing.
4. What is informal organization? Describe its benefits and limitations.
5. What is informal organization? What are the different types of informal groups?
6. Explain the concept of group dynamics. How does a matured group develop to perform in an organization?
7. What is group cohesiveness? Describe the factors that affect group cohesiveness.
8. What do you mean by span of management? Explain the factors which affect an effective span of management.
9. Describe the purposes of management by committees. What are the advantages and disadvantages of committees?
10. Describe the characteristics of an autonomous work team.

Short Notes

1. Closed systems and open systems
2. Types of informal groups

3. Explain flat organization structure and how does it form?
4. Describe the conditions of effective functioning of committees.

CASE STUDY

Dahiya Steel Company recently undertook a restructuring aimed at eliminating two management levels. This is primary aim to streamline decision making by reducing the number of layers from seven to five at GM through which decisions must travel. The changes affected about 100 employees including 15 managers. If one wanted to reduce the number of hierarchical levels in organization the only way to do so without reducing the number of employees at the bottom would be to increase span of control. Linking of activity at the top of organization with those at the middle and lower level as well as horizontal coordination are particularly useful because they facilitate the exchange of ideas across organizational units. GM wanted a structure that would enable authority to respond more quickly to the market and to measure more easily the performance of its organizational units. This structure facilitates the cut cost and shed extra flash (manpower) of the organization.

Questions for Case

1. How would you characterize the new changes in organization structure at GM? What difficulties in terms of employees' resentment might they face?
2. Suggest some future possibilities for using job enrichment to harmonize the situation and thereby enhancing results.
3. In view of new changes in organizational structure, what do you expect improvement in horizontal coordination?

Chapter 9
Organization Structure

9.1 CONCEPTS OF ORGANIZATION STRUCTURE

Organization structure is the formal hierarchical arrangement of positions with adequate delegation of authority and responsibility as well as uninterrupted communication designed by management to link the tasks of individuals and groups in achieving organizational goals. It is a tool through which management directs, co-ordinates and controls the business.

Organization chart is a line diagram that shows the superior-subordinate relationships that indicating the chain of command and the titles that have been assigned to the position holders. A tight chart creates a situation for employees which limits their interaction with a few persons and leads to routine and often impersonal behaviour. A loose, flexible structure, on the contrary offers a great deal of opportunities to expand interaction with large number of people and behave in innovative and personalized manner. The latter encourages individual employees to develop problem-solving orientation, to take initiative and to experience personal and professional growth. Organization structure varies with the following three main components:

1. departmentalization of positions and units,
2. methods vertical coordination, and
3. methods of horizontal coordination.

Departmentalization: It is the clustering of units into departments to achieve organization goals. Four of the most common pattern of departmentalization are **functional, divisional,**

hybrid, and matrix. Briefly, the functional structure groups positions into units on the basis of similarity of expertise, skills, and work activities (e.g., marketing, accounting, production or operation, and human resources). In contrast, the divisional structure groups positions into units according to similarity of products (e.g., a separate division for each of several products). The hybrid structure combines aspects of both the functional and divisional forms, with some jobs grouped into departments by function and others grouped by products. Finally, the matrix structure superimposes, or overlays, a horizontal set of divisional reporting relationships onto a hierarchical functional structure.

Methods of vertical coordination: It is the linking of activities at the top of organization with those at the middle and lower levels in order to achieve organizational goals. Vertical coordination can be achieve through formalization, span of management, centralization versus decentralization, delegation, and line and staff positions.

Methods of horizontal coordination: It is the linking of activities across departments at same levels. Horizontal coordination provides an additional means of processing information in course of producing their products or services in organizations. Horizontal coordination mechanisms supplement the basic hierarchy and related methods of vertical coordination. Such coordinating efforts with peers are particularly useful in promoting innovation/creativity across organizational units through direct contact, liaison roles, task forces, teams and managerial integrators.

Type of structure useful for a particular organization depends on a number of factors as shown below. In other words, what is called for is the *contingency view of organization.*

1. Environment: Managers play the role of 'boundary spanners', that is they must constantly have tab on the organization's environment. In order to cope with environmental change, the organization must adapt an open systems approach. All open systems share the following characteristics:

1. Open systems have permeable boundaries; hence they interact with the environment for survival.

2. Synergy is the 1+1=3 effect, i.e., an open system adds up to more than the sum of its parts. Only when all parts work in unison, the end result will be achieved.
3. Dynamic equilibrium of resources from environment is needed for survival.

Burns and Stalker (1961) suggested that two types of organizational structure are needed to deal with different environment conditions. These were **mechanistic** and **organic structures.** The mechanistic structure exists in a relatively stable environment with very little or no interaction with the environment. Such structure implies centralization of authority at the top, departmentalization of jobs, hierarchy of command, narrow span and intense division of labour. An organic structure, on the other hand, is more akin to dynamic environment. It has generally wide span of control which give rise to a flat form, more general supervision and more decentralization. Here more emphasis is placed on individual expertise and less on the formal hierarchy. These observations of Burns and Stalker suggest that different structures are successful in different environments.

The work of Burns and Stalker was expanded by Lawrence and Lorsch (1967). They suggested that the relationship between the environment and structure can further be extended to different attributes such as values, diversity of attitudes, perceptions, and interpersonal orientations among the members. These elements are relevant for their departments which may not always be congruent with organization goals.

2. Strategy: In recent years, organizations often change their strategies in order to better utilize their resources to fuel growth. The changes in strategy do not fit the current structures. Unless organizations subsequently make adjustments in structure, the new strategies cannot realize their potential and serious inefficiencies will result. To fit into the strategy, the structure will be redesigned taking into the components as mentioned in Fig. 9.1 and their relationships to the four types of organization structures: functional, divisional, hybrid and matrix.

3. Technology: Technology is defined as the process of transformation of inputs (materials, equipment, labour, etc.) into outputs (products and services). Technology results from a combination of knowledge, equipment, and work methodology used by an organization. Technologies are employed for different processes of production like batch production, mass production or tailor-made specialized production. The more complex the technology, the greater the number of levels in structure. Continuous process production technology was characterized by high vertical differentiation, low horizontal differentiation and low formalization.

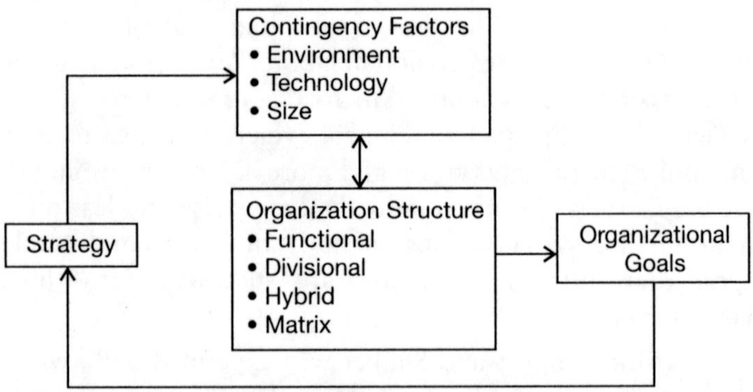

Fig. 9.1: Major components influencing the design of strategic organization structure

4. Size: As an organization grows from small to large, its organizational structure becomes more complex. Moreover, as the size increases, it tends to increase in specialization and functional differentiation.

The details of organization structures are as follows:

Functional Structure: It is a type of departmentalization in which positions are grouped according to their main functional (or specialized area of expertise) areas in a business organization. For example, production (operations), finance, marketing, human resources beside other relevant areas according to its own needs. Functional organization structure looks like as below:

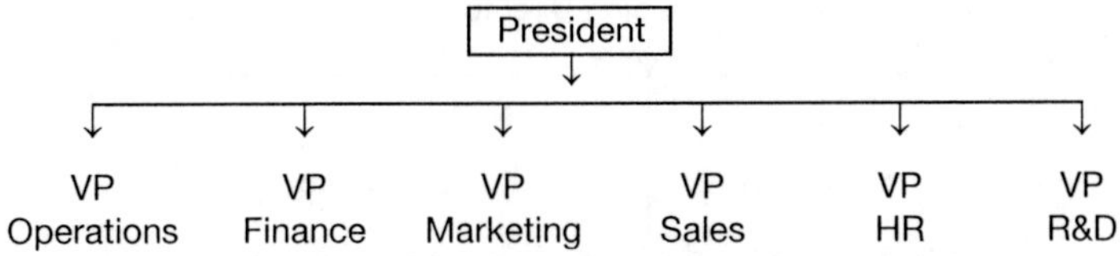

The functional form of organization has the following advantages and disadvantages as shown in table below:

Major advantages and disadvantages of a Functional Structure:

Advantages	*Disadvantages*
In-depth development of expertise	Slow response time across other functional problems
Clear career path within function	Delay in decisions as one function waits for another
Effective use of resources	Bottlenecks due to sequential tasks
Possible economies of scale	Restricted view of organization among employees
Technical advantage over competitors due to specialist managers	Difficult to measure performance of one function because various functions have a hand in organizational results
Ease of coordination within function	Narrow training for manager limited to his function

Functional structure is useful for firms (i) having a limited number of related products or services or deal with a relatively homogeneous set of customers or clients, (ii) operating in relatively stable environments in which change occurs at a slow enough rate for the various functions to adjust their efforts, and (iii) using by large organizations when considerable coordination is required among products.

Divisional Structure: It is a type of departmentalization in which positions are grouped according to similarity of products. In this, each division contains the major functional resources it needs to pursue its own goals with little or reliance on other divisions. The below shows the divisional structure for three divisions like product A, product B and product C. Here, each division can operate fairly independently.

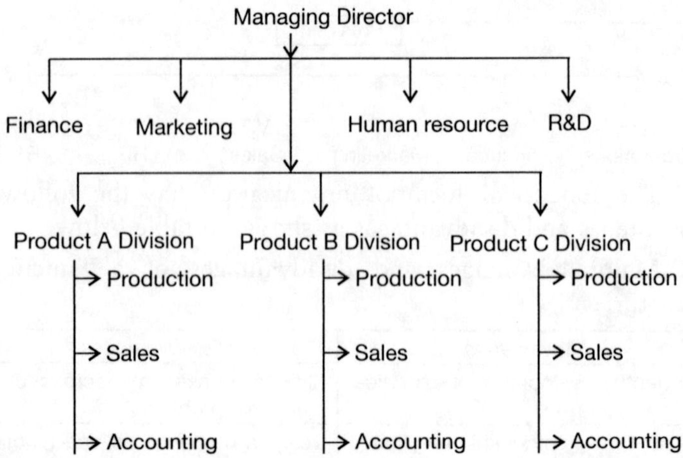

Divisional structures are also referred to as self-contained structures because the major functions are contained within each division. There are three forms of divisional structure: product, geographic and customer.

The **division by product** is shown above.

The **division by geography** is adopted when it is important to provide products that are tailored to the needs of different regions like eastern, central and western regions.

Advantages	*Disadvantages*
Fast response to environmental change	Duplication of resources in each division
Simplified coordination across functions	Reduction of in-depth expertise
Strong orientation to customer requirements	Strong competition among divisions
Accurate measurement of division performance	Limited sharing of expertise across divisions
Broad training in general management skills	Restriction of innovation to divisions

The **division by customer structure** is developed mainly when there are major differences among types of customers that preclude adequate coordination among the customers within a standard functional structure. In this, each division contains individuals who perform the necessary functions for a specific type of customer. For example, a bank is also provided services on the basis of customer needs like loans, term deposits, foreign exchange, savings, etc.

Hybrid Structure: It is a form of departmentalization that adopts parts of both functional and divisional structures at the same level of management. It attempts to incorporate advantages of both structures. Functional departments are usually created to take advantage of resource utilization, efficiencies, economy of scale, whereas divisional departments are used when there are potential benefits from a stronger focus on products, services, or markets. For example, IBM's hybrid structure has got functional departments of law and external relations, R&D, and personnel in which in-depth expertise is important, whereas divisional departments are divided into geographical regions to better serve differing customer needs throughout the world. The hybrid structure is used for medium-size or large organizations that have sufficient resources to justify divisions as well as some functional/staff departments.

Matrix Structure: It is a type of departmentalization which combine functional and divisional product pattern in the same organization structure. It becomes necessary when an organization has to manage a number of independent projects in mission mode. This kind of structure is advised for development of new product in research and development, in launching a weather satellite, in large engineering organizations or in management consulting firms in which professional experts work together on a project. Matrix organization structure as shown in Fig. 9.2 where functional departments of finance, marketing, operations, and human resources give the matrix a vertical structure, while the product divisions 1 and 2 give it a horizontal structure (thus, the simultaneous use of two superstructures).

To be effective, the product manager should be of same status that of functional departments. The product division is dissolved on completion of the product/project and members who are with product division return to the respective functional departments, hence in the matrix organization no fresh permanent structure is created. During product execution, they work under the product manager however they are also responsible to their functional head and their functional heads have authority over them thus, each functional staff has two bosses—his functional head and his product manager thereby unity of command is violated.

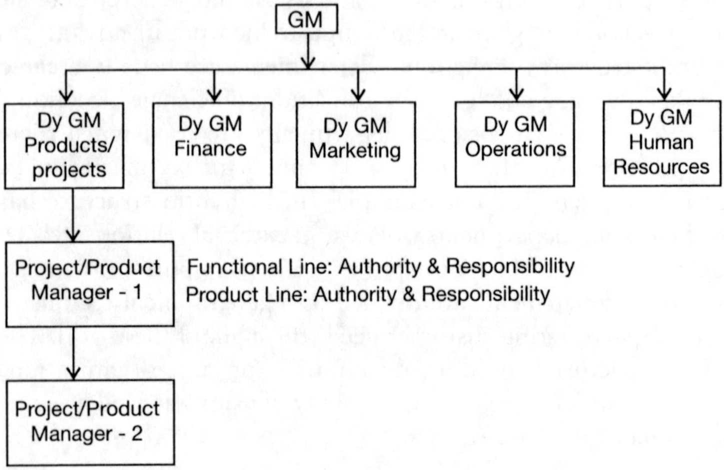

Fig. 9.2: Matrix structure

Steps for Making Matrix Structure Successful

1. Define the purpose of project or task.
2. Clarify the roles, authority, and responsibility of managers and team members.
3. Ensure members of task force thus developed are experts of their own field rather than on rank.
4. Provide the prime and equal importance to functional and divisional (product) managers.
5. There is pressure for shared resources. It needs flexibility in the use of functional resources across projects or products.
6. Management begins to decentralize decision making. This can be achieved by increasing the use of business teams and task forces that make decisions in such areas as product development and cost cutting, as well as

encourage greater cooperation among functional divisions.

7. As structure is cross-functional teams as well as dual reporting, it needs collaborative culture. Thus, managers require special training, particularly in interpersonal skills.
8. The demands of products placed on the organization are changing and unpredictable and also frequently making technological improvement by competitors making it important to have a large capacity for processing information and coordinating activities quickly.
9. Reward product managers and team members suitably.

Advantages of a Matrix Structure

1. Decision making is decentralized as it is made at the level of the divisional product manager and the functional manager. This allows upper-level management to concentrate on strategic issues.
2. Strong horizontal coordination to project or product beyond what is normally possible in the functional structure alone, increasing the probability of success.
3. Improve environmental monitoring.
4. Fast response to change because many decisions are made at lower levels.
5. Functional specialists can be added to or reassigned from projects/products as needed, allowing effective use of human resources.
6. Efficient use of support systems, such as computers, special equipment, etc. can be allocated among many projects as and when needed, thereby reducing the costs of such systems.

Disadvantages of a Matrix Structure

1. Increase administrative cost.
2. Potential confusion over authority and responsibility.
3. Heighten possibilities of conflicts due to dual-authority and responsibility of managers between product

managers and functional managers. Managers show greater loyalty to their parent department than project/product manager.

4. Excessive focus on internal relations at the expense of clients and project goals.
5. Encourage group decision making to the point where even relatively minor decisions are made in groups, causing a serious erosion of productivity.
6. Slow response to change due to poor interpersonal skills of participants or upper management attempts to retain centralized control.

REVIEW QUESTIONS

Long Answer Questions

1. Compare and contrast the pure line and line and staff organization structures.
2. Based on concepts of organization structure, draw line and staff organization structure of a medium-sized manufacturing unit.
3. "Sound organization structure is an essential prerequisite of efficient management." Discuss this statement and describe the various elements for development of organization structures.
4. "Drucker's statement—any work on structure must start with objectives and strategy." Discuss with its components.
5. Draw line diagram of divisional structure by product and describe its advantages and disadvantages.
6. "A matrix organization may be used to overcome some of the problems associated with the traditional forms of departmentation." Elaborate.

Short Notes

1. Limitations of traditional line and staff organization
2. Steps making matrix structure successful
3. Hybrid departmentalization
4. Product and process departmentation

CASE STUDY

The Mohan Foods & Beverages Ltd. is based at Gaziabad. It manufactures fast foods and beverages. The organization currently has a functional organizational structure with the following major positions reporting directly to the Managing Director (MD): GM (Production), GM (Finance), GM (Marketing), Dy. GM (Planning and Administration includes human resource function).

Because of changing conditions in the markets for the company's two main products—foods and beverages, Mohan Foods & Beverages is thinking about changing its organization structure to a hybrid design. In the process, the MD is considering adding two Sr.GM one for (Production) and another Sr.GM gets GM (Finance) and GM (Planning and Administration which has been elevated from Dy. GM to GM) further elevating marketing position as Sr.GM (Marketing). It is also decided that Sr.GM (Marketing) will have two wings—GM (Marketing-Delhi and Eastern Zone) and another GM (Marketing-other zones). Thus, there are three Sr.GMs who report directly to MD. Sr.GM (Production) has two wings—GM (Foods) and another GM (Beverages).

1. Draw an organization chart depicting Mohan Foods & Beverages' current organization structure.
2. Draw a chart showing the proposed change from Mohan Foods & Beverages' current structure to a hybrid organization structure.
3. Describe the pros and cons of the proposed new structure and some possible ways of promoting innovation.

Chapter 10
Authority, Delegation and Decentralisation

10.1 AUTHORITY

Authority is the right to make decisions, carry out actions, and direct others in matters related to the duties and goals of a position. In the organization structure, authority is to dispersed among its various positions.

Henri Fayol, "Authority is the right to give orders and power to exact obedience."

Louis Allen, "The sum of the powers and rights entrusted to make possible the performance of the work delegated."

Daris defines authority, "as the right of decision and command."

From the above definitions, the following characteristics of authority may be induced:

1. There is the existence of right in authority which puts the manager in a position by which he can get the things done from his subordinates.
2. The right of giving of order is legitimate.
3. Authority is exercised by making decisions and seeing that these are carried out.
4. The use of authority may control the negative aspects of behaviour.
5. The use of authority is determined by the personality factors of the possessor.

According to **classical authority theory,** authority originates at the top in formal structure in organization and managers at each level of organization derive their authority from the managers at the higher level. According to **human relations view,** the authority of a superior depends on the willingness of his subordinates to accept it. A subordinate accepts his superior's authority because he considers it to be legitimate, otherwise he will have to face several unpleasant consequences, such as dismissal, penalty, fine, etc. and hence the subordinate in his own interest accepts the authority of his superior.

Most subordinates are unwilling to accept the authority of the superiors outside certain limits which Herbert A. Simon refers to as areas of acceptance. These areas vary from worker to worker and from situation to situation. Hence, manager intuitively aware of their workers' areas, avoid overstepping them. Four conditions must exist to make an order acceptable to a person:

1. He must understand the order.
2. He must believe that it is not inconsistent with the purpose of the organization.
3. He must believe that it is not incompatible which is his own interest.
4. He must be mentally and physically able to comply with it.

It is essential for managers to have authority if they are to get tasks accomplished by their subordinates. Authority relationships ensure cooperative action and facilitate the achievement of organizational goals by stating each employee's responsibility.

According to H. Koontz, "authority in an organization is the right in a position to exercise discretion in making decisions affecting others."

Herbert A. Simon has described three functions of authority:

1. It enforces obedience to norms—otherwise sanction against him.
2. It secures expertise in the making of decision.

3. It permits centralization of decision making and co-ordination of activity.

Limitations of Authority: There are several restrictions and limitations to the concept of authority:

1. Executive's authority is restricted by the enterprise's objectives, policies, procedures, and programs.
2. It also limits as per Articles of Association of the Company Act, 1956.
3. The lower down in the managerial hierarchy there is more restrictions of the authority. The higher up in the managerial hierarchy there is less limitations and broader the scope of authority as shown below.

Responsibility arises from the superior-subordinate relationship. Résponsibility may be defined as the obligation of a subordinate to whom a duty has been assigned, to perform the duty. Authority should commensurate with responsibility.

Line, Staff and Functional Authority: There are three types of authority in organization: line, staff and functional. Line and staff structure is shown in Fig. 10.1. Broken lines indicate staff function related to line divisions:

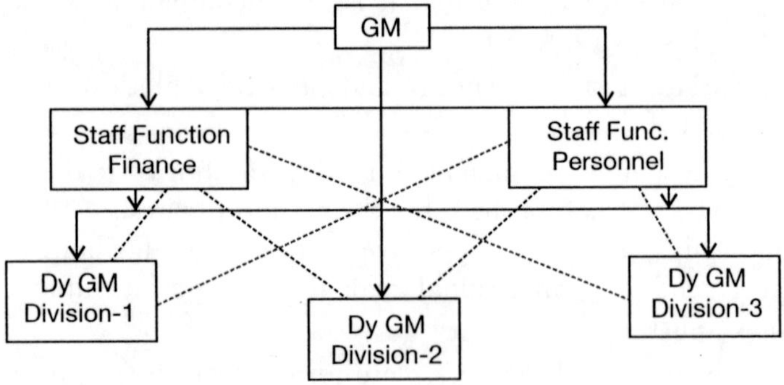

Fig. 10.1: Line and staff structure

Line Authority: A superior exercises direct command over a subordinate. Line authority is represented by the scalar chain of command from top to bottom levels in the hierarchy for decision-making. Similarly, communication channel is from top to bottom. Here authority relationship is direct line or steps. Line managers are those who are directly responsible for the achievement of organization objectives. For example, in manufacturing organization, production, sales and costing are line functions.

Advantages: (i) It is characterised by simplicity and clarity; (ii) chain of command ties the whole organization in a coordinated and unified whole; (iii) it can function with speed; and (iv) it is consistent with the principle of unity of command.

Disadvantages: Its disadvantages lie in the absence of staff specialists to advice, guide, and support line managers.

Staff Authority: Managers in staff capacity give advice to line managers. The staff managers are those who provide support in the form of advice and services to line managers to take right decision at right time. Personnel manager in staff capacity gives advice to production manager with respect to industrial relations problem so that line manager in this case production manager can take right decisions to circumvent the problem. Staff departments like personnel, finance, etc. have functional authority, which is authority over others in the organization in matters related directly to their respective functions. Here is in addition to line functions, staff functions are available for the management to advise/recommend on specialised functions in addition to their own functions to be performed. On the other hand, still, conflicts between line and staff managers frequently arise. Staff departments sometimes grow very large and began to oversee the line departments (that they are supposed to assist as a specialist) to such a point that they are counter productive. Thus, it is necessary to review the strength of staff personnel periodically. Certain line officers may place too great a reliance upon staff officers serving as their brains—not good relationship creating conflict. Although expert advice is available, it reaches the workers through line manager, may create confusion. To the contrary, the staff is unable to carry out its plans or recommendations because of lack of authority.

Advantages: The staff experts help line managers in the efficient performance of their functions by providing them support in the form of advice and services.

Disadvantages: (i) It complicates the problems of coordination, control and communication; (ii) staff specialists often infringe the unity of command; and (iii) line-staff relationships are often characterized by conflict.

Functional Authority: When a staff unit exercises command authority over specific matters relating to some aspect of line functions, it creates a functional structure. A functional structure is also created when the corporate executives exercise functional control over their respective counterparts in the semi-autonomous divisions of the company. It is generally delegated by corporate executive to those staff department which has special knowledge/specialisation and where there is danger of diverse interpretations of policies by line managers. As a matter of fact, the line managers are deprived of some authority.

Such functional authority (to draw from line authority) to a staff manager is always in specific matters and relates to his area of expertise and under specific guidelines. Functional authority should fulfil the following three conditions:

1. It should cover only a minor aspect of total job of line manager.
2. It should relate to area in which line supervisors do not have expertise. This means that functional authority should be restricted to a staff manager's area of speciality.
3. It should be granted only when company-wide uniformity is desirable. For example, centralized recruitment should be handled by personnel department. Similarly, safety director may have complete authority to issue instructions to all departments regarding installation and use of safety equipment.

Advantages: It makes possible the adoption and implementation of uniform systems and procedures throughout the company.

Disadvantages: (i) It creates dual accountability and weakens the unity of command and (ii) it causes conflict among line and staff managers.

Line and staff are often characterized more by conflict than co-operation. Staff specialists make complain that line managers are resistant to their ideas, and the line managers make complain that staff managers are sky-gazing specialists with no comprehension of practical situations.

10.2 AUTHORITY AND POWER

Authority in an organization is the right of a person occupying the position to exercise discretion in making decisions affecting others. It is of course one type of power within an organization.

Distinction between Authority and Power

Authority	*Power*
It is position of superior to provide the authority to subordinate to perform in accordance with authority delegated.	It is the ability of an individual to influence another individual to perform an act.
With the change in position, the authority of the individual also changes.	Power goes with the people. It is nothing to do with position.
Authority is delegated to a subordinate by his superior according to need to perform his duties.	Power cannot be delegated to any one, rather used by individual to influence anyone irrespective of his direct subordinate.
Authority increases as one goes up the organizational hierarchy.	Power will be with the expertise possessed by individual and goes without hierarchical position.
Authority may be legitimate because it is provided to the position.	Power may not be legitimate. Power of individual may not force one to accept it—extra constitutional.
Authority relationship one can see from organization structure.	Organization structure does not show power centers.
Authority is mostly well defined and commensurate with responsibility.	It is undefined and unlimited and only defined by his expertise, knowledge and charisma.
Authority flows downward to the subordinates.	Power flows in all directions. A expert gives advice to all present.
Narrow term—one source or subset of power.	Broad concept—can achieve results when authority fails.

Power, a much broader concept than authority, is the ability of a person to influence or to cause a person to perform an act.

(i) Power can be legitimate which normally arises from position.

(ii) Power may also come from the expertness of a person. This is the power of knowledge. Physicians, scientists and lawyers may have considerable influence on others, because they have expertise in their own fields.

(iii) Power exists as referent power to influence people because people believes in him and his ideas. Thus, Mahatma Gandhi had charismatic power but had very little legitimate power. By the force of his personality, his ideas, and his ability to preach, he strongly used to influence the behaviour of many people. Likewise, movie star or military hero might possess a considerable referent power.

(iv) Power arises from the ability of some people to grant rewards. University professors have to reward/grant or withhold higher grades.

(v) Coercive power is still another type—normally arising from legitimate power, it is the power to punish negative reward. For example, withholding increment, etc.

Empowerment means that employees, managers, or teams at all levels in organization have the power to make decisions without asking their superior for permission. Moreover, concept of delegation of authority are also closely related to empowerment. Both, delegation and empowerment, are matter of degree as shown below:

- Power should be equal to responsibility (P=R).
- If power is greater than responsibility (P>R), this could result in an autocratic behaviour.
- If responsibility is greater than the power (R>P), subordinates' frustration because they do not have the necessary power to carry out the task for which they are responsible.

10.3 DELEGATION

A manager cannot himself do all the tasks necessary for the achievement of objectives, his capacity to do work and to take decisions is limited. He, therefore, assigns a part of his work to his subordinates along with both the responsibility and authority necessary to achieve expected results. This downward pushing of authority to make decisions is known as delegation of authority. In the words of Louis A. Allen, "If the manager requires his subordinate to perform the work, he must entrust him with part of the rights and powers which he otherwise would have to exercise himself to get the work done." It should be remembered, however, that by delegating authority the manager does not surrender his authority rather retain the overall authority.

Principles of Delegation—(1) Functions defined—define clearly the functions to be performed by subordinates; (2) delegation by results expected—standards/norms of results to be decided; (3) parity of authority and responsibility—responsibility without authority makes a subordinate ineffective whereas authority without responsibility makes subordinates irresponsible; (4) absoluteness of responsibility—delegation is his responsibility. After delegating, he remains accountable for the activities of his subordinates; (5) unity of command—at one time, a subordinate should receive command and be accountable to only one superior. If a person reports two superiors for the same job, confusion and conflict will arise; (6) well-defined limits of authority—this will avoid overlapping of authority. This will allow the subordinates to take initiative within the ambit of authority. He will refer to superior those matters which are beyond the limit of authority; (7) authority level principle—avoid to refer the decision to his boss if it is within his jurisdiction of authority. Only matters outside the scope of authority should be referred to superior; (8) establish proper control by superior over delegated powers to subordinates. Time to time, these powers should be reviewed.

Process of Delegation—According to Peter Drucker, managers should do activity analysis, decision analysis and relationship analysis in order to decide what activities they should assign to their subordinates, how much authority they should delegate to them and what kind of accountability to accept to them.

The process of delegation involves the following steps:

1. **Determining the goals:** The manager assigns goals to his subordinates. Successful delegation is characterised as delegation by objectives.
2. **Defining responsibility and authority:** The person who has to perform a job efficiently should know what his job is and how much authority he has to perform it.
3. **Motivating subordinates:** The manager motivates the subordinates to do their assigned job with zeal and enthusiasm. He uses financial and non-financial incentives to motivates the subordinates.
4. **Holding accountability:** Whatever the nature and extent of delegation, manager always observes the activities of subordinates to review their progress and provides guidance whenever necessary. He holds them accountable for the work assigned but he will still be ultimately accountable or responsible to his superiors for completion of each task and coordination with the overall organizational work.
5. **Training of subordinates:** Authority must be commensurate with the responsibility. Managers, therefore, organize training programmes to enhance their knowledge of the job so that they carry out the delegated task.
6. **Establishing control:** Specific standards of performance are established and communicated to subordinates to enable them to assess their performance against standards and self-control their activities for ease of operations.

Advantages of Effective Delegation

1. Delegation helps the manager to distribute of his heavy workload to his subordinates. By reducing workload for routine matters, he can concentrate on more important policy matters.

2. It speeds decision making because subordinates need not approach the boss every time for a decision.

3. It leads to better decisions. As authority is distributed, an individual concentrates on a few matters facilitating him to take quality decisions.

4. It helps train subordinates and improve motivation and morale. Effective delegation develops subordinates to accept responsibility and exercise judgement. Seeing the results of his action, he gets motivated and his morale becomes high.

5. It serves as compensation to those employees who have the limited scope of promotions.

6. The process of delegation results in superior-subordinate relationship which gives rise to a formal organization structure. It ensures continuity in business.

Barriers to Effective Delegation

In spite of the above advantages, there are certain road-blocks for effective delegation:

1. Fear of loss of power—some managers feel uncomfortable when they see that their subordinates take decisions without their consultation. It hearts their ego.
2. Some managers do not develop the art and science of effective delegation hence they take the easy path not to venture for delegation.
3. The "I can do it better myself" fallacy—a manager has false confidence that he can do better than his subordinates. This may be due to lack of confidence in subordinates.
4. Fear of being exposed—some inefficient managers are afraid of their subordinates outshining them and exposed.
5. Difficulty in briefing (poor communicator)—many times managers are reluctant to delegate because they think it is easier to do a task themselves than to spend time on briefing the subordinates.

6. Inability to establish and exercise control through proper feedback of use of authority delegated to subordinates.

10.4 DECENTRALISATION OF AUTHORITY

Decentralisation of authority is much more than delegation. Delegation is a process or an act while decentralisation is the end result of delegation and dispersal of authority. Delegation of authority to subordinates at all levels denotes relationship between a superior and a subordinate, whereas decentralization of authority to a department functionally responsible for a particular function denotes relationship between the top management and various departments or divisions. According to philosophy of organization, decentralisation requires a careful selection of which departments to push down and which to hold near the top in the organization structure. This selective dispersal of authority is based on importance and specialisation, i.e., important departments are kept near the higher echelon. For example, personnel department is given the functions of personnel management wherein authority is vested in the head of department to deal with personnel matters.

Organizations vary in degree to which their departments and divisions are decentralised. Degree of decentralisation depends upon its external environment, to coordinate activities within its formal structure, to do its particular kind of work and to manage capabilities of its members. The appropriate degree of decentralisation enables an organization to (1) become more flexible and capable of greater speed as it reacts to changes in the external environment; (2) deal with complex combinations of business activities; (3) cope with growth and change; (4) placing managers who are familiar with the work in positions; (5) relieve managers of information and decision overload; (6) motivate and improve human resources; and (7) increase a sense of ownership for work and for the organization.

Manager must find the best match between the degree of decentralization and their organization's external and internal environments. The challenge facing managers is to balance the advantages of decentralisation without losing the coordination, integration, and control advantages provided by centralisation.

Determinants of Appropriate Decentralisation

1. When the external environment is more competitive, turbulent, hostile, and uncertain in order to compete with their competitors, it is necessary that increasing number of managers are equipped with decentralisation of authority.
2. Strategies pursued by organizations dictate a need for decentralisation because the complexity of doing business in many markets would overwhelm managers.
3. Size and complexity affect decentralisation. The larger an organization is, more it needs decentralisation. Large and complex organizations, such as Procter & Gamble and IBM, need high levels of decentralisation.
4. Interdependent task is also relevant to decentralisation because monitoring of the work must be done at lower-level. The same is true for tasks that involve uncertainty and non-routine technologies requiring frequent consultation, advice, or direction. For example, research and development is usually quite decentralised.
5. The decision to decentralisation of authority to lower-level managers is high enough. Decentralisation, however, helps lower-level managers learn to make necessary abilities or motivation to make the right decisions. Decentralisation often improves the quality of the decisions that managers make.

Managers should take all of the above considerations into account when making decisions to decentralisation.

Advantages of Decentralisation

1. Decentralisation reduces problem of communication and red tape.
2. It permits quicker and better decision making. It is nearer to work and situation to take better decision.
3. Decentralisation recognises and actually capitalizes on the importance of human element—more freedom to do the tasks.

4. Decentralisation leads to a competitive climate among departments to excel.
5. Decentralisation ensures the development of managers.
6. It facilitates diversification of products, activities and markets.

Disadvantages of Decentralisation

1. Duplication of efforts or resources.
2. Decisions are taken for the interest of one division/ location not for entire organization effecting morale of human resource.
3. Weak central leadership.
4. Decentralisation has disadvantages for lower-level managers. It places major responsibilities and the worries and burdens associated with this work directly on their shoulders. The result can be longer hours and more intense work, often increasing stress.

10.5 COORDINATION

When work is divided into departments, someone must integrate and coordinate the activities of departments. Coordination links two or more organizational members and/or departments so that they function well together. Coordinating, for example, links the production of stationery with the sale of stationery beyond organization structure.

A look at an organization chart reveals that organizational members and activities are separated both vertically and horizontally. All of these people and organizational activities need to be coordinated and integrated if the organization is to accomplish its goals in efficient and effective manner. Thus, organization have two basic coordination needs: vertical and horizontal coordination.

Herbert Simon, a Nobel laureate, notes that organizations are coordinated by programming and feedback. Coordination by programming reflects a blueprint for action. For example, rules, policies, procedures, plans, and schedules guide and govern organizational activities.

Organizational sociologist James D. Thompson notes that coordination by communication and interaction between two or more organizational members. In vertical and horizontal coordination, there are some of which are programmed (goal statements) and some of which are feedback (direct supervision). In addition, organization's culture plays an important role in the coordination activity. The shared belief and values that comprise the culture also brings about coordinated and integrated behaviour.

There are number of techniques which are being used for effective coordination. These are as given below:

The organization's **Vertical Coordination** needs can be achieved in a number of ways, including direct supervision, standardization, and goal statements.

Direct supervision: In small, uncomplicated organizations or within individual work units, managers, team leaders, and other unit members can meet face to face. This direct supervision facilitates communication, direction, and assistance, and integrates activities across organizational levels. Thus, GM of a paper firm might communicate directly with the Dy.GM of marketing who, in turn, talk to Sr. Manager of sales, thereby coordinating together different levels.

Standardization: Managers coordinate work across levels by standardizing activities. Large spans of control, high communication needs, desire for uniformity in operations, and physical dispersion all create pressure to standardize activities. Coordination would be smooth if rules and procedures are standardized, spans of control are optimum and proper feedback mechanism is developed.

Goal Statement: Goals of organization would be interwoven at vertical and horizontal hierarchy's goals. These interrelated goals guide the actions of lower-level employees, and the accomplish of the goals becomes the means through which the next higher-level achieves its goals, and so on back up to the top of hierarchy.

Horizontal Coordination occurs at a single hierarchical level. Horizontal coordination can be achieved in several ways. In many instances, managers can use the same direct supervision, standardisation, and goal statement techniques that bring about vertical coordination. Additional techniques include direct contact, liaisons, task forces/teams, managerial linking roles, and multiple command systems.

Direct Contact: Achieving horizontal coordination for two managers who have a common problem can be as simple as talking to each other. Using the Fayol's gangplank principle, the Dy.GM of purchasing asks the Dy.GM of finance for permission to review the budget. This eliminates the need to work through multiple layers of management for budget change. The reduction in hierarchical levels (avoid standard hierarchical relationship) is intended to speed communication and coordination for horizontally separated departments.

Liaison: When the volume of contact between two departments becomes extremely heavy, management may assign a liaison to facilitate communication between the departments. This person constantly moves between the two departments to facilitate joint planning and problem solving.

Task Forces and Teams: When problems of coordination arise involving a large number of departments, managers may form a task force. The task force is a temporary group, composed of representatives from the departments experiencing the difficulty, that tackles the problem and dissolves when the problem is resolved. If the problem persists, the task force becomes permanent and is referred to as a task team.

Managerial Linking Roles: When conditions are highly uncertain with heterogeneous interdependent departments, to coordinate with such departments, a linking manager may be nominated with formal authority to say, "we are going to solve it this way."

Multiple Command Systems: Coordination is sometimes difficult when two or more departments each have command authority over an activity. Creating two such command centres violates Fayol's principle of unity of command, yet there are times when adopting this strategy brings about appropriate integration of two activities to deal with a project.

REVIEW QUESTIONS

Long Answer Questions

1. Explain the line and staff authority. What are the causes of line and staff conflict?
2. Explain the terms authority and responsibility. Why can authority be delegated but not responsibility?
3. Power and authority are not one and the something. Comment.
4. What is power? State the different sources of power.
5. What is delegation of authority? What obstacles stand in the way of effective delegation of authority?
6. Distinguish between delegation and decentralisation. What are the limitations of decentralisation?
7. Define decentralisation of authority. What are the advantages and limitations of decentralisation?
8. What is delegation? Explain the process of delegation.
9. Explain the term 'coordination.' What are the various techniques of effective coordination?
10. Describe the various determinants of appropriate decentalisation.

Short Notes

1. Authority and responsibility
2. Expert and referent power
3. Delegation vs. decentralisation of authority
4. Advantages of delegation of authority
5. Types of coordination
6. Coordination is as important as delegation

Chapter 11
Staffing

Staffing is the management function as it is concerned with human resource planning, recruiting, selecting, appraising and training, and developing employees.

11.1 HUMAN RESOURCE PLANNING

Definition.—Human resource planning is a management process of analyzing an organization's human resource needs relative to an organization's strategic plan at some specified time in future under changing conditions and devising the steps necessary to satisfy these needs. The human resource planning process which can be divided into three parts: (1) resource demand forecasting, (2) resource supply forecasting, and (3) human resource actions if surplus or shortage.

HR planning may be attempted for short-term plan—one year or less, mid-range plan—five years while 10 to 15 years span could be used for a prospective plan which may be amalgamated with corporate plan of the enterprise. The long lead time is necessary as the selection process (hiring) and training and development of the employees take time before they are available to the organization in a real sense.

HR Demand Forecasting: Strategic plan depends upon the firm's long-range business decisions. It may depend upon the following:

(i) **Job analysis** is the assessment of job requiring knowledge, skills, and abilities needed to perform the job.

(ii) **Demographics:** The changing profile of workforce in terms of age, sex, literacy, technical inputs, and social background have implications for HR planning.

(iii) **Economy:** Movement from prosperity to recession and back to prosperity pose considerable problems for the planner. These may be the result of government taxation, policies, import restrictions or curtailment of transfer of know-how. Though economic predictions are considerably difficult to make with accuracy, some consideration must be given to the level of economic activity in planning for human resources requirements.

(iv) **Technological trends:** Advances in technology have definite effects on the nature and mixture of job available. For example, advances in computer technology resulted in a decrease in the number of book-keepers and an increase in the computer programmers. The use of automatic equipment including robots replaces human labour.

(v) **Social trends:** Government directives for special quota for SC/ST, OBC, and physically challenged personnel, son of the soil, recent amendments in labour laws and various social and political factors that will help shaping the future business environment.

(vi) **Expansion/modernization** programme.

In considering the above factors and making a specific long-range projection, one method that can be utilized is termed as **"Delphi Technique"**. Essentially, it is an iterative questionnaire technique in which a large number of recognized experts are asked to make separately specific estimates of human resources needs in the future. This is followed by feedback of summerised results, followed by a request for a new estimate. After three or four iterations, their trends to be some convergence in specific future estimates. In effect, it is a 'judgement refining' process but the numbers resulting should still be regarded with considerable suspicion.

Short-range plan: Though long-range planning may appear to be a luxury to most firms, the human resource department does require some lead time to provide the human resources required by the firm in the short-run. Specific sales forecasts for the coming year must be translated into production programme. Various techniques can be used in making a short-term projection of both the amount of work to be done and number of personnel necessary to do it. **Time-Series analysis** can be used to identify trends in the past. This should enable some understanding of how the organization has changed over time. The bias in such analysis is in favour of the past and must be altered by review of many of the long-range factors discussed above.

Various ratios can be computed, such as the number of sales personnel in relation to the level of sales. Further systematic time study can be done to determine the manpower demand forecasts with the help of departmental managers, personnel, O&M, or work study specialists.

The modelling techniques which seek to project organization change including succession analysis, probabilistic analysis (referred to also as Markov analysis of personnel flow based on probability theory) and regression analysis. Simulation model which seeks to represent role of important personnel decisions, the consequences of personnel performance measures and accomplishment of corporate goals merits special mention. Systematic time and motion study can be used to determine a more accurate time for manufacturing items. Motion study is a process of analyzing a job to find the easiest, most effective and most economical method of doing it. Then, time study is to measure the manpower to manufacture one unit of items with the most effective way of producing the items.

The implications of normal attrition and personnel policies concerning internal promotions, transfers, career development, etc. could also be gauged by building these variables into the models.

Relocations/plant closure—Due to market demand, recession, etc. plants are relocated and sometimes non-viable workstations are likely to be closed. With the result retrenchment, voluntary retirement measures are to be undertaken, hence excess of manpower is shredded out.

HR Supply Forecasting

Every organization will have two major sources of supply of human resources: internal and external. Internal sources are personnel already on the pay-roll of the organization, i.e., its present workforce. In projecting future availability, the following factors are usually considered:

(i) Current manpower skills inventory—Personnel records should be summarised in some systematic manner to indicate the talent available for various positions, e.g., name, designation, department, date of birth, marital status, education background, professional training and development, work experience outstanding strength and abilities, personal development need and remarks. The skill inventory record on computer would be useful for human resource planning.

(ii) Productivity level—Future projection of resource need are often made on the basis of past experience. For example, let us suppose that average sales per person last year was ₹ 2.5 lakh per year. Review of changes in productivity levels reveals that sales per person have been increasing at the rate of 10 percent per year due to technology improvement, etc. If next year's projected sales is ₹ 2.5 crore, we would not anticipate an increase for 100 sales person (₹ 2.5 crore divided by ₹ 2.5 lakh), but rather for only 91 sales persons since expecting an increase in productivity per person to ₹ 2.75 lakh.

(iii) Organization structure—With a view to improve the productivity, there is a need to examine the existing organization structure of the organization under the following principles: Unity of objectives—The organization as a whole and part of it must contribute to the attainment of enterprise objectives. Division of work—Structure of organization should be divided and grouped the activities of enterprise that they contribute most effectively and efficiently. Span of control—The limit to the number of sub-ordinates who can be effectively supervised by an executive is to be taken into account in grouping and organising activities. Scalar Chain of Authority—Every sub-ordinate position in the enterprise must be linked by a line of formal authority in the organizational structure to the source of ultimate authority. Unity of Command—In assigning activities, it is to be seen that sub-ordinates receive orders from one superior only. Principle of Responsibility—The responsibility of the sub-ordinate to his superior authority by delegation is absolute. Also, no superior can escape responsibility for the organization activities of his sub-ordinates. Based on the above, improvement in the proposed organization structure over existing one, provides enhanced efficiency and thereby marginal decline in proposed requirement of manpower.

(iv) Turnover rate—Turnover rate is defined as the percentage of total employees who separate within 12 months of the year. The particular system for calculating turnover rate is not important as long as the measurement is consistent over the long term. Turnover consists of resignation, death, termination, and retirement.

(v) Absenteeism rate—Absenteeism is the title given to a condition that exists when a person fails to come to work when properly scheduled to work.

Human Resource Actions

The matching of projected human resources needs with projected human resources demand as well as supply (already available in the organization after conducting measures indicated under human resource supply forecasting), provides the basis for undertaking various actions to ensure that supply will equal demand at the time specified. Such actions as the following can be undertaken:

(i) Recruitment—If projected supply is short of projected demand, the addition of new personnel is likely possibility. The sources of recruitment may be one of the following: (a) Advertising in appropriate media, (b) Promotion from within the firm, (c) Recommendations from employees and business associates, (d) Campus recruitment, (e) Executive search organizations, (f) Non-executives may be recruited from local employment exchange. If such skilled labour is not available through employment exchange, advertisement may be restored to. As regards executive cadre, open advertisement would be a right choice of recruitment provides internal potential candidates have already been covered through promotion. Generally, recruitment may be restored to at the lowest of executive cadre. However, about 2% positions at higher level may be filled from outside brilliant candidates to infuse new blood.

(ii) Training—With the change in technology and innovation in management concept, there is a need not only fresh campus recruitment but also a massive training of personnel. For example, change from electro-mechanical to electronic product, from manual processing of data to computerized management information system, etc. require training and retraining to personnel of various levels.

(iii) Succession plan/career management—Every well-managed firm should have a succession plan that identifies qualified subordinates who are ready to replace each key executive. Unfortunately, the matter of succession is often deferred and when circumstances force a change someone is thrust unexpectedly into a position for which he has not been prepared/trained.

(iv) Productivity programme—Various firms have been taken specific programme to increase the productivity. Improving productivity levels will increase the supply of human resources without increasing the number of personnel. The employee has also been involved in the process through participating in improved quality of work life programme and agreeing to alter various work rules that hold down productivity.

(v) Reduction in workforce—If the projected supply of human resources is in excess of projected demand, the firm may force to retrench personnel, otherwise they are to be involved to improve productivity in exchange for guarantee not to retrench manpower. To hope is that such reduction in costs will lead to greater sales. A reduction in force is always a difficult process for everyone—the employee, the management, the union, the government and the community.

(vi) Redeployment plan—This will set out programmes for transferring or retraining existing employees for new jobs.

(vii) Redundancy plan—This will indicate the following:

- Who is redundant, where and when;
- The plans for retraining, where this is possible; and
- Alternative programmes for voluntary separation (golden hand-shake), retrenchment, lay-off, etc.

(viii) Training plan—This will show:

- The number of trainees or apprentices required and the programme for recruiting or training them;
- The number of existing staff who need training or retraining and the training programme; and
- The new courses to be developed or the changes to be made in the existing courses.

Monitoring and Control

No manpower plan will be perfect unless it provides for continual process of monitoring and control. The significance of monitoring is that it helps to ensure that the right decisions are implemented and that the wrong ones are altered. Assumptions in planning process should be monitored.

REVIEW QUESTIONS

1. In making long-range demand forecasts of human resource requirements, what major subject areas require attention? How does the Delphi technique fit into such forecasts?
2. Why isn't a current inventory of human resources sufficient to determine the supply of human resources?
3. Outline the steps involved in the human resource planning process.
4. How can an organization's human resource supply be increased?

5. Describe the implications on HRP when an organization is in a surplus mode.

11.2 RECRUITMENT AND SELECTION PROCESS

Recruitment: Recruiting is the process of searching of right type of candidates for actual or anticipated organizational vacancies after off-setting these vacancies through internal search within the organization. A good recruiting programme should attract the qualified and not attract the unqualified. This dual objective will minimise the cost of processing unqualified candidates.

Recruitment Policy

(i) Recruitment activity may be centralised at corporate office or unit office level. For management trainees, it may be centralised at corporate office and for supervisory and workers level it may be undertaken at unit office.

(ii) Recruitment of employee may be decided for example management trainees, the first level as well as about 2% executives from the top level to infuse new blood may be the entry point for managerial cadre whereas unskilled workers, specified percentage of skilled worker and supervisory cadre as well as specialised categories like stenographers, timekeepers, etc. after taking care of internal candidates may also be the entry point for non-executive cadre.

(iii) Preferred sources of recruitment which would be tapped by the organization, e.g., for skilled or semi-skilled workers internal sources and employment exchange may be preferred for highly specialised categories and management personnel, other sources besides the former way be utilised.

(iv) Criteria of selection and preferences should be based on conscious thought and serious deliberations. In some cases, trade unions may be consulted in working out the recruitment policy. In others, management may take the unilateral decision.

(v) The cost of recruitment and financial implications of the same.

Sources of Recruitment

There are two categories of sources of supply of manpower—Internal and External.

Internal sources—These include personnel already on the pay-roll of the organization. In course of time, vacancies so generated are filled from within through transfers and promotions. Some organization keep "badli" lists or a central pool of persons quit earlier voluntarily or due to retrenchment from which vacancies can be filled for manual jobs.

External sources—Organizations may look for people outside it. Entry level jobs are usually filled by new entrants from outside. Also in the following circumstances, organizations may resort to outside sources, (a) When suitable qualified people are not available within the organization, (b) when the organization feels it is necessary to inject new blood into it for fresh ideas, initiatives, etc., (c) when it is diversifying into new avenues, and (d) when it is merging with another organization.

Methods of Recruitment

The methods of recruitment may include one or more of the following: (a) Direct, (b) Indirect, and (c) Third party.

Direct methods: These include campus interviews usually used for jobs requiring technical or professional skills. Organizations may visit IITs, IIMs and colleges, and universities and recruit persons for various jobs. These institutions usually have a placement officer or a teacher-in-charge of placement, who normally provides help in attracting employers arranging interviews, furnishing space and other facilities and providing students' resumes. For this purpose, carefully prepared brochures, describing the organization and the jobs it offers are distributed among students before the interviewer arrives.

Indirect methods: These involve mostly advertising in newspaper, on the TV, radio, in trade and professional journals, technical magazine, and brochures.

Nowadays companies develop their own websites so that at the time of vacancies, the profile required, is posted to the corporate website as well as other commercial web recruitment sites as www.Naukri.com, etc. Even the candidates place their brief bio-data on several websites that provide the facility of Internet data banks. These commercial Internet data banks facilitate companies to surf and choose the candidates whose profile is best suited to their requirement.

Third party methods—Various private employment agencies are used for recruitment of specific occupations like technicians, accountants, computer programmers, engineers, doctors, executives, etc. These agencies bring together the employers and suitable persons available for a job. Because of their specialisation, they can interpret the needs of their clients and seek out particular type of persons. In recent years, certain websites have been opened for employment of various categories of aspirants. These are www.timesjobs.com and www.monster.com. The individual may download the resume as per format in website and the same will be sent to various companies requiring such applicants. The concerned company communicates with applicants with its email address.

- Employment exchanges are the main agencies for public employment. They also provide a wide range of services, like counselling, assistance in getting jobs, information about the labour market, labour and wage rates, etc.
- Executive search agencies maintain complete information records about employed executives and recommended persons of high caliber for managerial, marketing and production engineers posts. These agencies are looked upon as "head hunters', raiders and pirates. Such organizations are like ABC consultants, Furguison India Ltd., etc.
- Indoctrination seminar for college professors; these are arranged to discuss the various topics related to the company to which professors are invited. Visits and banquets are arranged so that professors may

be favourably impressed and later speak well of the company and help in getting required personnel.

- Friends and relatives of present employees constitute a good source from which employees may be drawn. This, however, is likely to encourage nepotism, i.e., persons of one's own community or caste may only be employed. This may create problem for the organization.
- Trade unions are often called on by the employers to supply whatever additional employees may be needed. Unions are asked for recommendations largely as a matter of courtesy and an evidence of goodwill and co-operation.
- Professional societies may provide leads and clues in providing promising candidates for engineering, technical and managerial positions. Some of these maintain mail order placement services.
- Temporary help agencies employ their own labour force both full-time and part-time and make them available to their client organizations for temporary needs.
- Casual labour source is one which presents itself daily at the factory gate or employment office. The daily requirement of labour can be met through "sardar" casual jobseeker.
- Deputation; persons are requisitioned on deputation from another organization donee if he is spareable for certain number of years on the terms and conditions mutually agreed to by donor and donee. Ready expertise is available but for short duration only.

11.3 SELECTION

In human resource planning, selection is a part of recruitment. In the selection process, applicants are assessed against the criteria establish in job analysis in order to predict which job applicants will be successful, if selected. Selection process is a costly preposition hence proper selection of personnel is obviously an area where effectiveness—choosing competent workers who perform well in the position and remain with the organization thereby minimising turnover can result in large savings.

All selection activities, from the initial screening interview to the physical examination exist for the purpose of making effective selection decisions. Each activity is a step in the process that forms a predictive exercise seeking to predict which job applicants will be successful, if hired. Problems occur when we make errors by rejecting candidates who would later perform successfully on the job or accepting those individual who subsequently perform poorly on the job; such problem is, however, less in the selection decision. In actuality, the selection process represents an effort to balance the objectives of evaluating and attracting. The interview is an obvious example of an activity where both objectives must be served. At the same time, that the interviewer is attempting to acquire information about the candidate so an intelligent selection decision can be made. He or she is also informing the applicant about the job and the organization thus successful in selling his/her organization to the candidate. If the organization fails in selling itself to the candidates there is little likelihood that the applicant will accept the job even if it is offered.

The discrete **selection process** consists of seven steps:

1. Preliminary interview,
2. Completion of the application blank,
3. Employment tests,
4. Comprehensive interview,
5. Background investigation,
6. Physical examination, and
7. Final employment decision

Each of these steps represents a decision point requiring some affirmative feedback for the process to continue. Each step in the process seeks to expand the organization's knowledge about the applicants' background, abilities, and motivation and it increases the information from which decision makers will make their predictions and final choice.

Initial Screening/Preliminary Interview

Based on the job description and job specification, some of the applicants can be eliminated. Applicants with adequate experience and adequate education may be shortlisted. The screening interview is also an excellent opportunity for management to describe the job in enough details so the candidates can consider whether they are really serious about making application. The sharing of job description information with the individual can frequently encourage the unqualified or marginally qualified to voluntarily withdraw from candidacy with a minimum of cost to the applicant or the organization. Another important point during the initial screening is to provide details of full range of salary with basic and other perquisites so that applicants may decide not only for the sound opening but also to the pay package.

Completion of Applicant Blank

Applicants are asked to fill up the blank 6-8 pages comprehensive personal history profile such his qualification, specialization, experience, companies in which he has worked, etc.

From the analysis of the above application, management may be able to assess, prima facie which candidates will succeed on the job and which would not. In practice, most organizations use different application forms for managerial and technical post, for example, the form may require detailed answers to questions regarding the candidate's education and experience in the relevant areas of operation. For skilled jobs, the form might stress on tools and equipment the applicant has used.

After screening, the candidates go through a written test. These tests are screening devices and provide supplementary input in selection decisions.

Kinds of Tests: The various test used in selection can be put into four categories: (a) (i) Achievement and (ii) Intelligence Tests, (b) Aptitude or Potential Ability Tests, (c) Personality Tests, and (d) Interest Tests.

(a) **Achievement Tests:** These are also called proficiency tests. These measure the skill or knowledge which is acquired as a result of a training programme and on the job experience. These measure what the applicant cannot do. These are of two types:

Test for measuring job knowledge—These are known as "Trade Tests". These are administered to determine knowledge of specific skill such as typing, shorthand and in operating tools and mechanical equipment. **Work sample tests**—Work sample is an effort to create a miniature replica of a job. Applicants demonstrate that they possess the necessary talents by actually doing the tasks. By carefully devising work samples based on job analysis data, the knowledge, skills, and abilities needed for each job are determined. For example, a work sample for a typing job would provide the material to be typed and note the time taken and mistakes committed, work sampling provides actually hands-on experience.

(ii) **Intelligence Tests**: These measure the overall intellectual ability or the intelligence quotient (I.Q.) of a person and enable us to know whether he has the mental capacity to deal with new problems. These determine a person's fluency in language, memory induction, reasoning, speed of perception and spatial relation ability.

(b) **Aptitude Test**: This test measure the latest ability of candidate to learn a new job or skill. Aptitude tests do not measure motivation. On-the-job motivation is often found to be more important than aptitude of the job. That is why the aptitude test is supplemented by interest tests.

(c) **Interest Tests**: These are designed to discover a person's areas of interest and to identify the kind of work that will satisfy him. The interest tests are assessed in the form of answers to a well-prepared questionnaire. The two most widely used interest tests are the "Kuder Preference Record" and "Strong Vocational Interest Blanks".

Interview

The interview, along with the application form, is the most universal predictive tool for selection. The interview consists of interaction between interviewers and applicant. Thus, it can be a powerful technique in achieving accurate information and getting access to material otherwise unavailable.

Two kinds of interviews for selection have been identified. These are:

1. Stress interviews: Stress interviews are deliberate attempts to create pressure to observe how an applicant behaves under stress. Methods used to induce stress range from frequent interruptions and criticism of an applicant's opinion to keeping silent for an extended period of time. It should not be done at the beginning of the interview because this can make it impossible to compare a candidate's normal behaviour with his behaviour under trying situation. The applicant should be given a chance to recover from the stress before he leaves.

2. Depth interviews: These are designed to intensively examine the candidate's background and thinking and to go into considerable details on a particular subject of special interest to the candidate. The theory behind it is that if the candidate is found good in his area of special interest, the chances are high that if given job he would take serious interest in it.

These points are then weighted according to employer's requirement as well as level of position.

Limitations of Interviews

1. The Halo Effect: Under this type of error, one marked characteristic of the candidate (either favourable or unfavourable) may be allowed to dominate the appraisal of his entire personality. Physical appearance, his brilliant scholastic record, his fluency or lack of it in language, experience of living abroad, experience as a sportsman, etc. any one of these qualities may create a halo effect. The interviewers should assess the whole of the candidate's personality and should not be led away by any one trait or achievement. He should remember that good candidates come in all shape, size, ages, education, religion, caste, region, etc.

2. Leniency: When a candidate is rated by two raters, their ratings may be different. One may show consistent leniency by giving him high scores; the other may consistently rate him by giving low scores. Leniency is usually associated with lack of confidence and interest in rating. Toughness may be result of exaggerated expectation, lack of contact with people, and general rigidity of personality.

Physical or Medical Examination

Applicants who get over one or more of selection hurdles are sent for a physical examination either to the organization's physician or to medical officer approved for the purpose.

11.4 PLACEMENT

Once employment is accepted, the individual is placed in the department under a supervisor. A proper placement reduces employee turnover, absenteeism and accident rates and improves morale. The supervisor should provide all necessary help to the new employee to adjust in the environment and co-workers. To aid this process, organizations have orientation programme of six months or so which help the new employee to socialise the entire operation culture and relationships prevailing in the organization. If this does not happen at the initial months, new employees may intended to quit, which is a costly preposition for the company. In recent years in order to overcome placement problem, most of the large organizations appoint management trainees who undergo long and intensive (one or two years) in-company training in various departments. After completion of training programme, placement is scheduled so that both trainees as well as supervisors who are acquainted during training period will be able to accept each other on placement in the departments.

11.5 INDUCTION AND ORIENTATION

Induction and orientation covers the activities involved in introducing a new employee to the organization and to his work unit. It reduces the initial anxiety at the time of joining the new job. For example, an orientation programme should familiarise the new recruit with the organization's objectives, history, philosophy, procedures and rules; communicate relevant personnel policies, review the specific duties and responsibilities of the new member's job; provide a tour of the organization's physical facilities; and introduce the employee to his superior and co-workers.

Conduct orientation programmes for acquired organization's employees. It covers the "rules of the game" in the acquiring organization.

REVIEW QUESTIONS

1. What is recruitment? How do you proceed for recruiting management trainees for your organization?
2. What is the "dual objective" of recruitment?
3. What specific constraints may prevent a manager from hiring the best candidate?
4. The best candidates are the ones who are hard to find. That is why it is imperative to select the right kind of source of recruitment, even to pay for it. Do you agree or disagree? Discuss.
5. What could be the basis to identify the criteria for selection? How can its validity and reliability be established?
6. What is testing in selection? What types of tests do you adopt for selecting two-three years experienced mechanical engineers in a software organization?
7. Describe a three-days induction programme for Management Trainees (Technical) in a Cement Industry.

Chapter 12
Training and Development

12.1 INTRODUCTION

We are living in a world where only change is permanent. New technologies and other changes make existing structures and skills obsolete. Combining job/skill and elimination of wasteful work practices are also essential. In view of mediocre schooling and vocational education besides loopholes in the selection and recruitment, employee training is needed to make sure that enterprises are viable, competitive, productive and profitable. Training and development activities are the main mechanism through which individual's goals and aspirations can be integrated with the organizational goals and requirements.

Training is a learning experience to improve skills, knowledge and attitudes of an employee for doing his or her jobs. Training is short-term intervention utilising a systematic and organized procedure to improve operative employees' performance on the current job or prepare them for an intended job.

Development is a related process. It is a long-term educational process utilising a systematic and organised procedure for development of conceptual and theoretical knowledge of those employees who supervise the activities of other operative employees. Management development, in contrast to employee training is more future oriented and concerned with education. On-the-job management development technique includes: (a) Coaching, (b) Understudy-assignments, (c) Job rotation, and (d) Committee assignments. Off-the-job management development technique includes: (a) Sensitivity training,

(b) Transactional analysis, (c) Lecture courses, and (d) Simulation exercises.

Objectives of Training

Training is the cornerstone of sound management for it makes employees more effective and productive. A training programme becomes essential for the purpose of meeting the specific problems of a particular organization arising out of the introduction of new lines of production, changes in design, the demands of competition and economy improvement in product quality, improve in health and safety of its members, individual adjustments in the changed situation to take care of obsolescence, promotion and also improve their careers.

12.2 RESPONSIBILITY FOR TRAINING

Training is the responsibility of the following main groups:

(a) The top management which frames the training policy and approve training budget;

(b) The personnel department plans, establishes, and evaluates training programmes;

(c) The training department develops training programmes suitable for various groups, their administration conducts and follow up of training plans;

(d) Supervisors who impart bulk of teaching load and implement and apply developmental procedures; and

(e) Employees/trainees who provide feedback and suggestions for improvement of training modules.

12.3 LEARNING AND TRAINING

Learning is that human process by which skills, knowledge, habits, and attitude are acquired and utilised in such a way that behaviour is modified. Training is rooted in the learning process. Training is an organised procedure by which people learn knowledge and acquire the skills they need for a definite purpose. In other words, training causes learning—a process that takes place within the trainees, in which behavioural changes occur as a result of experience. Learning cannot be measured directly but the changes in behaviour that occur as a result of learning can only be measured.

Human being has greater capacity for adaptation. This is because of his learning capacity. Learning can be defined as a relatively permanent change in behaviour due to practice or experience. However, physical maturation would not be considered learning. The practice or experience must be reinforced on periodical basis in order for learning to occur. If reinforcement does not accompany the practice or experience, the changed behaviour will disappear. Learning improves in presence of motivation in terms of doses of rewards.

Learning will be facilitated by providing feedback through positive reinforcement. For instance, if workers are verbally praised when they have properly performed a task, they are likely to continue doing the task this way and be motivated to strive toward performing better work.

Learning Curves

Learning rarely takes place at a constant rate. It varies according to the difficulty of the task and ability of the individual. A usual method for demonstrating the rate of cumulative change of a specific criterion during a given period is the use of "Learning Curves". The progress of learning any skill can be obtained by presenting it graphically in the form of learning curve. The curves for individuals may differ widely because of individual differences in learning. The curve usually begins with a sharp rise in learning, then increases at a decreasing rate until a plateau is reached for less opportunities for improvement or task is becoming difficult. Plateaus often indicate crucial stages in learning, when the learners have to make extra effort and the trainer has to provide additional incentives to the learner. Other reasons that may cause plateaus are distraction during learning, lack of motivation, inefficient performance method or very often ineffective teaching or poor training.

Learning of a typist who is presently having a speed of 20 words per minute, in three months he increases the typing speed with sharp rise, then increases at a decreasing rate until a plateau is reached. This learning is depicted in a Learning Curve as given below:

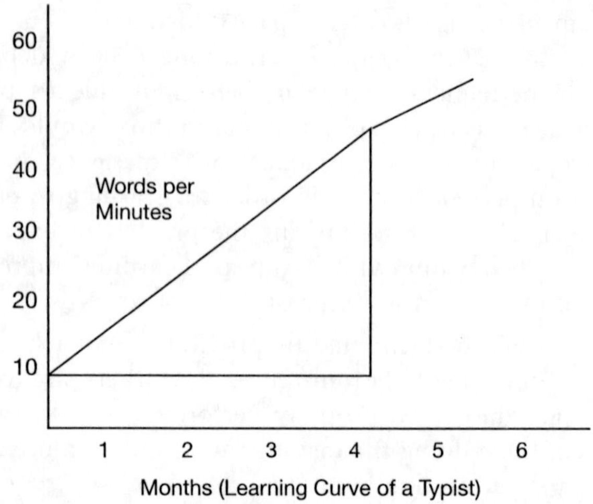

Learning must be transferable to the job in the workplace. It doesn't make much sense to perfect a skill in the classroom and then find that you can't successfully transfer it to the job. Therefore, training should be designed to foster transferability.

Training should focus on ways of orienting new employees, giving recognition, motivating a poor performer, correcting poor work habits, discussing potential disciplinary action, reducing absenteeism, handling a complaining employee, reducing turnover, and overcoming resistance to change besides improvement in existing job and prepare for future assignment.

12.4 ASSESSMENT OF TRAINING NEEDS AND PRIORITIES

Training is such to enable to meet the specific needs of both the organization and the individual employees. Thus, training needs are stated firstly the extent to which the skills required for a particular task or role have been acquired and utilised in improving one's performance and secondly the extent to which the individual interests, aspiration and potentials have been met and realized for ensuring job satisfaction and employee growth.

Management undertakes systematic training programmes in the following situations:

1. Drop in productivity, increased product rejection rate, inadequate job performance, etc.

2. Introducing new technologies for quantum jump in production and productivity.
3. Face stiff competition from similar industries.
4. Have a philosophy for better employee career development.

The most versatile model for identification of training and development needs are as follows:

Organization Analysis: This involves a study of the entire organization in terms of its objectives, its resources, the allocation and utilization of these resources.

Company objectives may be broken into specific goals and operational targets for various divisions, and sections of the organization.

The next step is to analyse (i) The manpower requirement to fulfil the business operation; (ii) The personnel performance to the required standard; and (iii) The working environment in their departments conducive to fulfilment of task.

Further diagnosing the organization climate is to understand express attitude towards employee training and development by top management, personnel department and line supervisors.

Task Analysis: The purpose of this exercise is to get as much information as possible about the nature of task and its various components leading to the performance standard to job information can be collected through questionnaires, interviews, personal records, production reports, etc. This information would be useful in establishing the training programme for the employees.

Man Analysis: Man analysis is the third component in identifying training needs. The focus of this analysis is on the individual in a given job, rather than on the job itself. Three basic issues are involved in a man analysis for training purposes. First, through appropriate observation, supervisory evaluation, and diagnostic testing we need to determine whether performance is substandard and training is needed. Second, we need to know whether current employees are capable of being trained, and the specific areas in which training is required. Finally, we need to ask whether current employees with substandard performance can improve their job through right type of training or need job rotation or job enrichment.

The information for such analysis may be collected through check-lists, merit ratings/performance appraisals, interviews, questionnaires attitude surveys and critical incidents.

The three kinds of analyses described above must be carried on continuously.

Having identified the training needs as above, the next step is to set up **training goals**. These goals should be tangible, verifiable and measurable. The goals are based on the following:

(i) Roles and tasks to be carried out by the target group.

(ii) Relationship with other positions and technological imperatives.

(iii) Relevance, applicability and compatibility of training to work situations.

(iv) Identification of existing and desired behaviour required after training to meet supervision, problem solving capability, innovation, quality, etc.

(v) Operational results such as productivity, cost, down time, turnover, etc. to be achieved through training.

Depending on goals set, the next step is to decide on **strategy of training** involving the following:

(i) Classification of objectives in terms of purpose: (a) Correction in skills, (b) Problem-solving capabilities, innovative ideas, quality, etc.

(ii) Classification of objectives in terms of levels of learning: (a) Skills of motor responses, memorisation and simple conditioning, (b) Adaptation to simple environment, (c) Interpersonal understanding and skill, (d) Values of individuals and groups

(iii) On-the-job or off-the-job training

(iv) In-house or external training

(v) Individual or group training

(vi) Horizontal, vertical or diagonal/mixed group

(vii) Changes required, if any, in the existing work roles, organizational relationships, work system requirements, process of supervision and alternative structures.

12.5 TRAINING METHODS AND TECHNIQUES

Training methods enable adult learners acquire desired knowledge, sharpen behavioural and performance skills and develop appropriate attitudes.

While exercising choice on selection of methods, it is to keep in mind that trainer trains adult who have reservoir of experience thus contributing a great deal to the learning situation. The trainees are likely to pay more attention to those aspects of learning which will help them advance their career and personal life goals. The choice of a method would depend on various factors such as competence of trainers, relevance of the participants, the programme contents and finally its cost implications.

Numerous training methods and techniques have been developed to meet certain specific needs however they inherit certain strengths and weaknesses. As such trainer should know their rationale before attempting to use any of them. Chart 12.1 gives the techniques mostly used for training of employees:

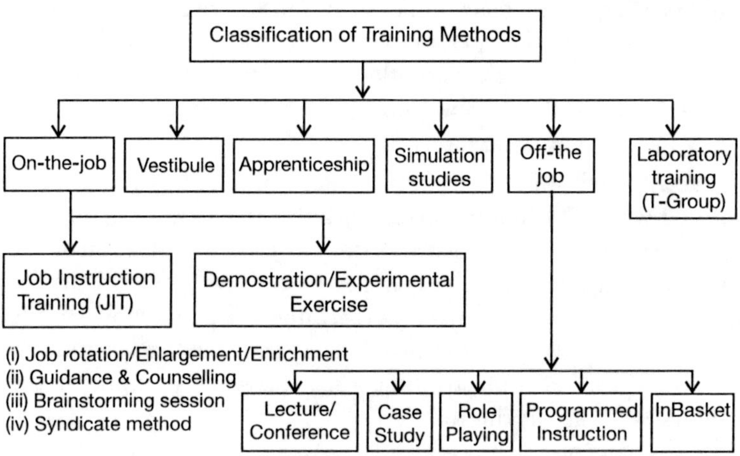

Chart 12.1

On-the-job Training: This training is learning on the job itself by a variety of ways. They embrace development through performance on the job, where organizational strength and constraints, human behaviour and technological systems have full and free play.

Job Instruction Training (JIT) is developed to prepare supervisors to train operatives for repetitive jobs. JIT consists of four basic steps:

1. Preparing the trainees by telling them about the job and overcoming their uncertainties.
2. Presenting the instruction giving essential information in a clear manner.
3. Having the trainees tryout the job to demonstrate their understanding; and
4. Placing the operatives into the job, on their own with the designated resource person to call upon should they need assistance.

Experimental exercises: Experimental exercises are usually short, structured learning experiences, where individuals learn by doing. For instance, rather than talk about interpersonal conflict and how to deal with them, an experimental exercise could be used to create a conflict situation where employees have to experience conflict personally and work out its resolution. After completing the exercise, the facilitator or trainer discusses and introduces theoretical concepts to explain the members' behaviour during the exercise.

Vestibule training or training center training: It is a classroom training which is often imparted with the help of equipment and machines which are identical with those in use at shop floor. This technique enables the trainees to concentrate on learning the new skill rather than or performing an actual job. While expensive, it minimises the problem of transferring learning to the job, since vestibule training uses the same equipment the trainees will use on the job.

It is very efficient method of training semi-skilled personnel particularly when many employees have to be trained for the same kind of work at the same time. It is often used to train clerks, bank-tellers, inspectors, machine operators, typists, etc. Besides use of prototype equipment in the training center, training is generally given in the form of lectures, conferences, case studies, role playing and discussion. By this method, training is imparted by experienced senior fellow workers and supervisors.

Simulation exercises: Any training activity that explicitly places the trainee in an artificial environment that closely mirrors actual working conditions can be considered a simulation. Simulation activities include case exercise, complex computer modeling and vestibule training. This training is essential in cases in which actual on-the-job practice might result in a serious injury, a costly error, or the destruction of valuable materials or resources. It is for this reason that the technique is a very expensive one. Simulation techniques have been most widely used in the aeronautical industry especially to train pilots for navigating new aircraft.

Apprenticeship: Persons seeking to enter skilled trades to become, for example, plumber, electrician, draughtsman, machinists are often required to undergo apprenticeship training. The duration is one year to three years with stipend. A major part of training time is spent on-the-job training on the shop floor. Each apprentice is given a programme of assignments according to a predetermined schedule, which provides for efficient training in crafts, trade skills. The merit of this method is that at stipend rate, skilled labour is available on the shopfloor.

Job rotation/enlargement/enrichment: These are the forms of on-the-job individual intervention with emphasis on providing the trainee experience in various types of jobs, locations and developments. Job rotation, we mean, change of job near to existing job create development, interest and fine tuning of attitude, thereby improve the performance. Job enlargement broadens the job horizontally and creating multiskilling providing satisfaction while job enrichment enriches the job by inserting the complexity and variation vertically thereby routine job becomes interesting thereby enhances satisfaction for a longer period of service.

Brainstorming session: It conducts on select members of the section. The problem of general interest is placed before the team. Members with their experience and knowledge generate original and creative ideas even difficult solutions to the problem. Then all the ideas are collated and by differential method reasonable solution is arrived. This exercise improves thinking process and leads to apply the mind in the existing job thereby improve the performance.

Off-the-job methods: Off-the-job training simply means that training is not a part of everyday job activity. The actual location may be in the company classrooms or in places which are owned by the company, or in universities or associations which have no connection with the company. These methods consist of:

1. Lectures/conferences
2. Case studies
3. Role playing
4. Programmed instructions
5. In-basket

1. **Lectures/conferences:** The lectures or conferences are imparting knowledge especially when facts, concepts or principles, theories, and problem-solving abilities to a very large groups which are to be trained within a short time, thus reducing the cost per trainee. They are usually interwoven with film shows, case studies, role playing and demonstrations. Audio-visual aids enhance their values. There are at least two variations of this method—talk and discussion which allow some participation of the trainees. In order to take active participation in this, the speaker encourages trainees to raise questions thus maintaining interest in the topic.

2. **Role playing:** This method is used to improve interpersonal communication with particular emphasis or empathy and listening. The trainees are assigned the roles on the basis of a written script of a live business situation. This exercise practices the trainees to understand the gap between existing behaviour and desired behaviour. Roles are often played spontaneously and unrehearsed.

3. **Case study:** The case situation is an actual situation which is written for training purposes. When the participants are given cases to discuss, they examine the cases in terms of defining the objectives dealing with the issues/problem identification and analysis of the situation and of its cases. There could be several solutions to the problem, and each of these alternatives and their implications need to be examined. In actual situation, on many occasions, a manager may not have all the relevant information with him before taking a decision. Similarly, the case method, decisions/solution of the case has to be taken with limited information.

The method is extensively used in business/law schools for improving conceptual and functional skills among senior-level executives. The Harvard Business School has been developing a number of case studies based on real life business situation, while in Administrative Staff College of India at Hyderabad, Indian Institute of Managements at Ahmedabad, Calcutta, Bangalore and Lucknow and other institutes of higher learning in management prepare case studies.

4. **Programmed learning:** A form of individual study, the programme learning is more suited to meet the behavioural objectives and when non-motor skill or knowledge is to be learned by a large number of trainees. The facilitators guide trainees' independent progress during the programme. This method is based on principle of positive reinforcement developed by B.F. Skinner. This allows the trainee to learn through a series of small steps in phases and at his own pace.

5. **In-Basket:** In-Basket or in-Tray is a simulation technique where the trainees are presented with pack of papers and files in a tray containing administrative problems. They are asked to take decisions within specified time limit. Their reactions and responses are taken down in writing, analysed and then compared with one another. Feedback on their decisions forces them to re-consider not only their administrative actions but also their behavioural style. Learning occurs as trainees reflect and evaluate the decisions taken on priorities, customer's complaints, superior demand, irrelevant information and the like.

Laboratory Training

It is often called sensitivity training or T-Group based on the principle of group dynamics. As the name suggests sensitivity training aims at developing sensitivity within people towards thoughts, feelings, behaviour of other persons, encourage conflict resolution and promote mutual trust.

T-Group: One of the methods of sensitivity training is the T-Group. Bethel Maine of USA was pioneer of the T-Group. This intervention is to develop normative behaviours among group members by infusing concepts and awareness regarding necessary behavioural skills. Sensitivity training has developed to the status of an intervention is Organization Development (OD). T-Group training is process oriented and not content oriented where people operate a feeling level of communication, observing, revealing, listening, and unravelling messages.

The trainer must be professionally trained to lead the groups.

Business Games: The game is built around the model of a business situation and trainees are divided into teams consists of two to six members representing the management of competing firms. They simulate the real-life process of taking operating decisions regarding production, prices, marketing, and attempt to maximize hypothetical profits in this simulated environment. Decisions taken are analyzed by a computer, and series of the implications of their decisions are feedback. The game is played in 6 to 12 rounds to take the time dimensions into account. At the end, the final results are worked out by each team and compared with those of others.

12.6 EVALUATION OF TRAINING

We need to evaluate the effectiveness of our training programmes. Evaluation of the training programme must be based on the following principles:

1. Evaluation specialist must be clear about the goals and purposes of evaluation.
2. Evaluation must be continuous and should be planned at the same time as the training programme.
3. Evaluation must be specific.

4. Evaluation must provide the means and focus for trainers to be able to appraise themselves their practices and their products.
5. Evaluation must be based on objective methods and standards.

It is difficult to claim that training programme is effective unless it is evaluated. To avoid the uncontrolled training costs, management must insist on a through costs-benefit evaluation to ensure that training rupees generate satisfactory returns.

Opinions of trainees or managers appear to more prevalent than rigorous evaluation. The feedbacks of participants, while easy to acquire, are the least valid. These opinions are heavily influenced by factors that may have little to do with the training's effectiveness—things like difficulty, entertainment value or personality characteristics of instructors. Therefore, let us direct our attention to three approaches to evaluate the training effectiveness each of which offers improvement over subjective opinions.

1. The most sophisticated evaluative approach is the Experimental Control Group method: The first step is to identify the areas of training to be evaluated. Two groups are earmarked depending upon their age, skills, intelligence and learning abilities. The control group works on the job but does not undergo training programme, whereas the experimental group is undergo training regime. The two groups are re-evaluated two to three months after completion of training. While evaluating the programme we should assess the following four areas:

(i) The reactions of participants are heavily influenced by subjective factors like difficulty, entertainment value or personality characteristics of trainer or even their opinion that programme is ineffective.

(ii) The learning criterion is to assess whether the skills and knowledge that were to have been taught were in fact acquired by the trainees during training programme.

(iii) The behaviour change criterion has changed because of training programme.

(iv) The fourth criterion is results. Whether the trainee's morale is better, productivity has increased and complaints about the manager have decreased significantly.

It is important in evaluation of training programme that data so collected may be interpreted well by eliminating factors other than training programme to arrive the correct assessment.

The other evaluation techniques are:

2. Test-retest method and
3. Pre-post performance method.

Test-retest method: Participants are given a test before they begin the programme. After the programme is completed, the participants retake the test. The method is having inherent defect as the test score increases due to causes other than the training given.

Pre-post performance method: It is designed in which each participant is evaluated prior to training and rated on actual job performance. After programme is completed the participant is re-evaluated.

12.7 MANAGEMENT DEVELOPMENT

Ingenuity of manager is unlimited. The technical, conceptual and human skill need to be developed on-the-job as well as off-the-job through human resource development (HRD) effort.

In analysing the skills of manager, Katz speaks of three types: technical, human and conceptual.

(a) Technical skills are to know the mechanics of the jobs.
(b) Human skills refer to the ability to work effectively with others. These skills include the ability to communicate, motivate and lead.
(c) Conceptual skills refer to the ability to sensitive to the complexities of his work environment. Such skills concerned with the ream of ideas and creativity.

These skills are required in varied degrees in three levels of managers—first level, middle level and top level managers.

Management development programme (MDP) is an educational process utilizing a systematic and organised programmes by which managerial personnel learn conceptual and theoretical knowledge for general purposes. These purposes concern for: (i) Productivity; (ii) Quality; (iii) Human Resource Planning; (iv) Motivation; (v) Indirect Compensation; (vi) Health & Safety; (vii) Technology Upgradation; and (viii) Quest for Excellence.

12.8 MENTORING

Mentoring is developing new entrants to mingle and grow in the organization. The mentor provides basic support to protégé (high flyer) in terms of: 1. Career development and 2. Psycho-social support. The role of a mentor is:

Under mentoring, a young promising manager (protégé) is assigned to a mentor who is fairly senior in levels above the protégé; not necessarily from the protégé is department. Mentors are selected on the basis of their interest, availability and mentoring competence. One mentor may not have more than five protégé (high flyer). The mentoring period typically is of one year period.

1. Teaching, 2. Encouraging, 3. Nurturing, 4. Managing the developmental relationship, 5. Offer mutual respect, 6. Respond to the protégé's needs.

Mentoring aims to improve some basic human process issues like competence, communication and reward and recognition and so on. It also gives relevant positive and negative feedback to improve the junior's performance and potential. It extends helpful guidance for exploring on the job as wall as personal dilemma.

12.9 TRANSACTIONAL ANALYSIS (TA)

It is an Organization Development intervention for developing maturity in human behaviour and leadership trait. Transactional Analysis (TA) refers to a method of analysing communication interaction between people and a theory of personality. TA was developed by Eric Berne for psychotherapy for his patients in the year 1950. The fundamental theory underlying TA holds that the individual personality reflects person's way of thinking, feeling and behaving at any time known as ego states. These ego states are: parent, adult and child. These states have nothing to do with age but person of any age may have these ego states in varying degrees. A healthy person is able to move from one ego state to another.

The parent ego state incorporate the attitudes and behaviours include being overprotective, distant, dominant and authoritative. There can be two types of parent ego states: nurturing and critical. The nurturing parent ego state reflects nurturing behaviour not only towards children but also to other people in interaction. Similarly, critical parent ego state shows critical and evaluative behaviour in interaction with others. Each individual may likely to have mixture of two in varied degrees.

The child contains all the impulses that are natural to an infant to the age of five years. The person in this ego state can be obedient or manipulative, charming at one moment and repulsive the next. Characteristics of child ego state include creativity, conformity, depression, anxiety, dependence, fear, and hate.

Adult ego state is objective and rational. It deals with reality and objectively gathers information. Since it reasons and is reasonable, its actions are based on information. He updates parent and child data to be logical (parent ego state) and keeps and controls emotional expression appropriately (child ego state).

Sometimes these ego states harmonise, sometimes they are in conflict. Some people respond more with one ego state than with others. When people interact with others a transaction is said to occur. The transaction is routed from ego state and fall into four categories as shown below:

<table>
<tr><td></td><td colspan="2">You are O.K.</td><td></td></tr>
<tr><td rowspan="2">I am O.K.</td><td>I am O.K. You are O.K.</td><td>I am not O.K. You are O.K.</td><td rowspan="2">I am not O.K.</td></tr>
<tr><td>I am O.K. You are not O.K.</td><td>I am not O.K. You are not O.K.</td></tr>
<tr><td></td><td colspan="2">You are not O.K.</td><td></td></tr>
</table>

I am O.K. You are O.K.—People with others solve the problem rationally. This is based on adult ego of person (transaction). Managers and employees at this position are able to express freely what they feel about others because it offers little threat to them. They delegate authority and feel comfortable with a spread of authority. This is an ideal ego state (transaction).

I am O.K. You are not O.K.—This life position is taken by people who feel victimised. They blame other for their miseries and consider themselves okay (right). The manager in the parent ego use I am O.K. you are not O.K. life position. The parent-parent transaction can be beneficial in cases whose employee joins forces with the manager and support him. There are certain disadvantages of this type of situation. This may lead to unnecessary competition between manager and the employee, because the latter will promote his own idea rather than those of manager.

I am not O.K. You are O.K.—This life position refers to persons who always grumble in comparison to other people around them. Run in inferiority complex. This is parent-adult transaction.

I am not O.K. You are not O.K.—This life position leads to lose interest in life. Managers operating from this position do not make decisions in time; make silly mistake or provoke others to give them negative reactions. This is child-adult transaction where employee controls child ego state manager.

Other transactions which are also not effective

(i) Adult-parent Transaction—Manager adult ego state, others-parent ego state

(ii) Adult-child Transaction—manager-adult, others-child

(iii) Parent-adult Transaction—Manager-parent, others-adult

(iv) Parent-child Transaction—Manager-parent, others-child

(v) Child-parents Transaction—Manager-child, others-parent

(vi) Child-child Transaction—Manager-child, others-child

Manager not capable for leading employees successfully and prove to be a liability to the organization.

One of those positions dominates each person's life. The desirable effective position of adult-adult transaction. That is "I am O.K. You are O.K." can be learnt through education, understanding and experiences. TA course may help managers understand and other better and assist them in altering their response so as to produce more effective results.

12.10 MANAGERIAL GRID

The "Managerial grid" is an organizational development technique developed by Robert R. Blake and Jane S. Mouton.

The grid represents five leadership styles based upon two factors—concern for people and concern for production. Concern for production means the attitudes towards production and productivity innovation and quality of work. Concern for people includes degree of personal commitment towards goal achievement, maintaining the self-esteem and good interpersonal relations of subordinates. Figure 12.1 shows below the five leadership styles:

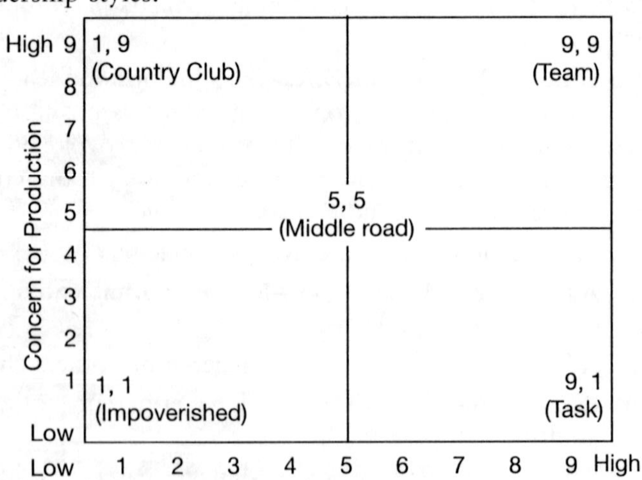

Fig. 12.1: Managerial Grid

1, 1- (Impoverished)—Apply minimum effort to get work done at the same time maintain morale.

1, 9- (Country Club)—Laissez faire leadership style.

9, 1- (Task)—High efficiency in work where human elements have little effect.

5, 5- (Middle Path)—adequate performance through balance of work requirements and maintaining satisfactory morale.

9, 9- (Team)—High task accomplishment from committed people.

The management training programme is built around this managerial grid to change managers towards 9, 9—the most desirable management style.

12.11 PLANNED ORGANIZATION CHANGE

In the dynamic society, change is necessary. Organizations those do not adapt to change find it difficult to survive. Since organizations must cope with change to survive, so too, must managers.

Reasons for Organizational Change: Some of the factors in the internal and external environment of the organizations necessitating change are as follows:

(1) Change in environment—Changes in social, political, economic, technological, and legal environment. Such changes may affect productivity, quality, labour management relations, nature of competition, economic constraints, organization methods, etc. In order to survive in the changing environment, organization must change.

(2) Change in managerial personnel—Because of retirement, promotion, transfer, new managers who fill up the positions, they bring new ideas, values, attitude, way of working and so on in the organization causing change.

(3) Deficiency in terms of organization structure, poor communication system, fewer delegation of powers, leadership styles not conducive to growth of organization and so on.

(4) To avoid developing inertia—Changes are incorporated to maintain flexibility.

Organizations adopt the strategies for planned change in all the related factors mentioned above simultaneously. It is observed that a change will bring disequilibrium in the organization. In order to achieve new equilibrium, the organization has to change factors effecting change.

Resistance to Change

The people generally dislike change. There are many factors responsible for resistance to change.

1. Perhaps the most important factor to resistance to change is the problem of adjustment. If one interprets the change affecting his position, status and authority adversely, he resists it. Moreover, in each change he has to change his way of working which he dislikes because it presents numerous difficulties to him.
2. Another factor which brings resistance to change is the effect of change on individual's level of need satisfaction. If change diminishes economic, psychological, and social status, he will resist the change.
3. Sometimes, individuals resist change because the group to which they belong resists it. Though each person interprets change individually, often he expressed it through a group. Generally, the members of a group are influenced by its codes, patterns and attitudes.
4. Besides logical resistance such as lack of confidence in the change agent (manager or consultant) or mode of introducing change, emotional reasons for resistance to change are also important. For example, if labour treats management as a different class in the organization, it will resist any change by the latter, whatever be the nature of change.

Dealing with Resistance to Change

Resistance to change can be minimized if not completely eliminated by adopting the following measures:

(i) The nature of change should be made clear to the people who are going to be affected by it.

(ii) Commonality of purpose and meaning of change can be achieved through education and communication.

(iii) The interest or pressure groups resisting change can be co-opted in the decision-making structures, thus absorbing their resistance and making them a partner in the change process.

(iv) People should be encouraged to actively participate and involved in deciding about the nature and direction of change.

(v) Change has to be initiated not on personal grounds or for personal benefits of a few individuals but for objective requirements of the organization.

(vi) The change is effected through already established institutions, norms, customs and social relations.

12.12 ORGANIZATION DEVELOPMENT

In the mid-1940s, some of the behavioural scientists thought that instead of emphasizing the skill development, why not we change the organizational climate. If this change could be brought about the members of the organization would be in a better position to solve problems, confront, conflict, formulate policies, and handle operational matters more effectively.

Organization development is the planned change in organization aimed at enhancing organization health and effectiveness by reorients the environment, structure, processes, and people. The goals of OD is to fight the past in the present in order to choose freely the future.

Objectives of OD—Some of the major objectives of OD are:

(i) Increase the level of trust and mutual emotional support among all organizational members.

(ii) Create a climate to confront with the organizational problems to solve with greater speed rather than keeping them under the carpet.

(iii) Create an environment in which the authority is based on knowledge and skill.

(iv) Increase the openness of communication, laterally, vertically and diagonally.

(v) Increase the level of enthusiasm and personal satisfaction among the employees and to develop a culture of consensual decision making.

OD programmes is also called interventions may be run through external change agent or consultant with a fresh perspective and knowledge of the behavioural science initially however, an effort is made to prepare a cadre of internal change agents from within the organization, who sustain, maintain and strengthen the change efforts.

The origanisation development approach places emphasis on making appropriate interventions in the on-going activities of the organization. The change agent establishes collaborative relationship with the clients and works jointly with them in diagnosing problem, setting change goals making intervention and evaluating the outcome:

Diagnosis → Intervention → Evaluation

OD Diagnosis

It is conducted by a management team and/or an outside OD consultant. After the relevant problem domain is selected, management and the consultant can turn to unfreeze the current situation, design the diagnostic strategy, and interpret diagnostic data. The diagnosis often focuses particular attention on the widely shared beliefs, values, and norms of organization members that may be interfering with maximum effectiveness. An OD programme should not be sudden introduction into organization. Some kind of announcement through meetings, newsletters or bulletin boards can be made to help start things. The employees now become aware and alert for the diagnosis. The change agents use multiple means of gathering data, such as interviews, questionnaire survey, observations of employee behaviours, and various internal reports and returns. The data are compiled and then feedback to employees in small groups to elicit further data for use in diagnosis.

Intervention

Once the situation has been properly diagnosed, OD interventions, or change strategies can be designed and implemented with the help of the change agent. The choice of intervention depends on the target group, that is, the level at which change is desired. The levels could be individual, groups or organization as a whole. Because of the interdependent nature of these levels, interventions must be directed at all subsequent levels. There are five popular OD interventions used by OD specialists as described below:

1. *Life and career planning:* Most employees do not have clear career plans—things just happen. OD consultants can help employees plan their careers carefully by allowing them to understand their own aptitudes and interests they can be transferred to a department of their liking.
2. *Process consultation:* The OD consultant observes the group and provides feedback regarding dysfunctions in such areas as interpersonal relations, communication patterns, handling of conflicts, and decision making. The goal is to help group members gain the skills they need to identify and resolve issues on their own.
3. *Team building:* It is aimed at helping work groups become effective at task accomplishment. Here OD consultants help in assessing group tasks, member role analysis, and strategies for accomplishing work tasks and job behaviour.
4. *Technostructural activities:* They are intended to improve work technology and/or organization structure. The OD consultants help organization members enhance their own work effectiveness by showing them how to evaluate and make appropriate changes in work methods, task design, and organization structure.
5. *Organizational culture change:* The OD consultants assist in developing methods for determining the current corporate culture, assessing its appropriateness, and planning necessary changes.

The most widely used OD interventions are sensitivity training (T-Group), process consultation and survey feedback.

Evaluation

The process is continuous and cyclical and therefore requires active involvement and commitment of both the change agents and the clients for a longer time duration. The data collected at diagnosis stage can then be used as benchmarks to make at least some evaluation of the interventions after they have been implemented. No one OD interventions necessarily produce results in all the targeted areas and in all situations. These facts reinforce the need to monitor and evaluate results.

Developing Awareness about Self

Personal effectiveness is increased through self-awareness of behaviour, feelings, attitudes, and competencies. However, understanding oneself alone does not make a person effective. Developing openness and trust between the manager and the subordinates are especially relevant for improving interpersonal relations. Joe Luft and Harry Ingham ('Johari'—it was developed by combining the first few letters of their names) examined the nature of self-disclosure in interpersonal relationship. According to the model, there are two dimensions for understanding the self—those aspects of person's behaviour and style that are known to him/her (self) and those aspects of his behaviour known to others—those with whom he/she interacts. A combination of these two dimensions gives four areas about self. It is shown in Fig. 12.2 to build upon relationships, this model is known as Johari Window. The model has four quadrants which together represent a total person in relation to others. The awareness of behaviour about self is dynamic. It keeps changing as awareness changes with parties to a relationship. The self-awareness of a person in relation to others is represented in the four quadrants:

1. **Open self:** This is a state where a person is known to himself and also others. The open self-arena includes information such as name, age, family, physical appearance, etc. are known to self and others. Arena area increases when the blind, closed and dark quadrants decrease.

2. **Blind self:** This represents a state where a person's behaviour and feelings are known to others but not to himself. As a matter of fact, he is blind about his behaviour.
3. **Hidden self:** The area involves that which is known to the person but not revealed to others; things in this area are secret. The person does not share it. For example, a manager may hide his anger from his subordinates.
4. **Unknown self:** The fourth area is the dark area, inaccessible both to the person and to others. This represents a state where a person does not know himself and others also do not know about him.

Known to Self-Unknown to Self		
Known to others →	A (Open Self) Arena	B (Blind Self) Blind
Unknown to others →	C (Hidden self) Closed	D (Unknown self—both Blind and Hidden) Dark

Fig. 12.2: Johari window model of self-awareness

Some psychologists believe that this is a very large area indeed thus by reducing the dark area, and increasing the area of open self the manager can give himself/herself and subordinates more information and more accurate information to respond to. This increase in accurate interpersonal information leads to better perceptual progress, greater trust, and more honest communication. Although it may not be advantageous to disclose everything about oneself, managers can overcome such weakness by encouraging the same openness and trust in the subordinates.

REVIEW QUESTIONS

1. Identify major categories of training methods. Give an example of each type of training method.
2. What is learning curve? How does it relate to training?

3. How do you assess the training needs of an electrician?
4. Why is the evaluation of training effectiveness necessary?
5. You cannot select a person to meet organization's requirement all the time and in all the positions, hence design the training module for skilled worker to take the skilled position.
6. Outline training objectives, strategies and mechanism.
7. Discuss the need for management development. Describe how such needs are assessed.
8. What criteria would you use to determine whether a management development programme was effective?
9. What are the techniques of OD for effecting change in the individual and the organization?

Short Notes

1. Transactional analysis (TA)
2. Planned organizational change
3. Management grid
4. Johari window

Chapter 13
Performance Appraisal

13.1 INTRODUCTION

Performance appraisal traditionally used as a mechanism of controlling employee through salary administration, reward administration, promotions and disciplinary action. Employees are evaluated or rated confidentially by one or more senior officers for their performance on some dimensions. The traditional performance appraisal function results in unawareness of employees of their strengths and weaknesses in relation to their capabilities in different positions in the organization throughout their career.

13.2 MEANING AND DEFINITION

Performance appraisal is evaluating the performance of an employee against the well-defined job standards in terms of quantitative, qualitative and behavioural aspects at the workplace.

Performance appraisal is a systematic and objective way of judging the relative worth or ability of an employee in performing his task. Performance appraisal helps to identify who are performing their assigned tasks well and those who are not and the reasons for such performance. Assessment should not be confined to past performance alone. Potentials of the employee for future performance must also be assessed.

The purpose of employee performance appraisal is:

(i) To provide a reliable index for promotions and transfers.

(ii) To determine increments and rewards.

(iii) To suggest ways of improving the employee's performance from the current level by assisting him/her with constructive criticism and guidance for the purpose of his/her development.

(iv) To identify the training and development need of the employee.

(v) To assess potential, latent skill to take up higher assignments.

(vii) To improve communication—performance appraisal provides means for greater understanding between the appraiser and appraisee—obviously for better performance in future.

(viii) Performance appraisal can be a useful tool for HRM activities such as selection, training, promotion, and transfers to determine whether they are effective or not.

13.3 APPRAISAL PROCESS

Figure 13.1 outlines the performance appraisal process. It begins with the establishment of key performance areas (KPAs). These should have evolved out of job analysis and job description while establishing these KPAs, rater will discuss these with the ratee so that these should be clear and objective enough to be understood and measured. Under each key performance area, it is further identified into tasks and targets, for example, a marketing manager has a key performance area of introducing a new product in a particular region, "to personally contact 10 major customers from each district and get their feedback on the product within a period of two months is a specific performance target." Tasks are specific measurable and observable activities to be completed during two months' time. Further whenever it is not possible to quantify efforts, the role occupant may define the specific tasks in qualitative terms, for example, improvement in customer relations and so forth.

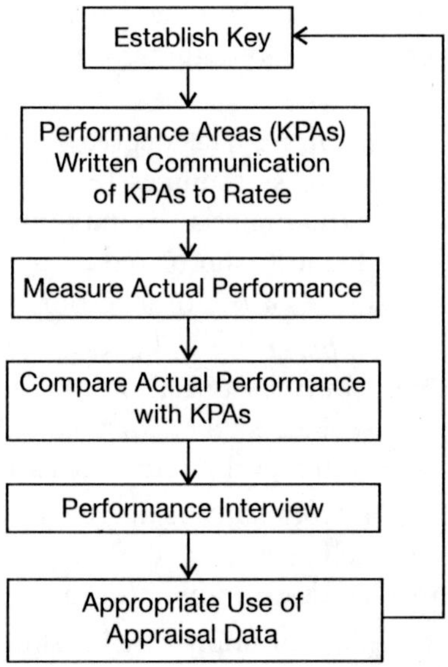

Fig. 13.1: Performance appraisal process

Once performance areas are established, the rater should communicate these expectations to the ratee. Such communication we mean that the expectations have been received and understood by the ratee (the subordinate). Therefore, feedback is necessary from the subordinate to the manager.

The third step in the appraisal process is the measurement of performance. To determine what actual performance is, it is necessary for the managers to use the information such as personal observation, statistical reports, oral reports and written reports. What we measure is probably more critical to the evaluation process than how we measure since the selection of the wrong criteria can result in serious dysfunctional consequences. So, the criteria must represent performance as stated and articulated in establishing KPAs.

The seven criteria for assessing performance are:

1. *Quality*: The degree to carrying out an activity approaches perfection.
2. *Quantity*: The amount produced expressed in monetary terms, number of units or number of completed cycles.

3. *Timeliness*: The degree to which an activity is completed or a result produced thereby the time available for other activities.
4. *Cost effectiveness*: The degree to which the use of the organization's resources (e.g., manpower, money, technology, and material) is maximized in the sense of getting the highest gain or reduction in loss from each unit or instance of use of a resource.
5. *Need for supervision*: The degree to which a job performer can carry out a job function without either having to request supervisory assistance or requiring supervisory intervention to prevent an adverse outcome.
6. *Interpersonal impact*: The degree to which a performer enhances self-esteem, goodwill and co-operation among co-workers and subordinates.
7. *Training need*: For improving his skills and knowledge.

The above criteria are related to past performance and behaviour of an employee. There is also the need for assessing the potential of an employee for future performance, particularly when the employee is tipped for assuring greater responsibilities.

There are four critical attributes required to handle higher level jobs.

1. Planning and organizing: Ability for anticipating work needs and development of effective action plans in relation to task assigned.

2. Team spirit: Co-ordination and co-operation with colleagues to achieve team objective.

3. Decision making: Ability to identify problems, priorities then analyse alternative and take decisions.

4. Initiative: Ability to determine and initiate actions that result in improved handling of jobs, without waiting to be told.

The fourth step in the appraisal process is the comparison of actual performance with established KPAs. The attempt in this step is to note deviations between KPAs and actual performance. While comparing, there is possibility that some kind of errors like leniency or severity, central tendency, halo effect and the like (the details of errors to be given in subsequent paragraphs) may be crept into evaluation.

The fifth step is the most challenging task, i.e., **performance interview**. The post-appraisal interview is a two-way discussion between a superior and a subordinate of latter's performance. The interview is a crucial step in the development programme for people in an organization, without the interview, the appraisal has little chance of succeeding in bringing about improved performance.

The emphasis in the interview should be on counseling and development and not on criticism, because of the significance of appraisal interview, every effort must be made to make it effective.

Appropriate Use of Appraisal Data

The final step in the appraisal process is the uses of evaluation data and information.

- In one way or another, **output of appraisal program** can critically influence the following areas of HRM.
- Remuneration administration including rewards.
- Validation of selection programs.
- Employee training and development programs thereby to learn, grow and make full use of their potential.
- Promotion transfer and lay-off decisions.
- Grievance and discipline programs.
- HR planning.

Thus, above action will reduce the gap between KPAs and the actual performance.

13.4 METHODS, TECHNIQUES OR TOOLS FOR PERFORMANCE APPRAISAL

Numerous methods have been developed to measure the performance of employee. These have been classified into two broad groups, i.e., traditional and newer or modern methods. Each group has several techniques as shown below.

The traditional methods lay emphasis on the rating of the individual's responsibility, creativity, integrity, leadership potential, intelligence, judgment, organizing ability, etc. On the other hand, newer methods place more emphasis on evaluation of job results/achievements than on personality traits. Result-oriented appraisal tend to be more objective and worthwhile especially for counseling and development purposes. Particular type of method could be effective for particular organizations, and for particular type of employees.

Methods of Performance Appraisal

Traditional Methods	*Modern Methods*
* Annual confidential report (ACR)	* Management by objectives
* Graphic rating scales	* Assessment centers
* Paired comparison method	* Human asset accounting method
* Check lists	* Behaviourally anchored rating scales (BARS)
* Forced choice description * Forced distribution method	* 360-degree (Feedback) appraisals
* Critical incidents method	
* Field review method	

Annual confidential Report (ACR): This is a traditional form of performance appraisal, found in most government organizations. A confidential report is a report on subordinate by the immediate superior raised once in a year and covers aspects like ability to work with others, leadership, initiative, job knowledge resourcefulness, decision making, etc. Rating on five-point scale, i.e., Outstanding, Very Good, Good, Average, Poor was given with the justification for rating as outstanding or poor. For integrity, there are special instructions to be recorded. Recommendations for promotion are also given.

The system is highly secretive and subjective. Feedback to the assessee is given only in case of 'Poor' and non-permotable rating. The confidential report is widely used for a variety of personnel decisions, particularly transfers and promotions.

Graphic rating scales: One of the oldest, simplest and most popular methods of appraisal is the graphic rating scale. It consists of several numerical scales, each representing a job-related performance criterion such as quantity, quality, job knowledge, dependability, initiative, attendance, attitude, co-operation, and the like. Each scale range from excellent to poor, numerically 5 to 1. The rater evaluates performance on each criterion, then add to total score for each employee as shown below.

Employee's Name..				Deptt..............................		
Rater's Name				Date.................................		
Sl. no.	Factors	Excellent 5	Good 4	Acceptable 3	Fair 2	Poor 1
1.	Quantity of Work	-	-	-	-	-
2.	Quality of Work	-	-	-	-	-
3.	Job Knowledge	-	-	-	-	-
4.	Dependability	-	-	-	-	-
5.	Initiative	-	-	-	-	-
6.		-	-	-	-	-
7.		-	-	-	-	-
8		-	-	-	-	-
9.		-	-	-	-	-
10.						
11.						
12.						
	Total	+	+	+	+	+
		Final Score----------------				

Source: W.B. Werther and Keith Davis, *Human Resources and Personnel Management*, p. 349.

The disadvantages of this method are rater's biases because of subjective criteria such as co-operation, attitude and initiative.

Paired comparison method: It is a relative ranking method. Under this, the rater compares each employee with every other employee on every trait one at a time. For example, there are five employees named A, B, C, D and E. The performance of A is compared with the performance of B and a ranking is made between A and B about whose performance is superior. Then A is compared with C, D and E in that order. The same procedure is repeated for other employees. The number of comparisons may be calculated with the help of a formula which indicates $N(N-1)/2$ where N stands for the number of employees in a particular group to be compared. If there are five employees, the maximum number of comparisons will be $5(5-1)/2$ or 10 pairs.

For the trait 'Quality of Work'					
As compared to	A	B	C	D	E
A		+	+	-	-
B	-		-	-	-
C	-	+		-	-
D	+	+	-		-
E	-	-	+	+	

For the trait 'Creativity'					
-	A	B	C	D	E
A		-	-	-	+
B	+		-	+	-
C	-	+		-	+
D	-	-	-		+
E	+	-	-	+	

After the comparison, the score is tabulated and a rank is established based on the number of time a worker is considered superior than the other. One obvious disadvantage of this method is that in a large group of employees, the number of permutation and combination increases requiring more time from the evaluator. To solve this problem, the group may be divided into subgroups for ranking purpose.

Forced distribution method: This method was developed by Joseph Tiffin. One of the errors in rating is leniency thereby clustering a large number of employees around a high point on a rating scale. The forced distribution method seeks to overcome the problem by compelling the rater to distribute the performance on all points on the rating scale.

The method operates under an assumption that the employee performance level conforms to a normal statistical distribution. Generally, it is assumed that employee performance levels conform to a bell-shaped curve. For example, the following distribution might be assumed to exist-excellent 10 percent, good 20 percent, average 40 percent, poor 20 percent and unsatisfactory 10 percent. Figure 13.2 shows the forced distribution on bell-shaped curve.

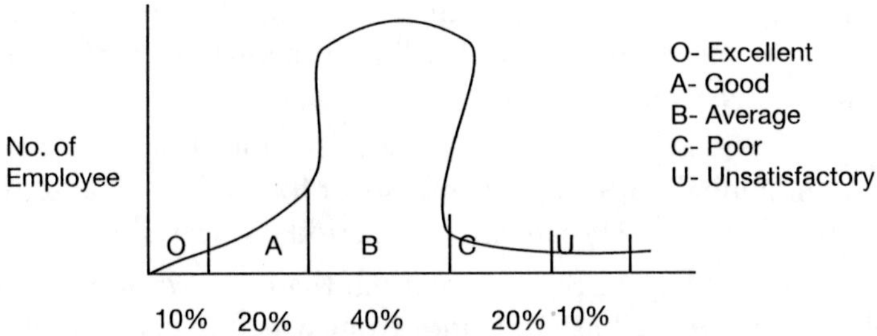

Fig. 13.2: Forced distribution on bell-shaped curve

The disadvantage of this method is that in the organizations that have done a good job of selecting and retraining only the good performance, the use of forced distribution approach would be unrealistic/unacceptable, as well as possibly destructive to the employee morale. The good point of this technique is that the problem of different raters using different parts of the scale is avoided. This method is very simple to understand and very easy to apply in organizations.

Critical incidents method: The critical incidents method has generated a lot of interest these days. The basis of this method is the principle that there are certain significant achievements of an employee during appraisal period which make all the difference between effective and non-effective performance of job/position. Such incidents are recorded by the supervisors as and when they occur.

The recorded incidents are then ranked in order of frequency and importance. Advantage of this method is here specific behaviours are cited not vaguely defined personality traits. A behaviourally-based appraisal such as this should be more valid than trait-based appraisal because it is clearly more job related. It also reduces the recency bias, if rater records incidents throughout the rating period. Finally, this approach can increase the chances that the sub-ordinates will improve because they learn more precisely what is expected of them.

13.5 MODERN METHODS OF APPRAISALS

Management by objectives (MBO): The MBO concept, as was conceived by Peter F. Drucker, way back in 1954, reflects a management philosophy which values and utilizes employee contributions. Application of MBO in the field of performance appraisal is a recent origin.

MBO is a process that converts organizational objectives into individual objectives. It consists of four steps—goal setting, action planning, self-control, and periodic reviews.

Goal setting: In the goal setting, the organization's overall objectives are used as guidelines from which departmental and individual objectives are set. At the individual level, the manager and subordinate jointly identify those goals that achievable with some extra efforts for the subordinate. The goals are tangible, verifiable and measurable. These goals are agreed upon and then become the standards in a previously arranged time period by which the employee's results will be evaluated.

Action planning: In action planning, realistic plans are developed to attain the goals. This step includes identifying the activities to accomplish each goal, time require for each activity and determining the resource required to complete each activity.

Self-control: Self-control refers to review his own performance. During the performance period, he judges his accomplishment against the goals and indicates in the form of self-appraisal. The superior also guides the sub-ordinate and modifies the goals for the next period. The MBO program is built on the assumptions that individuals can be responsible, can exercise self-direction and do not require external controls and threats of punishment to motivate them to work towards their objectives. This is in line with the motivational point of view representative of McGregor's theories.

Periodic progress reviews: Corrective action including setting of new goals is initiated when actual performance deviates from standards. Reviews are not meant to be little the individual but to add in future performance. These reviews should take place at least two or three times a year.

MBO program focuses attention on the results that are accomplished and not on personal traits or operational methodology. This method is largely applied to managerial personnel and employees who have a fairly wide range of flexibility and self-control in their jobs. On the other hand, assembly line worker usually has so little job flexibility where the performance standards and objectives are already fixed is not compatible with MBO. In India, MBO principle is limited to a few companies such as Indian Tobacco Company (ITC), Larsen & Toubro (L&T), etc.

Assessment centre method: Mainly used for executive hiring. Assessment centres are now also being used for evaluating managerial personnel potential. Assessment centre provides HR personnel and psychologists. Generally, middle-level managers are come together to assessment centre to have their participation in job-related simulation exercises. A few numbers of experienced with proven ability managers from the organization are drafted and train them as observers to assist in evaluation process. The principal idea is to observe and evaluate managers over a period of time, say two to three days their behaviour and performance across a series of select exercises such as in-basket exercise, business game, role playing and other similar activities which require revelation of attributes like assertiveness, persuasive ability, communication skill, planning and organization ability, resistance to stress, decision making, creativity and so on. After recording their observations of ratee behaviours and subsequent personal interview, the raters meet to discuss their observations for each ratee. This primary evaluation is further subjected with self-appraisal and peer evaluation to arrive on final rating as excellent, good and fair as well as suggest development need of each appraise.

Advantages: A well-conducted assessment of this nature can and does achieve better forecasts of future performance and progress than other methods of appraisal. Also, reliability, content validity and predictive validity are said to be high in the assessment centre.

Problems: Assessment centre ratings are said to be influenced by the participant's interpersonal skills, judges tend to evaluate the quality of the individual's social skills rather than quality of decision themselves.

The approach also involves real hazards. One of the most obvious is the examination-taking syndrome. Solid performers in day-to-day operation at shop floor feel suffocated in the simulated environment. Employee who gets a poor report becomes demoralized and chances are there that he becomes liability who was once an asset. Other problems include strong and unhealthy sense of competition among the assessees and the possibility of over emphasizing the test performance.

Behaviourally anchored rating scales (BARS): BARS is tailor-made for the job and has the following steps. A set of performance dimension say five in number for particular job/ position is identified. These may be specific to the job. For example, out of five performance dimensions one knowledge and judgment's critical incidents in descriptive form ranging from 7 to 1 from extremely good performance to extremely poor performance is indicated in the rating scales.

The scales are anchored by descriptions of actual job behaviour that supervisors agree represent specific levels of performance.

BARS are developed to provide results which subordinates could use to improve performance. Superiors would feel comfortable to give feedback to the ratees. Further, BARS help overcoming rating errors. Unfortunately, this method too suffers from distortion inherent in most of rating methods.

360-degree feedback: This method involves a manager rated his performance and potential by his superior, colleagues, internal customers and subordinates.

Such multi-rater assessment involves collecting responses through structured assessment forms about a manager from his bosses, peers and subordinates and self. The technique spans over several parameters: performance as well as behaviour, his approach to work, how effectively he handles his boss and his juniors, communication, delegation, values, ethics, fairness, balance, courtesy and other critical attributes—nothing is excluded from the ambit.

The forms are designed in a way to elicit one of the three responses to the subject's rating on a parameter—significant, strengths, weaknesses, development required, leadership styles, etc. cannot be rated but they are verbally pictured.

Each manager is assessed by a minimum of nine colleagues—at least two of them being his bosses, two to three of them peers, and two to three of them subordinates. While giving the superiors a distinct advantage to evaluate, peer rating provides a comparative and at times competitive perspective.

Usual performance appraisal method judges the outcome of a manager's efforts but ignore the road taken. They focus on achievements rather than intrinsic qualities that a manager must have in order to lead. However, these qualities are what the peer appraisals reveal.

In this method, assessment form consists of seven main factors which are divided into various sub-factors and each sub-factor is to be assessed on scale 'High, Medium and Low' with assigning score which will be analyzed and graphed by computer, the responses are presented collectively to the appraisee.

Depending on the interpretation of the data and the findings, counseling sessions are held to solve the specific problems and weaknesses identified. This is a powerful tool for self-development especially at the senior level which is where one tends to get insulated.

Benefits: If 360 degree assessment is done in a systematic manner, it will contribute to motivation of employees, reveal role of employees, provide scope to express individual views and opinions—recognize talents, placement requirements, training need and career planning. The technique is particularly helpful in assessing soft skill possessed by employees. This method is used by software companies like G.E.C., WIPRO, Reliance Industries, Infosys, etc.

Though there are conflicting views and opinions on the performance appraisals, one thing universally accepted is that appraisal system is most essential in the absence of which it is difficult to control people.

Problems in Performance Appraisal

None of the appraisal methods is accurate or reliable. As it is difficult to quantify all the ingredients of performance, subjectivity is crept in thereby individual rater falls into rating errors. The most common rating errors are as under:

1. *Leniency or severity*: Every rater has his own value system which acts as a standard against which appraisals are made. Besides this, the rater may feel that anyone under his jurisdiction who is rated unfavorably will reflect poorly on his own worthiness or if unfavorable rating is known to ratee, his relation may deteriorate with him. High rating is termed as leniency, whereas low rating denotes severity.
2. *Central tendency*: It is the most commonly found error. Raters who are prone to central tendency error are those who continually rate almost all employees as average or middle of scale. For example, if manager rates all subordinates as 3 on a scale of 1 to 5, then no differentiation among the subordinates exist which is incorrect. Failure to rate subordinates as 5, for those who excel in his performance and as 1, if the case warrants it, is due to the rater who would like to play safe. The above two errors can some extent overcome by providing forced distribution wherein rater is asked to categories the ratees into the blocks of 20% as outstanding/good, 40% average, 10% fair and 20% poor/unsatisfactory. Rating scales with clear-cut anchor points and defined categories in between can also check those errors.
3. *Halo effect*: A tendency to allow the assessment on one trait to influence assessment on other traits. For example, if ratee is good in interpersonal relations; he may be rated high on other traits like leadership, motivation, production. This error arises when traits are unfamiliar, ill-defined, and involve personal reactions. Character traits cause this error more after than the others. The halo effect can be minimized by providing a short training programme to the evaluators.
4. *Rater effect*: This includes favoritism, steriotyped and hostility. Excessively high or low scores are given only

to certain individuals or groups based on the rater's attitude towards the ratee, not on actual outcomes or behaviours, sex, age, race, and friendship biases are example of this type of error.

5. *Recency effect*: The rater's rating is influenced by performance/achievement by the ratee just near the end of the review period, i.e., during writing of appraisal, this tendency may inflate his rating or mar the same by one activity by chance happened at the end of the appraisal period thereby ignoring the commonly demonstrated behaviours during the entire appraisal period.
6. *Horn effect*: Basing the evaluation on the basis of one negative quality of feature perceived. This results in an overall lower rating than may be warranted. He comes in 'chappal' regularly. He must be careless at work tool.
7. *Spillover effect*: Allowing past performance to influence how present performance is evaluated. 'The person who has done good work in the distant past is assured to be okay at present also.'
8. *Similarity error*: This type of error occurs when the evaluator rates other people in the same way he perceives himself. Those who show this characteristic may be benefited while other may suffer. For example, the evaluator who perceives himself as aggressive may evaluate others by looking for aggressiveness.

Another source of error in performance evaluation is criterion contamination and **bias**, because of a variety of factors beyond the control of rater and ratee. Blum and Nylor indicate the sources of bias:

(i) *Opportunity bias*: When performance result of ratee is influenced by factor beyond the control of him. For example, ratee's performance is enhanced by better working conditions, supportive supervisors, more experienced co-workers as compared to other employee (ratee) as such his rating will be bias to that extent.

(ii) *Group characteristic bias*: The characteristics of an individual's group make a dent in his performance. Cohesive groups with high morale can produce more than the cohesive groups with the low morale. Since the individual's performance is greatly influenced by the group. This bias must be eliminated while evaluating the individual performance.

(iii) *Knowledge of prediction bias*: A ratee's past achievement can influence his present appraisal rating. An employee who topped in the selection list or got outstanding reward might leave the impression that he is the best among the employees and hence may be rated better than his other colleagues, though both have comparable performance during current appraisal period.

13.6 CAREER PLAN

Define Career

The term career means "advancement" in an organization. A career can be defined as actual series of job positions held by the individual over the span of one's service life. It consists of a sequence of role experiences leading to an increasing level of responsibility, status, power, and rewards.

In order to develop one's career, there is a need to examine two processes: how individual plans and implements his own career goals (career planning) and how the organization designs and implements his career development programmes (career management).

Career Planning is a deliberate attempt by an individual to become more aware of his own skills, interests, values, opportunities, constraints, choices, and consequences. He identifies career-related goals and programs accordingly of work, education, and experiences to achieve those goals.

Career Management is an ongoing process that involves preparing, implementing, and monitoring career plans undertaken by an individual alone or within the organization's career systems.

Organizational Career Development is a formal, organized, planned effort to achieve a match between individual career needs and organizational needs. For example, the organization has needs for competent staff and employees have needs to effectively utilize their personal skills.

Career Development Practices are designed to enhance the personal and professional satisfaction of employees and at the same time to improve organizational competitive advantage. However, it may be difficult to completely match individual and organizational career efforts because the rate at which an individual grows and develops may not parallel an organization's needs.

Career Development Cycle

For analyzing career development, it is important to understand that one may pass through various phases of his career. These are identified as:

Early career phase: up to 28 years

- learning how to fit into the organization
- becoming productive on the job

Transition stage: 29-32 years

- the individual may become uneasy about his career progress
- Job hopping is more common during this phase

Establishment/Settling down career phase: 28-40 years

- locating one's career anchor and building one's career around it
- stabilizing in his jobs by spending time to grow through promotions
- most of the energy is directed to career-oriented objectives

Maintenance career phage 40-50 years

- maintain specialization and a name in the department
- face one's mid-career-crisis: To those who make the successful transition go greater responsibilities and rewards. For others, it may be a time of reassessment,

job changes, adjustment of priorities, or the pursuit of entire different career

Late career phase 50-65 years

- continue to grow and enjoy becoming a mentor
- using one's experience and wisdom resting on one's laurels
- letting go and planning for one's retirement.

13.7 PROMOTIONS

Promotion is the upward advancement of an employee in an organization's hierarchy which covers a change in duties and higher level/degree of responsibility and usually involves higher pay, carry higher designation and better terms, and conditions of service and therefore, a higher status or rank. It is considered good personnel policy to fill vacancies in a higher job through promotion within. Such promotions provide an inducement and motivation to the employees, remove feelings of stagnation and frustration and inculcates, a sense of growing up with the organization reinforcing common goals between the individual and the organization. Sometimes outside recruitment is sought, a minor percentage of vacancies are filled if suitable candidates within are not available or with the view to infuse new blood with the experienced persons from other similar industries.

Promotions have a salutary effect on the satisfaction of the promoted person's needs to esteem, building up morale, loyalty and a sense of belonging and security. They also afford an opportunity for greater self-actualization through more varied and challenging assignments.

We shall examine two criteria—seniority and merit:

Seniority systems—Seniority is a factor which can be measured quantitatively; it is easily explained and understood and therefore free from changes of favoritisms and discrimination.

Promotion by seniority is not only preferred by trade unions but also from very senior officers belonging to defence services, judiciary, civil services and most employees of industries, since it is an objective and impartial method of judging employees for promotion in India. This system will be preferred till a full-proof system of assessing the merit is developed for promotion.

Merit systems—Merit is taken is to mean an individual performance in existing job and potential to excel in future assignment. Management prefers merit system of promotion, since only deserving employees are promoted who in turn will enhance the profitability of the enterprise. Using merit as the sole basis for promotion is subject to criticism. The devices used for judging merit such as performance-appraisal ratings and confidential reports has biases, hence are not above subjectivity.

Another view is advanced that alone merit is not the sole criterion for success in the promoted post but it involves other traits not reflected in the devices chosen for deciding merit of the individual.

Merit vs. Seniority

If seniority is regarded as the sole criteria for promotion, there is no incentive for employee to learn or improve. Their only response will be to stick around and accumulate years of service. In this system, efficiency is marred. Further, if an unqualified and dull person is promoted only because of his seniority, it may undermine the morale of others. With the passage of time, efficient employee may leave the organization—a total loss to the organization. On the other hand, seniority develops loyalty among employees who think that promotion will come to him automatically when it is due.

From the point of view of organizational efficiency and maximum utilization of talent, merit seems to be the logical basis of promotion. It brings rewards for meritorious work, extra competence, achievement and initiative. It encourages employees to work hard to get advancement in shorter possible time.

We have so far discussed the two conflicting factors of promotion—seniority and merit. Each has its pros and cons besides the situational factors like size, technology, and unionization which decide the use of one or the other for effecting promotion.

As each criterion suffers from certain limitations, perhaps the following types of broad options in promotion policies are:

- Time scale promotion (based merely on seniority)
- Merit promotion (based mainly on merit)
- Merit-cum-seniority (combination of merit and seniority)
- Adhocism (no policy, only adhocism based on expediency).

The National Commission on Labour (NCL) has suggested that as a general rule, particular non-executive categories in the lower rungs, seniority should be the basis for promotion. In respect of middle management executives (technical, supervisory and administrative), seniority-cum-merit should be the criteria. For higher managerial positions (technical and administrative), merit should be the sole criterion. While formulating a promotion policy for the enterprise, care should be taken to see that it is simple, rationale and free from discrimination. Such promotion policy can withstand in the court of law.

REVIEW QUESTIONS

1. What do you mean by performance appraisal? Discuss its objectives.
2. Discuss the two important methods of performance appraisal—one based on traits of employees and another is 360 degree assessment.
3. Why is performance evaluation of employees important? What are the essentials of a sound appraisal system?
4. Pros and cons of appraising employee's performance through forced distribution method—elaborate and discuss.

Short Notes

1. Career planning
2. Seniority vis-à-vis merit promotion
3. Career anchors
4. Common errors in performance appraisal with special reference of item—Horn Effect.

CASE STUDY

You are the GM of a FMCG company. There are hundred employees working under you. Out of which twenty are managers reporting in line and staff. Performance appraisal is the process of defining expectations for employee performance; measuring, evaluating, and recording employee performance relative to those expectations; and providing feedback to the employees. Its employees are annually rated by means of a graphic scale. The rating factors are dependability, initiative, quality of work, quantity of work, relationship with people, and job knowledge. Resulting rating are used to influence promotions, salary adjustments, and as criteria for training.

At this time, some trouble has arisen. On receipt of their final ratings from personnel department, three of the company's managers have expressed their dissatisfaction with ratings and prepare a memorandum describing fallacy in the designing the performance appraisal. They have insisted that bell-shaped normal distribution might be 20 percent (excellent and good), 60 percent (average) and 20 percent (poor and unsatisfactory) as against presently provided as 30 percent (excellent and good), 40 percent as average and 30 percent (poor and unsatisfactory). These present criteria of 30, 40 and 30 create a lot number of managers non-promotable for a longer period. The non-promotable managers are having equal level of educational qualification, potential to grow and length of service.

1. What should now be done to overcome this situation?
2. Would you suggest an another performance appraisal system using Behaviourally Anchored Rating Scales (BARS) or the 360 Degree Performance Appraisal System? Critically analyse.

Chapter 14
Work Motivation

14.1 INTRODUCTION

Most human resource management strategies are meant to improve the capabilities of individuals and groups as well as canalize their energies towards achievement of organizational objectives. In fact, job performance of an individual is a function of his ability and willingness or desire to use his ability in achieving personal or organizational goals. This willingness or desire to act, and to behave, is what may be called motivation.

14.2 DEFINITION

Motivation may be defined as an inner force that impels human beings to behave in a variety of ways.

Koontz and O'Donnell observes "Motivation is a general term applying to the entire class of drives, desires, needs, wishes and similar forces that induce an individual or a group of people to work."

Motivation is a basic psychological process consisting of primary, general, and secondary motives, drives, desires or willingness of an individual to behave in a certain manner at a certain time and in a certain situation. Being motivated means that a particular behaviour has to follow.

Motivation is the willingness of people to respond to the organizational needs. The more positive the individual's motivation towards the organization, the more effective is his performance.

Motivation and Behaviour: Motivation has come from motives which are the expression of human needs. Motives can be simple or complex. Simple motives originate from physiological needs, such as thirst, hunger, shelter, and sex. Most motives, however, are not very simple and originate to get affiliation, status and power. The human behaviour is caused by motives as needs and behaviour is rarely determined by a single motive or need. Unsatisfied needs produce tension in the mind of individual. When the individual is unable to satisfy needs, frustration is the result. At that point of time, motivation (incentives) causes goal-directed behaviour. Such desired behaviour tries to satisfy his desired needs and tension is released. However, satisfaction of one need leads to feeling of another different need or the same need after lapse of certain time. Thus, this process is continuing one.

14.3 THEORIES OF MOTIVATION

Many theories of motivation are generally revolved around the following three major approaches. The content theories go as far back as the turn of the 20th century when pioneering scientific managers such as Fredrick W. Taylor, Frank Gilbreth, and Henry L. Gantt proposed sophisticated wage incentive models to motivate workers. In this approach, workers were regarded as a factor of production; little importance was paid to the potential influence or importance of human factors upon work performance.

Next came the human relations movement mainly emerged from the Hawthorne experiment which indicated that the personal and social needs of employees are very important as is the case with production/productivity, material and environment issues. In the meantime, professor Douglas McGregor based on his experience and exploratory research on the nature of man at work has presented two opposite set of assumptions as Theory X and Theory Y. At the same time came the content theories of Maslow, Herzberg, Alderfer and McClelland's need for Achievement Theory. It follows the process theories. Based mainly on the cognitive concept of expectancy, the process theories are most closely associated with the work of Victor Vroom, Porter and Lawler and so on. More recently, equity and its derivative procedural/organizational justice theories have received the most attention in work motivation.

14.4 MCGREGOR'S THEORY X AND THEORY Y

After viewing men at work, D. McGregor proposed two sets of assumptions about human nature. The first set of assumptions, basically negative based on traditional theory of human behaviour, McGregor labeled Theory X; and the second, basically positive, based modern concept, he labeled Theory Y. Under Theory X, assumptions are as follows:

1. The average men dislike work as by nature they are indolent and will avoid work whenever they can.
2. Since people dislike work, they must be coerced, controlled, or threatened with punishment to achieve the objectives of the organization.
3. Most people are basically lazy, have little ambition, shirk responsibilities and place security above all other factors associated with work and seek formal direction whenever possible.
4. He is inherently self-centered, indifferent to organizational need.
5. He is by nature resistance to change.
6. He is gullible, not very bright, the ready dupe of the charlatan and the demagogue.

Propositions of Theory X

(i) Management is responsible for organizing the elements of production—money, material, machine, man, and methods in the interest of economic gain.

(ii) Management is responsible for directing the efforts of people, motivating them, controlling their action and modifying their behaviour to fit the needs of the organization.

(iii) People would be passive unless management intervenes. Even they are resistant to organizational needs. They must be persuaded, rewarded, punished, and controlled.

Theory X supports the authoritarian view which is not desirable in the present-day economy. The man at work is not a cog of a machine, he is a human being required to be managed with care. Later McGregor himself denounced the theory by saying, "The conventional approach of Theory X is based on mistaken notions of what is called cause and effect analysis. An organization built upon theory X notions will be one in which there is clear supervision and control of subordinates and high centralization of authority. Leadership will tend to be autocratic and workers will have very little to say in decisions affecting them."

McGregor recognized certain needs that theory X fails to take into account, for example, self-fulfillment, ego-satisfaction and social needs of individuals. Thus, it pleads for a humanistic and supportive approach to managing people. Management tries to provide an atmosphere of peace and discipline within the organization, without the oppressive measure. Hence, people with interest and simultaneously enjoy the benefits of congenital relationship.

Accordingly, McGregor listed the following assumptions that he called Theory Y:

1. Employees can view work as being as natural as rest or play. The average human being does not inherently dislike work.
2. People are not by nature passive or resistant to organizational needs. The average person within a favorable human relations climate, learns not only to accept but seek responsibility. Avoidance of responsibility, lack of ambition, and emphasis on security are generally consequences of experience, not inherent human characteristics.
3. Employees will exercise self-direction and self-control if they are committed to the objectives. External control and the threat of punishment are not the only means for bringing achievement.
4. Under the conditions of modern industrial, the intellectual potentialities of the average human being are only partially utilized.
5. Creativity that is the ability to make good decisions is widely dispersed throughout the population and not

necessarily the sole province of those in managerial functions.

McGregor's assumptions in terms of theory X are based in the beginning when the concept of 'economic man' was accepted wherein emphasis was given on the satisfaction of physiological and safety needs. These were also the basic constituents of Maslow's need hierarchy model. Subsequently, prospective findings of the Hawthorne Experiments, higher order needs were emphasized and these needs mostly replaced lower order needs. Thus, assumptions under theory X are being replaced by assumptions under theory Y being replaced in the managerial styles and techniques.

McGregor had further clarified his theories in the following terms:

(i) Theory X and Theory Y are not the only two possible theories of management. These were examples of two among many managerial cosmologies.

(ii) The two theories are not managerial strategies. It is the nature of man and compelling situation that influence managers to adopt one strategy rather than another. As such it is not appropriate to say that in all situations theory Y would be more effective.

(iii) Man is not economic man but he is an organic system where behaviour is affected not only by external force but by intrinsic one. Theory X and theory Y are not, therefore, polar opposites; they do not lie at extreme of a scale. They are simple different cosmologies.

14.5 THEORY Z

Much after the prepositions of theories X and Y by McGregor, Urwick, Rangnekar and Ouchi and others have evolved alternative theory under the caption Theory Z. Among others, a Japanese researcher, Ouchi's theory Z has attracted a lot of attention of management practitioners as well as researchers. There are four postulates of theory Z. These are:

1. Strong bond between organization and employees.
2. Employee involvement.

3. No formal structure.

4. Co-ordination of human beings.

1. Strong Bond between Organization and Employee: Ouchi has suggested certain methods as under:

(i) Lifetime employment.

(ii) Stability of employment by slowing down of evaluation and promotion which brings saturation in employee's prospects very soon. As against vertical movement of employees, more emphasis should be placed on horizontal movement which reduces stagnation. A career planning for employees should be prepared so that every employee is suitably places.

2. Employee Involvement: The involvement comes through meaningful participation. This means involvement in decision making thereby their commitment and giving due reorganization to them.

3. No Formal Structure: It supposes no formal structure for the organization. Instead it must be a perfect team work with co-operation along with sharing of information, resources and plans. Example is of a basketball team. It places emphasis on rotational aspect of employee placement which provides opportunities to him, to understand how his work affects others or is affected by others.

4. Co-ordination of Human Beings: The leader's role is to co-ordinate people and not technology to achieve productivity. This involves developing people's skills and also the creation of new structures.

The leader must develop trust which means there should be a complete openness and candour in the relationship. This develops a common culture and imbibes the class feeling in the organization. This can be achieved by a common canteen, similar uniform and involve at least in such decisions which effect them.

Theory Z may be implemented as a motivating instrument in India with a pinch of salt. Some of the methods like lifetime employment, no formal structure and perfect participation may not be feasible in Indian context.

14.6 THE CONTENT THEORIES OF MOTIVATION

The content theories of work motivation focus on needs that people have and how are these needs prioritized.

Maslow's Hierarchy of Needs: Abraham Maslow was the pioneer in arranging the needs of a person in a hierarchical order. In essence, he believed that once a given level of need is satisfied, it no longer serve to motive. The next higher level of need has to be activated in order to motivate the individual. Maslow identified five levels in his need hierarchy. They are basic needs:

(i) Physiological needs: Includes hunger, thrust, shelter, sex and other bodily needs. They are relatively independent of each other and in some cases can be identified with specific location in the body. These needs are cyclic. In other words, they are satisfied for only a short period, then they reoccur. For example, a hungry person will strive for food. However, after eating it, he will not hanker for food till he will not feel hungry and will be motivated/inspired only by the next level of needs.

(ii) Safety needs: This needs is roughly equivalent to the security needs. Maslow stressed emotional as well as physical safety. The whole organism may become a safety-seeking mechanism. Like physiological needs, these become inactive once they are satisfied, i.e., they no longer motivate the person. An individual who is safe, feels endangered no longer and hence makes no attempts to ensure security. In employment, safety needs are of primary importance to employees, because they are dependent on others (supervisors) for safety.

(iii) Social needs: Refer to belongingness. Man is a social animal. All individuals want to belong with others to gain acceptance and to give and receive friendship and love from them. After the first two needs are satisfied, social needs become dominant in the need hierarchy, a person will strive for meaningful relations with others. In the organization, workers form informal group of like-minded colleagues. It is seen that during free time, these informal group members meet, play, and socialize. This is the index of belongingness of individual in society. The person who already met physiological and safety needs need love from society and strive for it.

(iv) Esteem needs: Represent the higher needs of humans. The need for self-respect, power, achievement, self-confidence, competence, knowledge, independence, and status can be considered part of this level. Maslow carefully pointed out that the esteem level contains both self-esteem and esteem from others. Competitiveness and a desire for the acceptance of one's performance by peers are important esteem needs from the point of view of an organization. They can be utilized by efficient managers to achieve organizational goals and also to create feelings of worth, and of being useful and necessary for employees.

(v) Self-actualization needs: Persons who have become self-actualized, self-fulfilled, and have realized all their potential, he becomes everything that he is capable of becoming. In effect, self-actualization is the person's motivation to transform perception of self into reality. Maslow's need hierarchy theory observes the following premises:

1. Maslow's need hierarchy theory can be converted in the content model of work motivation shown in Fig. 14.1a. If Maslow's estimates are applied to an organization, example, the lower-level needs of personnel would be generally satisfied (85 percent of the basic needs and 70 percent of security needs), but only 50 percent of the social needs, 40 percent of the esteem needs and a mere 10 percent of the self-actualization needs would be met. The percentage will vary from individual to individual, situation to situation and in the same individual in different situations:

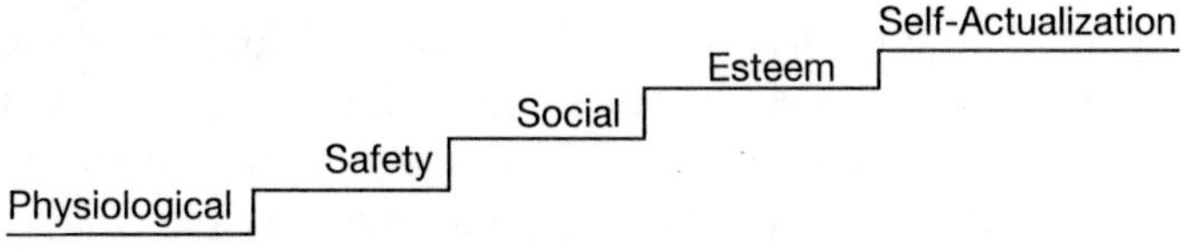

Fig. 14.1a: Hierarchy of work motivation (Model I)

Unless the lower-order needs are first (though partially) satisfied the satisfaction of higher order needs will not be possible. Thus, physiological needs have to be satisfied before the security needs will emerge. Security and physiological needs have to the satisfied before one moves up to the social needs and so on. For example, when man's physiological and safety needs have been satisfied, his social needs becomes dominant and come at the top of the hierarchy as shown in Fig. 14.1b.

Maslow's theory has stood the test of time and still makes a contribution to the study and application to work motivation. In particular, Herzberg's two-factor theory and Alderfer's ERG theory, covered next, are based on Maslow's concept of needs.

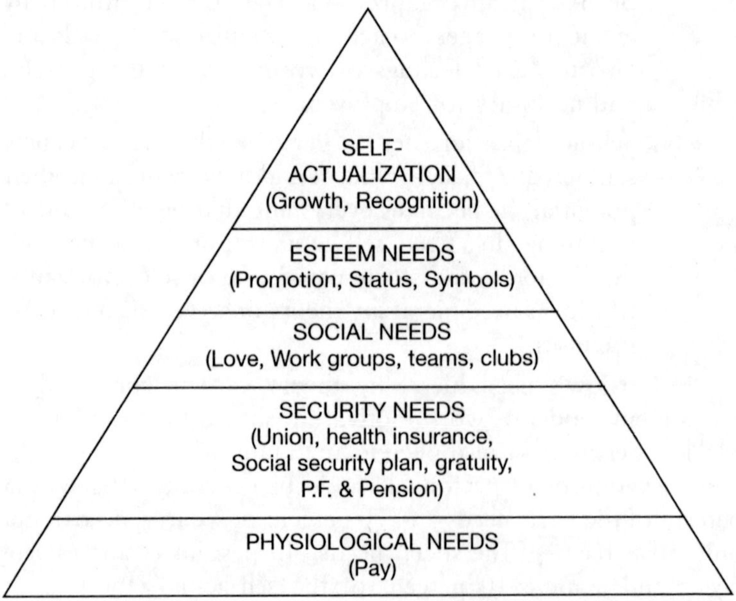

Fig. 14.1b: Pyramid of work motivation (Model II)

14.7 HERZBERG'S TWO-FACTOR THEORY

Herzberg extended the work of Maslow and developed a specific content theory of work motivation. He proposed that there were two categories of needs essentially independent to each other. The first of job conditions has referred to as maintenance or hygiene factors and second set of job conditions as motivational factors.

Herzberg labeled the hygiene factors as the dissatisfiers. There are ten maintenance or hygiene factors. These factors are preventive and environmental in nature see Fig. 14.2. These hygiene factors prevent dissatisfaction but they do not lead to satisfaction. They serve as a take-off point for motivation. By themselves, the hygiene factors do not motivate. These maintenance factors are necessary to maintain a reasonable level of satisfaction/output in employees. Any increase in providing maintenance factor beyond certain level will not provide any satisfaction to the employees and no increase in output is reflected, however, any cut in these factors below this level will dissatisfied them resulting in loss in output.

Hygiene Factors	Motivators
1. Company policies and administration	1. Achievement
2. Supervision	2. Recognition
3. Working conditions	3. Responsibility
4. Salary	4. Advancement
5. Relationship with peers	5. Work itself
6. Personal life	6. Growth
7. Interpersonal relations with subordinates	
8. Status	
9. Security	

Fig. 14.2: Herzberg's two-factor theory

Motivational factors—These factors are capable of having a positive effect on job satisfaction often resulting in an increase is one's output. Most of these factors are related with job contents. Herzberg includes six factors that motivate employees (Fig. 14.2). There are: achievement, recognition, work itself, responsibility, advancement and growth. Any increase in these factors will satisfy the employees; however any decrease will not affect their level of satisfaction. Since these increase level of satisfaction in the employees; these can be use in motivating them for higher output. Thus, individual must have a job with a challenging content in order to be truly motivated.

Herzberg maintains that potency of various factors is not entirely a function of the factors themselves. It is also influenced by the personality characteristics of the individuals. From their point of view, individuals may be classified into two—motivation seekers and maintenance seekers. The motivation seekers generally are individuals who are primarily motivated by the 'Satisfiers' such as advancement, achievement and other factors associated with work itself. On the other hand, maintenance seekers tend to more concerned with factors surrounding the job such as supervision, working conditions, pay, etc.

Comparison of Herzberg and Maslow Models:

> Herzberg's theory is closely related to Maslow's need hierarchy. The hygiene factors are roughly equivalent to Maslow's lower-level needs. On the other hand, motivators are roughly equivalent to Maslow's higher-level needs. There are some divisions of esteem need: some part coming under maintenance factor, e.g., status and others, advancement and recognition going under motivational factors (Fig. 14.3). There is a particular difference between two models. Maslow emphasizes that any unsatisfied need whether of lower order or higher order will motivate individuals irrespective of level of employees. On the other hand, Herzberg has suggested two independent factors, therein any lower order need is provided these are hygiene factors which fail to motivate workers.

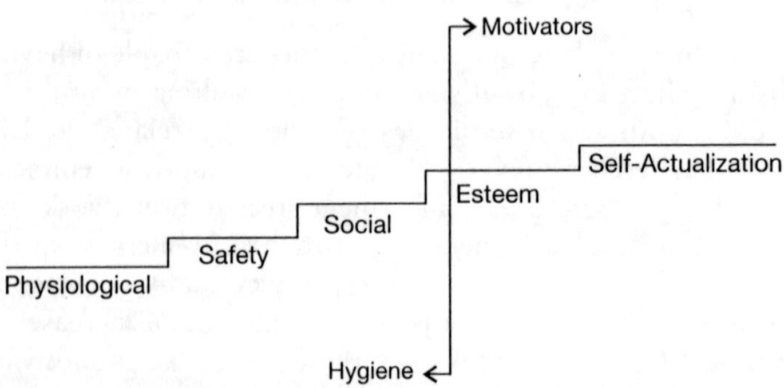

Fig. 14.3: Relationship between Herzberg and Maslow models

Following points have further thrown light on two-factor theory:

1. The theory oversimplifies the complexities of work motivation. While establishing the theory, probably, the complexity of job, age of employees, environment/situational conditions were not kept constant leading to simplified assumptions which are not validated in subsequent research studies. There seem to be job factors such as pay that lead to both satisfaction and dissatisfaction. For example, pay can be dissatisfying if not high enough but also satisfying as a form of achievement and recognition.

2. The job design technique of job enrichment is one of Herzberg's contributions. The job enrichment applies to improvement of jobs in such a way that they have more motivators than before. This idea behind job enrichment is to keep maintenance factors constant or higher while increasing motivational factors.

3. There is difficulties in applying the theory in letter and spirit. For example, there is considerable amount of mixing of maintenance and motivating factors. Therefore, these finding suggest that various factors relating to jobs, may not be classified into maintenance and motivating factors. This classification can only be made on the basis of level of person's need satisfaction and relative strength of various needs.

4. Herzberg says, "Money and fringe benefits are known as negative motivators," for their absence from a job unquestionably will make people unhappy, but their presence does not necessarily make them happier or more productive.

5. According to Herzberg, the opposite of satisfaction is not dissatisfaction, as was traditionally believed, i.e., removing dissatisfying characteristics from a job does not necessarily make the job satisfying, or vice versa.

6. Job content and job context factors are discrete aspects of work and are neither different points on the same continuum nor different levels in the motivation hierarchy. Absence of one does not mean the presence of another.

Vroom believes that "Herzberg's inference regarding differences between 'dissatisfiers' and motivators cannot be completely accepted and that the differences between started sources of 'satisfaction' and 'dissatisfaction' may be the result of defensive processes within those responding. People are apt to attribute the causes of satisfaction of their own achievements, but more likely to attribute their satisfaction to obstacles presented by company policies or superiors than to their deficiencies."

14.8 ALDERFER'S ERG THEORY

Alderfer formulated a needs category model consisting of three groups of core need: existence, relatedness, and growth (hence ERG theory). The existence needs are concerned with survival (physiological well-being). The relatedness needs stress the importance of interpersonal and social relationships. The growth needs are concerned with the individual's intrinsic desire for personal development. Figure 14.4 shows how these groups of needs are related to the Maslow and Herzberg categories. Though they are very close, yet the ERG needs do not have strict lines of demarcation.

Alderfer's EGR Needs	Maslow's Hierarchy of Needs	Herzberg's Two Factors
Growth needs	Esteem and Self-Actualization	Motivators—Advancement, achievement, work itself
Relatedness needs	Social	Hygiene
Existence	Physiological and Safety	Factors—working conditions and salary

Fig. 14.4: Relationships—ERG, Maslow and Herzberg's theories of motivation

Alderfer is suggesting more of a continuum of needs than hierarchical level or two factors of prepotency needs. Unlike Maslow, he does not contend that a lower-level need must be fulfilled before a higher-level need becomes motivating or that deprivation is the only way to activate the need. For example, according to him, the person's background or cultural environment may dictate that the relatedness needs will take precedence over unfulfilled existence needs. Unlike Maslow, according to ERG theory, if a higher order need is not satisfied, the individual would fall back on the lower-level need (frustration and regression). When higher order growth needs cannot be met due to lack of ability, the individual is inclined to regress back to lower order relatedness/existence needs. For example, when a person cannot get promotion, according to Alderfer's ERG model, the individual would turn towards social relationships or become more eloped with pay and benefits.

14.9 MCCLELLAND'S NEED FOR ACHIEVEMENT THEORY

David C. McClelland, a psychologist at Harvard University has proposed that there are three major relevant motives or needs in workplace situations. These are need for power (n/Pwr), need for affiliation (n/Aff) and new for achievement (n/Ach). Considerable research was done by McClelland and his associates, particularly on achievement motive.

Power Motive (n/Pwr): The ability to induce or influence behaviour is power. McClelland has found that people with high power need have a great concern for exercising influence and control. Such individuals are generally seeking position of leadership; they involve in conversation, they are forceful, outspoken, hard headed and demanding. These institutional managers are interested above all in power, they focus on building power through influence rather than through their own individual achievement. They are low in affiliation motivation. However, the need for power must be disciplined and controlled so that it is directed toward the benefit of the institution as a whole and not toward the manager's personal aggrandizement. Moreover, the top manager's need for power ought to be greater than his need to be liked. Managers in this category, exercise their power impulsively. They are more often rude to other people, they drink too much, they try to exploit others sexually and they collect symbols of personal prestige such as fancy cars or attractive offices.

Affiliation Motives (n/Aff): Since people are social animals, most individuals like to interact and be with others in situations where they feel they belong and accepted. Sometimes affiliation is equated with social motives. People with high need for affiliation usually derive pleasure from being loved and tend to avoid the pain of being rejected. They are concerned with maintaining pleasant social relationships, enjoying a sense of intimacy and understanding, and enjoy consoling and helping others in trouble.

Affiliative managers need to be liked more than they need to get things done. Their decisions are aimed at increasing their own popularity rather than promoting the goals of the organization. According to sociologists, the person whose need for affiliation is high does not make a good manager. This kind of person creates low morale because he does not understand that the other people in the office will tend to regard exceptions to the rules as unfair to themselves.

Achievement Motive (n/Ach): According to McClelland, the need for achievement is a distinct human motive that can be distinguished from other needs. It can also be isolated and assessed in any group. McClelland has identified four basic characteristics of high achievers.

(i) Moderate risks: Set moderately difficulty but potentially achievable goals.
(ii) Immediate feedback: Work for situation where they can get a concrete feedback in order to know, how well they are doing.
(iii) Accomplishment: Interested in personal achievement rather than the reward of success.
(iv) Preoccupation with the tasks: The person lends to be totally preoccupied with the task until it is successfully completed. This type of commitment often reflects on his outward personality, which frequently has a negative effect on those who come in contact with him.

Managers motivated by the need to achieve are not worried about what people think of them. They focus on setting goals and reaching them, but they put their own achievement and recognition first.

Development of achievement motive: Achievement motive can be developed not only at early age, but also at later date. Number of workshops were conducted with managers in the

U.S.A., Italy, Poland and India and were successful in increasing individual need for achievement. These workshops have four primary goals:

1. To teach participants how to think, talk and eat like a person with high achievement.
2. To simulate participants to set higher, but carefully planned and realistic work goals over the next two years.
3. To give the participants knowledge about themselves.
4. To create group esprit de corps from learning about each other's hopes and fears, success and failures and from going through an emotional experiences together, away from everyday life, in a retreat setting.

It was found that after two years those who had undergone such courses, made more money, were promoted faster and expanded their business faster than comparable men who had not taken some similar management workshop.

Further, McClelland in his theory seems to be more concerned with motive than behaviour which is rather narrow in its scope. In work situations, it is the behaviour that is given greater significance rather than the feelings of the people. Finally, all of the content theories direct managers to share responsibility and empower employees in addition to recognizing their achievement.

14.10 VROOM PROCESS THEORIES OF MOTIVATION

Although the early motivation theories offer insights into motivation no single one offers a valid explanation for why some people exert a high level of effort on their job while other don't. What is needed a theory to also consider the contingency aspects relevant to particular people in particular situations. Victor H. Vroom proposed his expectancy theory as an alternative to content models, which he felt were inadequate explanations of the complex process of work motivation. The model is built around the concepts of valence, instrumentality, and expectancy and is commonly called the VIE theory as expressed by:

$$\text{Motive Force} = \Sigma \text{ Valence} \times \text{Expectancy}$$

Algebraic sum of products of valences is multiplied by expectations.

Valence: The strength of an individual's preference for particular outcome in the case of valence is positive the individual must prefer attending the outcome to not attending it. A valence to be zero when the individual is indifferent toward outcome, the valence is negative when the individual prefers not attaining the outcome to attaining it.

Another input into valence is the instrumentality of the first-level outcome in obtaining a desired second-level outcome. For example, a person would be motivated towards superior performance (+1 Valence first-level) because of the desire to be promoted. The superior performance outcome (first-level outcome) is being instrumental in obtaining a promotion (+1 Valence second-level outcome). Instrumentality refers to the degree to which a first-level outcome (superior performance) will lead to a desired second-level outcome (promotion).

1. Expectancy is the probability (believe) (ranging from 0 to 1) that particular action or effort will lead to a particular first level outcome. Although the Vroom model does not provide specific solution to motivational problems facing a manager, it is of value in understanding organizational behaviour. It can clarify the relationship between individual and organizational goals. Vroom feels that anyone or a combination of these possibilities will result in a low level of motivation to perform. The model is designed to help management understand and analyses employee's motivation and identify some of the relevant variable, it does not suggest on what motivates organizational member as the Maslow and Herzberg models do.

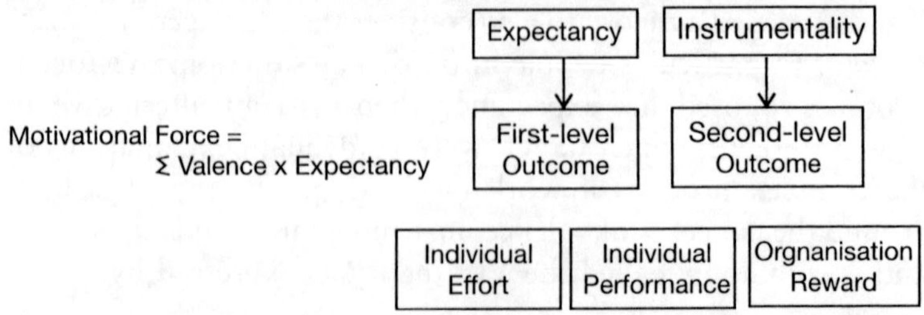

Fig. 14.5

It is important to determine what needs each employee seeks to satisfy. This knowledge will be valuable to management to design the awards to suit the need of the employee since rewards that are valuable to employee X may not be attractive to employee Y, it is necessary to individualize rewards to each employee. Employee assigns the following relationship:

Effort ⇒ Performance ⇒ Rewards ⇒ Satisfying personal goals

Porter and Lawler has refined and extended Vroom's model therein relationship between satisfaction and performance are expressed diagrammatically rather than mathematically, these are more variables, and the cognitive process of perception play a central role.

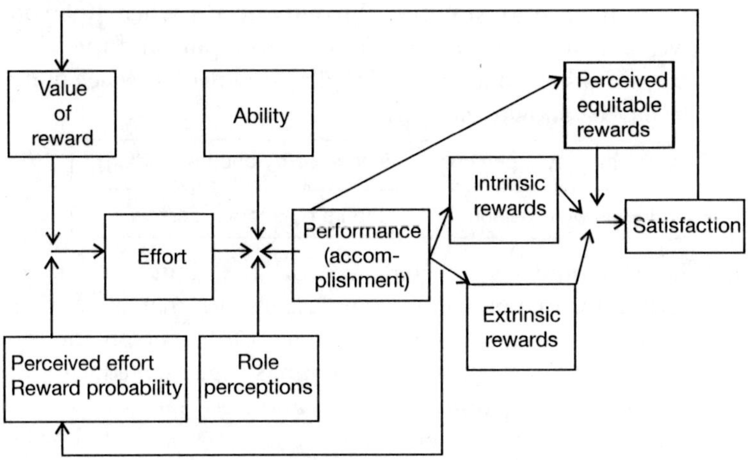

Fig. 14.6: Porter and Lawler model

Porter and Lawler start with the premise that motive force does not equal satisfaction or performance. Motivation, satisfaction, and performance are all separate variables and relate in ways different from what was traditionally assumed. This model suggests the importance of rewards in the relationship between performance and satisfaction. Specifically, it is prescribed that performance and satisfaction will be more strongly related when rewards are made contingent upon performance than when they are not.

Though Porter and Lawler's model is more application oriented than Vroom's model, it is quite complex. The model recommends that managers should examine and understand such variables as the values of possible rewards, the perceptions of effort-reward probabilities, and role perceptions. Thus, accordingly they should change reward policies.

14.11 ADAMS EQUITY THEORY OF MOTIVATION

The theory of Stancy Adams argues that employees are not only concerned with the absolute amount of their efforts, but also with what others receive for the same efforts. The theory put forward that a major input into job performance and satisfaction is the degree of equity (or inequity) that people perceive in their work situation. Inequity occurs when a person perceives that the ratio of his outcomes to inputs and the ratio of a relevant other's outcomes to inputs are unequal. The equity theory may be shown as follows:

$$\frac{\text{Outcomes by a person}}{\text{Inputs by a person}} = \frac{\text{Outcomes by another person}}{\text{Inputs by another person}}$$

There should be a balance of the outcomes/inputs relationship for one person in comparison with that of another person. Both the inputs and the outcomes of the person and the other are based on the person's perceptions. Age, sex, education, social status, organizational position, and how hard the person works are examples of perceived input variables. Outcomes consist primarily of rewards such as pay, status, promotion, and intrinsic interest in the job.

If the person's perceived ratio is not equal to the others, he will strive to restore the ratio to equity. To store equity, the person may alter the inputs or outcomes, cognitively distort the inputs or outcomes, leave the field, act on the other, or change the other.

It is important to note that inequity does not come about only when the person feel cheated. For example, Adams has studied the impact that perceived overpayment has on equity. His findings suggest that workers prefer equitable payment to overpayment. In case, workers who feel under paid (outcomes) or overworked (inputs), in relation to other, in order to restore inequity; the workers may reduce their productivity in order to restore equity. The dictum "a fair day work for fair day pay" denotes a sense of equity felt by employees. When employees perceive inequity, it can result in lower productivity, higher absenteeism or increase in turnover. Hence, the most significant contribution of the equity theory that management must know is that if rewards are to motivate employees, they must be equitable and fair.

14.12 FINANCIAL AND NON-FINANCIAL MOTIVATORS

Management generally uses financial and non-financial motivation tools to motivate their employees.

A. Financial Motivators. Money is a universal motivator. Wages and salaries, bonuses, fringe benefits, etc. are most important motivators. It is not only satisfying lower order needs such as physiological needs, security needs, but also provide a position of take-off for prestige, recognition, and a visible symbol of achievements. Pay can be dissatisfying if not high enough but also satisfying as a form of achievement and recognition. Saiyadain and Monappa in his studies found that only 33 percent of Indian managers chose their jobs for the remuneration. Several other studies on Indian samples are suggesting that money alone cannot motivate in most cases. Gellerman points out that in organization money is actually used as a means of keeping an organization adequately staffed and not as a motivator. This can be seen in the practice of making wages and salaries competitive between various organizations so as to attract and hold people. As per equity theory, people are concerned not only with absolute amount of money they are paid for their efforts; the relationship of this amount to what others are paid is also important. Although money was probably over emphasized in classical management theory and motivation techniques, the pendulum now seems to have lowing too far in the opposite direction. Money remains a very important but admittedly complex potential motivator. Money can be used as an effective positive reinforcement intervention strategy to improve performance.

The more some people get the more they seem to want. The idea here is that once money satisfies basic needs, people can use it to get ahead, a goal that is always just out of their reach, so they strive for more. Conversely, there is evidence that shows that if an organization reduces its pay, morale may suffer so pay more. Sieve Kerr of GEC noted that, "Nobody refuses money, nobody returns money and people who have more that they could ever use to do dreadful things to get more".

B. Non-Financial Motivators. Management in addition to financial incentives provides non-financial incentives to motivate people in the organization. The connotation of non-financial incentives does not mean that organization has nothing to spend on these. For example, if the individual gets promotion, he gets better status more challenging job, etc., he also gets more pay. Given the significance of motivating employees to result in productivity and satisfaction, a large number of non-financial motivational interventions have been tested and tried out which are as under:

1. Promotion, status and recognition
2. Job enrichment
3. Job enlargement
4. Job rotation
5. Quality circle
6. Others

1. Promotion, Status and Recognition: Promotion to a higher level of echelon satisfies the needs of human beings in the organization as well as in the society. Since the promotion depends upon capabilities and good performance and it enhances status, authority, recognizing of his good work, higher wage, etc., people will try for that. Status may also be improved if the individual get attractive office, out of turn allotment of bigger house, day time work, etc.

2. Job Enrichment: For the first time while enunciating his two-factor theory of motivation, Herzberg has mentioned the job redesign technique of job enrichment. Subsequently, at later date, a group of researchers provided an outline of successful job enrichment programs. They are of the opinion that an employee is motivated to perform his work if the activity is meaningful to him, if he is responsible for its completion; and if he has knowledge of result in reasonable time. **Job Enrichment** is the process of upgrading the job-task mix in order to increase significantly the potential for growth, achievement, responsibility, and recognition. Job enrichment increases *job depth,* the degree to which individuals can plan and control the work involved in their jobs.

According to them, these are following five core job dimensions to tackle the job enrichment (Fig. 14.7).

Fig. 14.7: Five core job dimensions in job enrichment

(i) Skill variety: The extent to which a job requires a worker to perform activities that challenge his skills and abilities, making repetitive, dull unstimulus jobs less boring and more satisfying.

(ii) Task identity: The extent to which a job requires completion of a whole and identifiable piece of work (moderating the job content). It means enhancement of planning and controlling of their work.

(iii) Task significance: The extent to which a job has a substantial and perceivable impact on the lives of other people in the organization or the work at large. The extent of discretionary power to handle the task.

(iv) Autonomy: The extent to which a job gives a worker freedom and independence—usually with less supervision and more self-evaluation. It amounts to cover some to supervisor's job to subordinate worker (vertical loading).

(v) Feedback: The extent of the knowledge of results within a reasonable time in order to correct their own performance.

A successful job enrichment programme should ideally increase employee satisfaction, though stagnation is there in the organization. At the same time, direct benefits to the organization in terms of lower absenteeism and reduced turnover besides reasonable improvement in production/productivity and quality of products. The more these core characteristics are reflected in job enrichment exercise, the more likely individuals are to feel motivated by job changes.

3. Job Enlargement: It is adopted as a means of motivating people in the organization. As against job enrichment which involves vertical loading, job enlargement involves horizontal enlargement to a wider variety of similar tasks to a job in order to make it more challenging. It improves worker's skill so that they are more able to help satisfying their needs. Job enlargement reduces the monotony of repetitiveness. It increases efficiency and interest in work because fatigue is lessened. However, Herzberg feels that merely giving a person different kind of jobs is not enough and have somewhat limited success in motivating employees because the basic nature of the job remains the same. Job enlargement is also being used as multi-skilling by combining a few related skills.

4. Job Rotation: It is a motivation technique therein the employees are rotated in different sections to perform different skilled jobs for certain period of time. Such horizontal job transfers can breakup the monotony and at the same time provide opportunity for diversity to learn new skill, change supervisors, relocate or make new job acquaintances, can deter or slow up the onset of boredom from job that have become habitual. Job rotation therefore can renew enthusiasm for learning and motivate workers to high performance. The bank makes a regular practice of rotating managers through various departments. As a result, the managers tend to be more cooperative with one another because they either have been or will be in the other person's job at some point. Job rotation across different units may also help stimulate innovation, since it promotes the exchange of ideas. However, there are certain problems in this technique. First productive work may suffer because of the obvious disruption caused by such changes. Second, job rotation becomes less useful as specialization proceeds, for few people have the breadth of technical knowledge and skills to move from one job to another job. Third, there is no appreciable change in personal satisfaction unless the jobs are such that the person is really interested in them. Potential problems with job rotation are that departments may view the rotating individuals as temporary help and give them only trivial things to do and may also question their departmental loyalty. For this purpose, the job rotation is not required. Thus, the role of job rotation in motivating people is limited.

14.13 BEHAVIOURAL SCIENCE APPROACH TO PARTICIPATION AND MOTIVATION

The behavioural sciences support the application of participative management through their concepts, theories and models. The experiment conducted by behavioural scientist, Elton Mayo, in the early thirties emphasizes values of cooperation and partnership between subordinates and supervisors, or between employers and employees. This has been reinforced by the findings of McGregor's theories of openness and trust shown by management to its employees. Further, Maslow has suggested the hierarchy of needs which culminates in a need for self-actualisation. It includes people being active, independent, capable of self-control through awareness of their potential; engaged in a variety of behaviours; having long-range perspectives; and seeking equality. Theory Y supports participative management, whereas theory X goes against the philosophy of the participative management which supports the autocratic style of managing people. In terms of motivation hygiene theory, participative management could provide employees with intrinsic motivation by increasing opportunities for growth, responsibility, and involvement in the work itself.

Participation is assumed to increase general satisfaction or morale, improve group commitment towards issues on which people are allowed to participate, provide more accurate information about such issues and increase productivity. These behavioural and social sciences theories and research contributed to the growth of participative management worldwide.

14.14 MORALE

Meaning: Morale is highly relative concept. It is generally refers to esprit de corps. Morale is the mental attitude or bearing of a person or a group regarding his confidence, discipline, and attitude towards work, peer group, superiors, and subordinates, for accomplishment of individual and organizational goals. It represents satisfaction that a person derives from his work and work environment.

Definition: Edwin B. Flippo defines, "It is a mental condition or attitude of individuals and groups which determines, their willingness to co-operate. Good morale is evidenced by employee enthusiasm, voluntary conformance with regulations and orders and willingness to co-operate with others in the accomplishment of an organization's objectives. Poor morale is evidenced by surliness, insubordination, a feeling of discouragement and dislike of the job, company and associates."

Jucius Michael has described, "Morale is a state of mind and emotion affection willingness to work which in turn affects individual and organizational objective." He elaborates it that it is an attitude of mind, and 'esprit de corps', a state of well-being and an emotional force.

Milton L. Blum observes that the individual morale is a group phenomenon incorporating four elements: group solidarity, group goal, observable progress towards the goal and individual participation in reaching the goal.

Characteristics of Morale

1. State of Mental Health: Morale is related to the state of mental health which is closely associated with loyalty, egoism, enthusiasm, etc.
2. Identification of Group Interest: Morale is an identification of group interest and that of the interest

of the enterprise, fellow workers and requirements of the job.

3. Subjective feeling: Morale is the subjective feeling of the employees. The morale of a group is said to be high when the group shows an attitude of satisfaction.
4. Affects Behaviour, Performance and Discipline: Morale affects human behaviour, performance and discipline. It cannot be measured directly but is reflected in productivity, employee discipline, absenteeism, turnover, etc.

Importance of Morale

1. Morale plays a significant role in the organization success. High morale keeps the employees loyal to the job, profession and organization. This leads to employee commitment and sincerity. The commented and sincere employees plan not only their individual work, but also the work of the group and the entire department. High morale yield more production and high quality at lower cost.
2. According to Keith Davis, "Never underestimate the power of morale."
3. It stimulates a feeling of togetherness, a sense of identification with elements of one's job, working condition, fellow works, supervisors and the company which is conducive to the achievement of company's goals. It is an index of good industrial relations.
4. High morale helps the management to reduce labours turnover, team spirit, absenteeism and, grievances and improve discipline.
5. In recent times, researches indicate that higher morale has direct correlation with job satisfaction, hence importance is given to maintain it at appropriate level by the organization. In recent past, government has also introduced several labour welfare and social security measures to improve the morale of the industrial workers.

Individual and Group Morale

An individual's morale is related with knowing one's own expectations. If one is clear of his own needs and how to satisfy them most of the time, his morale is high. It relates to the individual perceptions of the existing state of well-being in the organization as it pertains to him. Whereas the group morale depends on the interactions among individuals in the group, such as a football team, a military unit or a work group. It is synonymous with 'team spirit'. Guion describes morale from the point of an individual worker. He defines it as the degree to which an individual's needs are satiated and the degree to which the individual derives satisfaction from his total job situation. Scott and Mitchell describe morale as one's overall feelings towards one's job. They use job satisfaction (job attitudes) and morale interchangeable. Another finding in terms of individual's morale is derived from studies conducted by the University of Michigan. Under it, morale is considered as the combination of attitudes towards the company, the job and the immediate supervisors.

Group morale and the morale of the individual are interrelated but not necessarily identical. They have an effect on each other. It is conceivable that an individual's own personal perception of existing conditions as they relate to himself may be high, and the group perception of conditions may be low, or vice versa, but more usually the two share common feelings.

Factors Affecting Morale

Employee morale is a very complex phenomenon and is influenced by many factors such as:

(i) The attitudes of executives and managers towards their subordinates

(ii) Service conditions like promotions, pay and reward, safety, security of job and other rules and regulations affecting employees

(iii) The nature of work

(iv) General quality of supervision

(v) Level of the intrinsic job satisfaction

(vi) Level of participation, consultation and delegation

(vii) Interpersonal relations within the group

(viii) Employee's age

(ix) Employee's educational level and occupational level

14.15 MORALE AND MOTIVATION

Morale and motivation in industry are often used interchangeably, though they refer to different kinds of phenomena. Motivation refers to the propensity towards a particular behaviour pattern to satisfy a need or deficiency. Morale describes an employee's state of attitudes, feelings and judgments about his work, peers, supervisors, subordinates and his organization.

Management relies on morale measurement as a basis for estimating motivation level of employees because direct measurement of motivation has several complications. As morale is an overt manifestation of the level of motivation, its measurement providers proper assessment of motivation in organizational settings. A management, while seeking optimal motivation among its workers, tries to take several steps to improve morale. It is assumed that this can help enhance job performance, job satisfaction and employment stability.

According to Mrityunjay Banerjee, "Motivation is intimately connected with the morale. Good motivation leads to high morale. Poor morale is the manifestation of defective motivating process." Thus, morale is a state of mental health which is closely related to motivation. Morale is willingness to work. Job satisfaction and dissatisfaction create the problem of morale among the employees. If an employee is satisfied with his work, his morale will be high. If he is dissatisfied his morale will be low.

Morale can be measured by assessing attitudes and job satisfaction. 'Attitude Survey' is most popular method of morale measurement. Morale can be improved by adapting several other measures, such as contest programmes among employees, special recognition and awards to long service.

Morale and Productivity

Since morale manifests itself in the attitudes of workers, it is important to know about the results of high morale and low morale upon his productivity. The review of the research studies do not show a direct relationship between morale and productivity. For example, Herzberg found that in 54% of the studies, high morale was related to high productivity while in 35% morale and productivity did not reveal relationship. In 11% of the studies, high morale was associated low productivity. Further, on the basis of several research studies Miller and Form have given four relationships between productivity and morale, viz.: (i) high productivity-high morale; (ii) low productivity-high morale; (iii) high productivity-low morale; and (iv) low productivity-low morale.

The first situation is likely to occur when group goals such as pride in work groups, group recognition, etc. are achieved, and where willing workers are satisfied with their job due to motivation. There is a circular relationship between morale and productivity. High morale pushes up productivity and high productivity in turn, pushes up morale and so on.

The second situation may occur when individual goals, other than performance are fulfilled and where supervisors lack technical and administrative skills. In such situation, morale of the workers may be high at the cost of productivity.

In third situation, supervisor is only able to increase productivity his skills or planning ability rather than through motivation to the employee.

The fourth situation occurs where factors obtained in combination of high productivity-high morale are lacking. Here also circular relationship exists between two. Low morale pulls down the productivity and low productivity shrinks the morale of the employees.

Indices of Low Morale

Indices of low morale are generally not noticed till it is obviously low or when something has gone wrong. Among the more significant of the indices of low morale are:

(i) Employee unrest

(ii) High rate of absenteeism and tardiness

(iii) High labour turnover

(iv) Grievances
(v) Need for discipline
(vi) Fatigue and monotony
(vii) Lack of pride in work
(viii) Wastage and spoilage

REVIEW QUESTIONS

1. Briefly discuss the importance of motivation to organizations.
2. Describe the theoretical development of work motivation. How it is applied to a person who is type Y according to McGregor's theory?
3. Compare Maslow Hierarchy of need with Herzberg theory of motivation.
4. Discuss briefly the various process theories of work motivation.
5. Money is the universal motivator however describe the conditions where it does not serve the purpose.
6. Distinguish between job enrichment and job enlargement.
7. State the various theories of motivation. How do need theories differ from behavioural theories?
8. What is morale? How is it different from motivation? How does morale affect productivity?

Short Notes

1. Theory Z
2. McGregor's Theory X and Theory Y of motivation
3. Financial and non-financial motivators

CASE STUDY

A plastic extrusion company manufacturing briefcase, suitcase and other accessories with a brand for last 20 years of existence. The company has decided to acquire a garment company stock and barrel which has not been performing above break-even point. In order to achieve performance, Managing Director of the garment company appoint 20 percent fresh blood to rejuvenate the organization. In the process, he poached a

Personnel Manager named Suresh Gangwar who is an engineering graduate with MBA degree, a fast-track personnel from FMCG company. For a week, he critically examined the existing situation and decided to pin point the issues like organization structure vis-à-vis reporting relationship, job description vis-à-vis job enrichment and a fresh incentive scheme/reward scheme. MD took a meeting with senior managers and Suresh Gangawar. The outcome of meeting among other issues decided to hire a management consultant who should have the background of industrial engineering. After a few sittings and field work, consultant came out with the following recommendations:

(i) Organization structure is to be revised by delayering from seven to five hierarchical levels thereby improving communication in the organization. The present designations are changed to high sounding designations which are appealing to clients.

(ii) Job descriptions/position description of manager and above officers are revised with job enrichment wherever required. This was necessary because of reducing the number of levels. This will also improve the morale of employees.

(iii) He designed the most sophisticated incentive scheme in order to motivate the employees. It would improve the productivity vis-à-vis higher pay packet of personnel. He also developed a non-financial incentive for sr. officers to achieve the overall objectives of the organization.

Questions for the Case

1. Explain the hierarchy of needs theory. How could this theory help you motivate individuals at garment company?
2. To what extent are goals set in the incentive plan that are specific and challenging? Do these goals improve organization effectiveness?
3. What were the indicators to show that morale of employees has improved?

Chapter 15
Leadership

15.1 INTRODUCTION

The exercise of power and authority may not be having long-term effect as the people may not be enthusiastic to contribute willingly for the achievement of organizational objectives. Such a willing effort can be achieved through right leadership which has a long-term effect on the people. Thus, leadership is an essential ingredient for successful organization. Infosys is one of the most unique organizations in India which set a unique leadership given birth of three basic beliefs: customer service, dedicated happy knowledge employees and a strive for excellence.

15.2 DEFINITIONS AND CHARACTERISTICS OF LEADERSHIP

Social scientists, business executives, theorists, management consultants and administrators have defined leadership in the way they see through the leadership dilemma. All agree that leadership is important, but no one can define it to the satisfaction of everyone.

Glover defined, "Leadership is that outstanding aspect of management which manifests ability, creativeness, initiative and inventiveness, and which gains the confidence, co-operation and willingness of the people to work by organizing and building employee morale."

Peter F. Drucker states, "Leadership is a human characteristics which lifts man's vision to higher sights; raised man's performance to higher standards and builds man's personality beyond its normal limits."

According to Hersey and Blanchard, "Leadership (L) is a function of leader (l), the followers (f) and situational variables (s), who exercises this influence is leader whether he is a manager in formal organization or an informal leader in an informal group or the head of the family." It can be depicted in the following equation form: L = f (l, f, s).

Characteristics Leadership

Leadership recognizes the following characteristics:

1. It is an attribute of personality; sometimes it is used as if it was certain positions, and sometimes as an attribute of behaviour of leader.
2. Leader influences the followers in such style so as to accomplish the objectives willfully. A reciprocal relationship between the leader and his followers is another characteristic of leadership. A leader not only influences his followers but is also influenced by it. As such followers should also have an attribute of behaviour amenable to be influenced. This relationship may be formal or informal. In formal organization, the leader gets the authority because of the position he holds. When such leadership is absent, informal leadership automatically develops. Reciprocally, group tends to create group loyalty and team spirit—which encourages leadership roles. According to Douglas McGregor, the attitudes, needs, and personal characteristics of followers are variables of leadership.
3. Leadership process is dynamic in nature to the extent the situation and attributes of leader and the group vary.
4. Communication process—specific attribute is important for successful leadership.
5. The nature of the specific situations such as the characteristics of the organization and its social, economic and political milieu are variables of leadership.

6. Feedback—It is concerned with the way a leader behaves in his man-to-man relationship with his followers. The above characteristics leadership functions hold good in any organization whether it be a political, religious, business or any other organization. Mahatma Gandhi had learnt social leadership in South Africa and used it in India as he got right kind of followers and compelling situation, thus becoming successful in freeing the country from the sickle of British Emperor.

15.3 DIFFERENCE BETWEEN MANAGEMENT AND LEADERSHIP

Leadership may be viewed as the process of influencing behaviour of an individual or group regardless of the reasons. It may be for one's own goals or a friend's goals, and may or may not be congruent with organization's goals. On the other hand, there can be managers only where organized structures create such roles.

Another difference in the two concepts lies in the context of scope of functions performed. A manager has to perform all the five functions—planning, organizing, staffing, directing, and controlling. Leadership function comes under directing through which behaviour is directed to get maximum use of subordinates' ability. However, in this process, subordinates may work about 60-65% of their capacity. Managers must exercise his leadership quality to raise the level of their efforts.

Bennis once commented, "There are many institutions, I know, are very well managed but very poorly led." This statement clearly demonstrates that managing and leading are not the same. Leadership and managership are not synonymous, though effective management requires effective leadership.

Managers work with people while leaders relate ideas to people in more intuitive and empathic ways.

Managers cope up with change whereas leaders bring change. Leaders develop a vision and direction for the future.

The business psychologist Abraham Zaleznick made a point in contrasting leaders and managers, "Managers prefer working with people; leaders stir emotion."

Warren G. Bennis views the differences between manager and leader as shown below:

Managers	*Leaders*
Administers	Innovates
A copy	An original
Maintains	Develops
Focusses on systems and structures	Focusses on people
Relies on control	Inspires trust
Short-range view	Long-range perspective
Ask how and when	Ask what and why
Eye on the bottom line	Eye on the horizon
Imitates	Originates
Accepts the Status Quo	Challenges the status quo
Classic good soldier	Own person
Does things right	Does the right thing

Adopted: Warren G. Bennis, "Managing the Dream: Leadership in the 21st Century."

15.4 LEADERSHIP THEORIES

Many of the researchers carried out in-depth studies to find the answer of the question: what makes an individual effective in his area of operation? Is his success due to his personality, or his behaviour, or the types of followers he has, or the situation in which he works, or a combination of all these? These researchers, however, could not give a satisfactory answer of the question. Instead these researchers have resulted in various theories, the prominent among these traditional theories being trait theory, behavioural theory, and situational theory. Each theory has its own contributions, limitations, assumptions, and framework of analysis. The understanding of various theories of leadership will provide a guideline to judge as to how a leader emerges.

Trait Theory

Trait is defined as relatively enduring qualities or characteristics of an individual. The method of study was to select leaders of eminence and their characteristics were studies. It was the hypothesis that the persons having certain traits could become successful leaders.

Although no set of absolute traits may be identified, the individuals who possess ability to lead others must have certain attributes to help them in performing their leadership roles.

We give below the qualities which, according to various authorities, should characterize a leader.

Authorities	*Qualities*
1. F.M. Viscount Shim	i. Courage, ii. Willpowers, iii. Judgements, iv. Flexibility, v. Knowledge, and vi. Integrity.
2. Ordway Tead	i. Physical and nervous energy, ii. Enthusiasm, iii. Sense of purpose and direction, iv. Technical mastery, v. Integrity, vi. Technical skill, vii. Friendliness and affection, viii. Decisiveness, ix. Intelligence, and x. Faith.
3. Henry Fayol	i. Health and physical fitness, ii. Intelligence and natural vigour, iii. Moral qualities, iv. Knowledge, and v. Managerial ability.
4. Chester I. Bernard	i. Vitality and education, ii. Decisiveness, iii. Persuasiveness, iv. Stability, v. Intellectual capacity, and vi. Knowledge.
5. R.M. Stogdill	i. Physical and constitutional factors—(height, weight, physique, energy, health, and appearance), ii. Intelligence, iii. Self-confidence, iv. Sociability, v. Will (initiative, persistence, and ambition), vi. Dominance, and vii. Surgency (talkative, cheerfulness, geniality, enthusiasm, expressiveness, alertness, and originality).
6. E.E. Ghiselli (Studied in year 1971)	i. Supervisory ability, ii. Achievement, iii. Motivation, iv. Self-actualising, v. Intelligence, vi. Self-assurance, and vii. Decisiveness.

It can be seen from above that there is a wide variation in traits to be possessed by successful leaders. Further, traits can be classified into Innate and Acquirable traits, on the basis of their source. According to Professor Argyris, some of personality traits of 'successful' executive are 'High Frustration Tolerance', understanding of the 'Laws of Competitive Warfare', or that he 'Identifies with Group'. Innate qualities are those which are possessed by individuals since their birth. These qualities are natural and often known as God-gifted. On the basis of such qualities, it is said that 'leaders are born and not made'. These qualities cannot be acquired by the individuals. The following are the major innate qualities in a successful leader.

(i) Intelligence, to a very great extent, is a natural quality in the individuals because it is directly related with brain.

(ii) Imagination, perception and intuition are also considered as natural traits.

Acquirable qualities of leadership are those which can be acquired and increased through socialization and identification process over a period of time. There are some psychologists who believe that most of the human qualities are partly natural and partly a matter of acquisition which can be acquired/ increased through practice however, the major role is played by environment and the various training methods.

1. Emotional Stability: A leader should have high level of emotional stability. He should be free from bias, is consistent in action, and refrains from anger. He is well-adjusted and self-confident to meet most situations brilliantly.
2. Human Relations: A leader should have adequate knowledge, how he should deal with human beings.
3. Empathy: A feeling for people and an understanding of a particular person's emotional reactions will enable any leader to adapt his approach to achieve a more favourable response however, the leader attempt to remain objective so that sentiment does not blind him to other requirements.
4. A genuine respect for people, coupled with deliberate effort to bring out the best in each person rather than to focus upon his weaknesses will encourage people to grow and to live up to the expectation in them. Again, train-then-trust is recommended as a philosophy to guide much leadership behaviour.
5. Integrity: Basic honesty and fairness, acting from conviction as to what is right rather than who is right, and setting high standards for oneself as well as for others—is perhaps the most essential of all leadership qualities. At the same time, integrity must be combined

with patience, understanding and a good sense of timing.

6. Determination to get results very often proves to be the real measure of successful leadership however, it no way a person is required to become ruthless, unscrupulous, or inconsiderate of others.
7. Motivating Skills: Not only a leader is self-motivated but he has requisite quality to motivate his followers.
8. Technical Skills: Technical competence of a leader depends upon his ability to plan, organize, delegate, analyse, seek advice, make decisions, control, and win co-operation from others.
9. Communication Skills: A leader uses communication skill in getting the acceptance of his plan of action from the followers. Normally, a successful leader is extrovert as compared to introvert.

The above qualities may be only suggestive and not comprehensive. Moreover, it is not necessary that all these qualities are possessed by a successful leader in equal quantity.

Critical Analysis

The trait theory is very simple. However, this fails to produce clear-cut results. It does not consider the whole environment of the leadership, of which trait may be only one factor. Moreover, no generalization can be drawn about various traits for leadership as there were considerable variations in traits established by various researchers. Effective leaders normally possessed emotional intelligence, integrity, commitment, motivation, self-confidence, intelligence and knowledge of the business.

There is a problem of measuring the traits. Though there are various tests to measure the personality traits, however, no definite conclusion can be drawn. Even in the same organization different traits appear necessary for different roles. Whereas technical knowledge is important at lower levels, conceptual skill is required at top level. On the other hand, in some organizations, especially in small organization, it demands multiplicity of roles because one manager has to do many jobs, hence combinations of traits are required to accomplish his duties.

Behavioural Theory

Behavioural theory attempted to explain the leadership phenomenon in term of behaviour of the leader. There are four basic elements determining suitable behaviour leaders, followers, goal, and environment. Leader's action may be viewed in two ways—functional (favourable) and dysfunctional (unfavourable) to leadership. The dysfunctional acts are inability to accept subordinates' ideas, display of emotional immaturity, poor human relations, and poor communication. These are also important in leadership because they demotivate employees to work together. The functional behaviour for successful leader includes setting goals, motivating employees, raising the level of morale, developing teamwork, effective communication, etc.

The difference between trait and behavioural theories is that former emphasizes some particular trait to be possessed by leader while latter emphasizes use of particular behaviour by leader. It is true that favourable behaviour provides for greater satisfaction to both the followers and the leaders.

Behavioural theory suffers from shortcoming, that is, a particular behaviour at a time may be effective, while at other times may not be effective. This means the time factor which is an important element is here ignored.

To support this theory, the research conducted by Likert and his associates at Social Research Centre of University of Michigan in the year of 1950 suggested that there are two dimensions of leadership behaviour, viz., employee-oriented and production-oriented. Employee-oriented leaders emphasise inter-personal relations, whereas production-oriented leaders emphasise technical or task aspects of the job. Though both employee-oriented and production-oriented leaders is to accomplish and get the jobs done by the group members, the Michigan studies favoured employee-oriented leadership to achieve the goals of both higher productivity and higher job satisfaction. Subsequently, the researchers in Finland and Sweden felt that the leaders should exhibit development-oriented behaviour in a developing economy.

Contingency Theory of Leadership: Fiedler developed a contingency model of leadership. According to him, leader's effectiveness depends on the leader's ability to act in terms of situational requirements (factors). These are:

1. Leader-Member (Follower) Relations: When relations are strong, the leader has a great influence on his followers/subordinates. When the leader-followers relation is weak, leader influences only through factor like the authority provided by his position in the organization.
2. Task Structure: When task of employees is highly structured and routine, leader has a great influence on his followers. If the task is complex, non-routine and unstructured, managers need to use a democratic consultative leadership style.
3. Leader's Position Power: Leader obtains power through organizational position. Managers higher in the hierarchy have higher authority.

To measure leadership styles, Fiedler used a testing technique a **least preferred co-worker role (LPC).** The LPC score reflects a leader's underlying disposition towards his subordinates. The LPC is the employee with whom the person could work least well. Those managers, who describe their LPC in favourable terms, are managers who have a great concern for human relations. They are described as relationship-oriented leaders who are relatively permissive and considerate. On the other hand, those managers who described their LPC in an unfavourable manner tend to be task-oriented and autocratic in their leadership style. In Fig. 15.1, the combination in situation 1 is very favourable to the leader.

If all the three dimensions are high, i.e., the leader is accepted by his followers (leader-member relationship is good), if the task is very structured, and a great deal of authority is available to the leader, the situation is very favourable. If the opposite exists, the situation is very unfavourable to the leader.

Fiedler felt that the group performance would be contingent upon the appropriate matching of leadership style and the degree of favourableness of situation which enables the leader to exert influence over followers. According to Fiedler, "a leader who achieves results in one situation when all the factors are good is termed as good leader, however, may not be effective in another situation when factors are not good is termed as bad leader." This stipulates that there is no "one best way" to lead in all situations. He assumes that managers can enhance the followers effectiveness if they carefully choose the situations that are favourable to the followers.

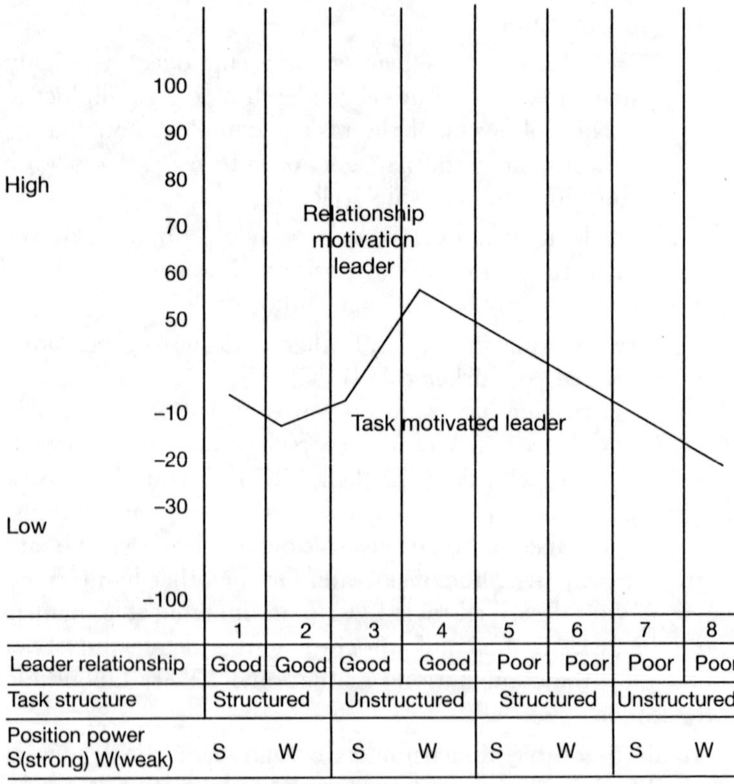

	1	2	3	4	5	6	7	8
Leader relationship	Good	Good	Good	Good	Poor	Poor	Poor	Poor
Task structure	Structured		Unstructured		Structured		Unstructured	
Position power S(strong) W(weak)	S	W	S	W	S	W	S	W
	Favourable for leader				Unfavourable for leader			

Fig. 15.1: Fiedler's situational determinants of effective leadership style

Fiedler's theory has been challenged on empirical, methodological, and theoretical grounds. Its empirical validity is said to contain serious flaws, e.g., sample sizes have been criticized as too small, creating statistical errors. Fiedler has developed only a simple generalization, since the theory's ability to predict is weak. Fiedler's model, however, seems to be reverting back to a single continuum of leadership style, suggesting that there are only two basic leadership styles; while most studies indicate that leadership styles can be plotted on two axes. Thus, it is not necessary that a leader who is high on one dimension (factor), is low on the other dimension. Rather, a combination of the two is found. Despite these observations, Fiedler's theory continues to be a dominant input in the development of a contingency explanation of leadership effectiveness.

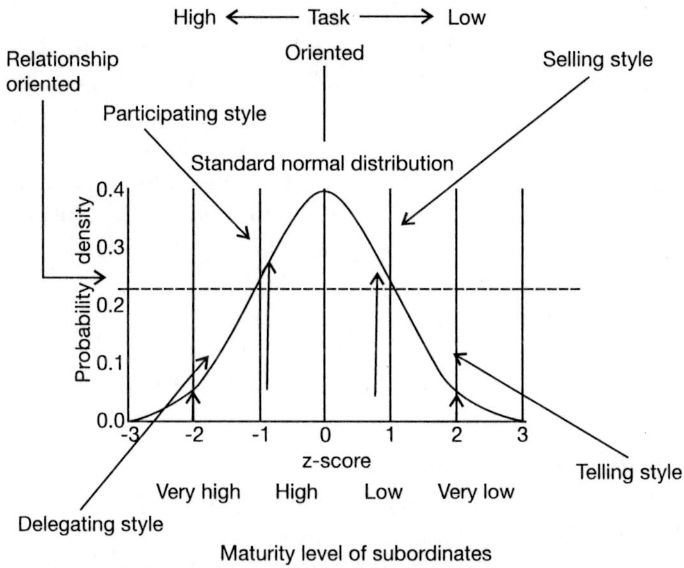

Fig. 15.2: Hersey and Blanchard's situation leadership model

Hersey and Blanchard's situational theory: Another contingency theory is the situational leadership theory developed by Hersey and Blanchard in the year 1982. It is based on premise that leaders need to change their leadership style depending on one major situational factor—the maturity of their subordinates/followers. Here, a leader must assess the maturity of subordinates.

They defined 'maturity' of subordinate as ability for achievement and willingness to accept responsibility. Ability is subordinates' knowledge, skill and competence to do a task and willingness is the motivation and desire to do the task. The theory states that the relationship between leaders and followers move through phases as subordinates 'mature', and that managers need to alter their leadership style with each phase. Figure 15.2, the bell-shaped curve, shows the four quadrants of maturity levels of followers vis-à-vis the appropriate leadership style.

When the employees first join the organization who have low level of maturity at that time, leader needs a high task and low relationship orientation when the leaders provide specific instructions and closely supervise performance. This is known as the **telling style.** As new employees become familiar with tasks and procedures who have moderate level of maturity, i.e., high task and high relationship behaviour. The leader provides direction and leads with his ideas, but also hears their suggestions however up to this level decision-making remains with the leader. The leader should have to adopt the **selling style**. Employees are still on the lower side of maturity. As employees become familiar with the work and culture of organization, they seek more responsibility and leadership style can become **participatory style.** A phase may be reached when the leader adopts a low-task low relationship orientation where subordinates are at a very high level of maturity and turn over responsibility for decisions and implementation, the leader adopts a **delegating style.**

Path-Goal Leadership Theory

This contingency theory was developed by Robert House, and it was further refined by House and Mitchell in 70s. It suggests that a leader's behaviour motivates and satisfies his followers in such a way so as to clear the path of achievement of their goals. It uses Victor Vroom's Expectancy Theory of Motivation. The path-goal theory states that there are four basic styles leadership behaviour. These are:

1. Directive Leadership: Here the subordinates know exactly what is expected of them, i.e., specific directions

are given by the leader. There is no participation by the subordinates.

2. Supportive Leadership: The leader is friendly and approachable and shows a genuine interest for subordinates.
3. Participative Leadership: The leader asks for and uses suggestions of subordinates but takes his own decision.
4. Achievement-oriented Leadership: The leader sets challenging goals for subordinates and shows confidence in them to attain these goals and perform well.

The theory suggests that these four leadership styles can be and actually are used by the same leader in different situations. Two of the situational factors that have been identified are:

(i) Personal characteristics of subordinates, and

(ii) Leader's behaviour will be motivational to the extent it satisfies subordinates' need.

Using any of the four leadership styles, contingent upon the above two situational factors, the leader attempts to define tasks and motivates the subordinates to perform best with greater satisfaction.

Modern Theories of Leadership

These include Charismatic leadership theory and Transformational leadership theory.

Charismatic Leadership Theory: Charismatic leaders are born with a combination of characteristics and have the spark to understand the situation and psyche of followers and motivate and modulate accordingly to achieve the results. M.K. Gandhi, Mao Tse-tung and W. Churchill are some of the charismatic leaders of world has. According to theorists, charismatic leaders have following behavioural dimensions.

According to House, the characters of the charismatic leaders include: self-confidence, confidence in subordinates, high expectations for subordinates, ideological vision, and use of personal example. The characters of the followers of the charismatic leader include: identification with the leader's mission, exhibit extreme loyalty to and confidence in leader, emulate the leader's values, behaviours and derive self-esteem from their relationship with the leader.

According to Jane M. Howell and Bruce J. Avolio, Ethics of charismatic leaders are:

- Uses power to serve others.
- Aligns vision with followers' needs and aspirations.
- Considers and learn from criticism.
- Stimulates followers to think independently and to question the leader's view.
- Open, two-way communication.
- Coaches, develops, and supports followers; shares recognition with others.
- Relies on internal moral to achieve organizational and societal interests.

Transformational Leadership Theory: Warren Bennis has a good metaphor for the transforming leader as "social architect." The inbuilding of purpose is a challenge to creativity because transforming followers from neutral, technical units into participants who have a particular stamp, sensitivity, and commitment. The art of the creative leader is the art of institution building, the art of fusion with value beyond the technical requirements of the task. The transformational leader, then, is primarily an expert in the promotion and protection of values. He creates environments in which followers can blossom, develop self-esteem, and otherwise be excited participants in the business and society as a whole. He stirs the emotions of followers to accomplish whatever goals he and they share.

B.M. Boss has characterised the transformational leader as under:

- Charisma: Provides vision and sense of mission, instills pride, gains respect and trust.
- Inspiration: Communicates high expectations, uses symbols to focus efforts, expresses important purposes in simple ways.

- Intellectual Stimulation: Promotes intelligence, rationality, and careful problem solving.
- Individualised Consideration: Gives personal attention, treats each employee individually coaches, advices.

Eclectic Approach to Leadership

Sanford has developed the eclectic approach to leadership. He contends that leadership depends upon traits of leader, situational variables and types of followers. As such, these three factors should be integrated to study leadership pattern. In fact, this is not a new theory but integration of various theories. As a matter of fact, no single theory satisfies the problem of leadership. From this point of view, eclectic approach is nearer to realism and answers the question: how leadership develops?

15.5 LEADERSHIP STYLES

Leadership styles are the patterns of behaviour which a leader adopts in influencing the behaviour of his followers (subordinates). These patterns emerge in the leader as he begins to respond in the same fashion repeatedly under similar conditions; he develops habits of actions that become somewhat predictable to those who work with him. Leader develops styles having dominance either individual personality, human relations, or task orientation, or a combination of them in varied degree. However, there cannot be a single best style which can always be adopted.

Styles based on Traditional Theories: Different types of the leadership styles are derived from the leadership theories. There are three leadership styles, viz., autocratic, bureaucratic, participative, and free-rein.

Autocratic Style: This style of leadership is characterized by leaders exercising high degree of centralized control and discipline coupled with autocratic decision making. The leader is highly task oriented and structures the whole work situation leaving nothing to the imagination of the subordinates. They believe that their subordinates lack the requisite intelligence or skill to take decisions of their own, and also lack work motivation. Hence, constant directive and strict control has to be maintained to extract work from them. The workers are not treated as rational and logical human beings who have their own needs, aspirations and goals. Such leaders see the 'stick' as the only task achieving factor.

The basic assumptions which are the core of any organization's culture would be:

- The boss is always correct,
- People are basically incapable of governing themselves, and
- Relationships in an organization are basically formal, each persons' relationship extents to, and ends, at the job.

Thus, given the set of assumptions, the artifacts, perspectives and the values of the organization (which forms its culture) reflects a work force bound by the strict rules and regulations, without any motivation to work, lack of creativity and innovativeness, a general sense of apathy and indiscipline and lack of mutual trust.

Autocratic leaders are classified into: (a) Strict autocrat who follows autocratic style completely where the method of influencing subordinates is thoroughly negative; (b) Benevolent autocrat who typically gives awards to the followers; and (c) Incompetent autocrat who adopts autocratic style with a view to hide his incompetency.

Considering the organizational efficiency and employees' satisfaction, autocratic style generally is not suitable.

Bureaucratic Style: Here the leader is more concerned about the procedures and rules than motivating or getting task done by his subordinates. He is obsessed with paper-work and maintenance of records. Even the smallest decision has to pass through the various levels of the bureaucracy before action is taken on it. The leader is basically a status-quo and believes in traditions and precedents. This also has a negative effect on employee creativity.

The culture prevalent in the organization is one in which the element of artifacts (tangible things) are given more importance.

The employees lack the values of hard work, honesty, etc., and there is a general lack of apathy towards work. A sense of lethargy creeps in among the employees.

Participative Style: In this style, the leader decentralizes his decision-making process. He considers the valued suggestions and ideas of subordinates before formulating decisions. This satisfies subordinates as they feel elevated when their ideas and suggestions are given weight in decision making.

The participative methods are democratic supervision, production committees, suggestion schemes and multiple management. However, this style has certain shortcomings which are as follows:

- Complex nature of organization requires a thorough understanding of its problems which lower-level employees may not be able to do. As such, participation does not remain meaningful.
- Some people in the organization want minimum interaction with their superiors or associates. For them, participation technique is discouraging instead of encouraging.
- Participation can be used covertly to manipulate employees. Thus, some employees may prefer the open tyranny of an autocrat as compared to covert tyranny of a group.

Free-rein or Laissez-faire Leadership Style: This is often described as no leadership at all. Here the leader will give or rather depend a lot upon the group to establish its own goals and work out its own problems and avoid power and responsibility. This attitude of the leader may greatly demotivate the subordinate who looks up to the leader for guidance and support.

Lack of motivation, group conflict, and disruptive attitude are some of the characteristics prevailing. People have least respect for authority and responsibility as the authority figure is weak and himself lacks the sense of responsibility. Hence, this style is used very rarely in business organizations.

Figure 15.3 shows a wide variety of leadership styles moving from a very authoritarian style at one end to a very democratic style and laissez-faire at the other end.

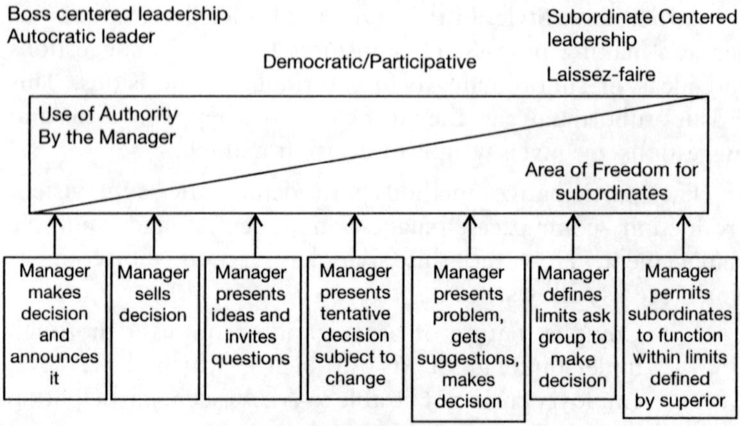

Fig. 15.3: Continuum of various characteristics of different leadership styles (R. Tannenbaum and W.H. Schmidt)

15.6 BLAKE AND MOUTON'S MANAGERIAL GRID

One of the most widely known approaches of leadership styles is the managerial grid developed by industrial psychologists Blake and Mouton. They set out leadership styles of dimensions of two specific behaviours of concern for people and concern for production in a framework, i.e., the Managerial Grid. It composed of horizontal and vertical axes in a nine-point scale. Within this nine-point scale there are 81 (9×9) different positions in which a leader's style may fall depending upon his leaning towards particular behaviour. Concern for people conveys degree of personal commitment toward goal achievement, maintaining the self-esteem of workers, responsibility based on trust, and satisfying inter-personal relations.

Concern for production includes quality in all activities relating to production, creativity, work efficiency, and volume of output. The managerial grid identifies five leadership styles based upon these two factors found in organizations, as shown in Fig. 15.4:

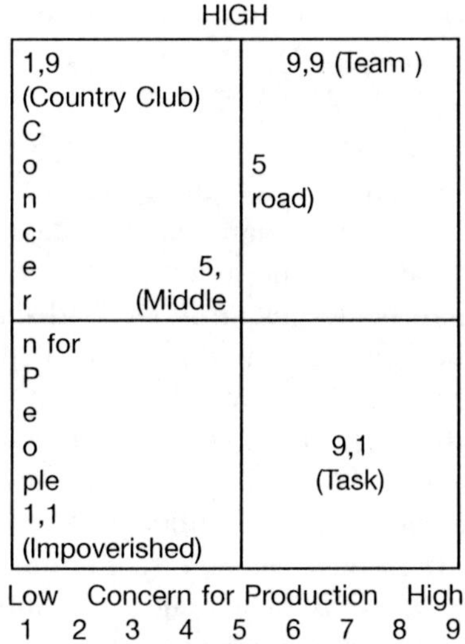

Fig. 15.4: Managerial grid

Blake and Mouton have described the five styles as follows:

The style 1,1 is impoverished management—low concern for both people and production. Extension of minimum effort is required to get work done and sustain organization morale. The attitude is laissez-faire. The 1,1 style manager does not exercise power or authority to get work done or to maintain a unity of command. He relieves himself of responsibility and is ready to blame his subordinates if something goes wrong. He has no clear idea of the goals to be attained. He is more security conscious than status conscious. The 1,1 manager is not willing to communicate with his superiors and subordinates unless it is absolutely necessary to do so. There is no place for creativity in this style.

The style 1,9 management is country-club management—high concern for employees, but low concern for production. Thoughtful attention is needed of people leads to a friendly and comfortable organization atmosphere and work tempo. The attitude is democratic enabling him to maintain a high level of morale; and the involvement of his employees in the decision-making process giving them a sense of belongingness.

By and large, the 1,9 manager acts on the assumptions of Theory Y, that "people are capable of doing work and assuming responsibility if they are given opportunities and incentives."

The 9,1 style is autocratic—high concern for production and low concern for employees. Efficiency results from arranging work in such a way that human elements have little effect. By and large, he operates on the assumptions of Theory X, that "an average human being has an inherent dislike of work and will avoid it if he can." He assumes that if his subordinates were intelligent enough, they would not be in that subordinate position. Hence, he must be constantly watched and supervised in course of his work. Here, the manager's goal is likely to be very high; but the goals of the subordinates are more or less ignored. He practices only one-way communication from top to bottom. In the 9,1 style of management, morale is low and creativeness is absent among subordinates.

The 5,5 style is middle-of-road management. Attitude is practical. Equal weight is given to concern for production and concern for employees, and extreme positions are avoided. It keeps adequate performance through balance of work requirements and maintaining satisfactory morale. In this style, manager is to achieve organizational goals with minimum effort in the shortest time, and ensure the utmost employee satisfaction. There is a suitable two-way communication thereby eliciting suggestions from the employees.

The 9,9 style is team building management. Attitude is mature, desirable and meaningful. Here, a high concern for people (9) is coupled with a high concern for production (9). Work accomplished is from committed people with interdependence through a common stake in organization purpose and with trust and respect. This style aims to the manager's prime responsibility is to see to it that each and every activity leads to the attainment of organizational goals. For this purpose, the manager delegates adequate authority to subordinates and makes them accountable for the work allocated to them.

Communication in this style of management aims at promoting an understanding of problems and a sharing of information, thoughts and ideas thus creativity is spontaneous.

Blake and Mouton argue that the 9,9 management style is the most effective type of leadership style. In fact, they have developed training programmes that attempt to change managers towards 9,9 management style. Managerial grid is similar to Ohio State University studies with one basic difference that managerial grid is an attitudinal model that measures the predisposition/concern about something of manager, while Ohio State framework tends to be a behavioural model that examines how leader's actions are perceived by others.

Managerial grid is a useful device to a manager for identification of managerial style. However, it does not tell why a manager falls in one part or the other of the grid and his style is influenced by many factors, including the superior, the kind of subordinates he supervises, and the situation in which he finds himself. In managerial grid, although the four corners and the mid-point of the grid are emphasized, these extreme positions are rarely found in their pure form in actual work situation.

Transfunctional Leadership (TL): We have to take a cue from Machiavelli or Bernard Bass. The characteristics of the transfunctional leadership (TL) are: Charisma (provides vision, instills mission trust), Inspiration (expresses important purpose in simple ways), Intellectual stimulation (offers challenge), Individual consideration (gives personal attention and advice). A manager is to reposition himself to integrate technical, political and cultural strands.

A constituent confers authority to a manager, not the other way around. Constituents can be employees, customers, shareholders, etc. The credibility of a manager will define his effectiveness. For developing credibility, six exercises are needed to be practiced: discovering yourself, appreciating constituents and their diversity, affirming shared values, developing capacity, serving a purpose, and sustaining hope.

15.7 LEADERSHIP STYLES IN INDIA

In order to analyse leadership style in Indian organization, we have to see the educational background, culture and religion outfits of manager. It also depends upon age and hierarchical level of manager. C.A. Myers from his interview with industrialists, government officials, labour leaders and managers in both Indian and foreign owned organizations, concludes that barring a few, most Indian top managers are relatively authoterian in their relationships with lower management and labour. Similar result has also been highlighted by Dr. H.C. Ganguli in his study of leadership behaviour in a State-owned engineering company. G. Rangaswamy, in year 1976, in his study of leadership behaviour of 56 top-level managers have found that Indian managers are more employee-oriented as compared to their American counterpart. Though this result is quite unexpected, he explains that this is due to Indian cultural and religious pattern which influences towards helpfulness and peaceful co-operation. D.N. Elhance and R.D. Agarwal conclude that 67 percent executives in private sector and 57 percent of them in public sector units have democratic leadership style. P. Singh and G.S. Das studied 280 managers from two public sector units and four private sector units and found that bureaucratic style is the most pre-dominant followed by the benevolent autocrat, developer and democratic in that order. The executives who are exposed to some formal management education are more democratic as compared to those who do not have such exposure. Further, leadership styles are determined by host of factors such as top leader, subordinates and situations. From this point of view, leadership style may be classified in (a) family-managed traditional organizations, (b) professionally managed Indian organizations and multi-nationals, and (c) public sector organizations. In family-managed traditional organizations, there is management by inheritance with the result that these organizations are highly centralized in their organization structure and are authoritarian in their approach. Moreover, A. Dasgupta points out that the proprietary character of business and large-scale participation of family members in it have made the attitude of the head of the business, who is also the head of the family, highly paternalistic. Now this approach is slowly vanishing, particularly in large organizations due to influence of labour leaders, globalization of economy, competition in business, invent of knowledge workers and professional input in business. On the other hand, there are many organizations in the private sector owned by Indians or by multinationals who have appreciable degree of participation or democratic leadership. For example, ITC Limited believes that the best results are achieved through participative management accompanied by authority with control. The third category of organizations are in public sector. Here, initially, public sector units were manned by civil servants who brought a bureaucratic culture with them. Its implication is status differentials, class distinctions, and impersonal relationships which work against participative style. With the passage of time, public sector units are headed by technocrats and professionals coupled with lot of management programmers who are supposed to give positive results accordingly they are changing the entire spectrum of leadership style to reasonable degree of participation or democratic leadership.

In order to know a right leadership style for Indian managers, it is necessary to examine the facets of Indian society. Here power and authority is considered an important characteristic. There are three important aspects of Indian society, viz., joint family, caste system, and ritualism. Accordingly, Indian manager adopts leadership style contingent upon the culture and other situational variables in his organization. The above does not mean that Indian societal system is the only factor which effects the style but the style is also effected due to technological advancement, industrialization, increasing amount of professionalism of management and policies of the government. Such situation demands greater consultation and participation on the part of managers. Therefore, a move towards participative style has already begun in enlightened companies both public and private sectors in India.

REVIEW QUESTIONS

1. 'A good leader is not necessarily a good manager'. Discuss.
2. Discuss the trait and behavioural approaches to study leadership. How are the two schools of thought essentially different?
3. What do you understand by leadership style? In your opinion, which one is the best style and why?

4. Bring out the various behavioural theories of leadership. Explain the Blake and Mouton's Managerial Grid.
5. Describe the contingency leadership style with special reference of Fiedler Contingency Theory.
6. Examine the leadership styles being followed by Indian managers, can you suggest a right style?

Short Notes

1. Leadership continuum
2. Autocratic and participative leaders

CASE STUDY I

Steve Jobs Bill Gates

'Steve Jobs' leadership style was **autocratic**; he had a meticulous eye for detail, and surrounded himself with like-minded people to follow his lead.

Steve Jobs could stand at the intersection of humanities and sciences and had a mind of creative design. He was both admired and criticised for his consummate skills and salesmanship. Jobs was perceived and demanding perfectionist who always aspired to see that his products were at the forefront of information technology industry.

Steve Jobs had an ability to recognize the beneficial skills in people. He was a true motivational speaker. He developed a working atmosphere that was created through positive thinking and innovative design. While this style of leadership may seem harsh to some it has opened a door to success for Steve Jobs.

Through his innovative ideas, Jobs has created one of the most successful tech companies on the globe—Apple, the biggest technology game changers in the market today. He was a genius in his own way and entrepreneur of the decade 2011.

Jobs understood the importance of taking risks and could be considered one of the biggest risk-taking leaders in the world. Even though during his career he made mistakes, he was always the first to learn from them and grow with what was necessary to succeed. He wanted to develop his products he knew the consumers want.

Although a billionaire, Jobs made it known that like Bill Gates, he had stipulated that most of his monetary fortune would not be left to his children. Among others, he was posthumously honored with an Edition Achievement Award for his commitment to innovation throughout his career.

Bill Gates Leadership Style

Bill Gates offers a more participative leadership style. He believes in the value of input from his employees for overall company success. The driving force behind the success of Microsoft is the enthusiastic and hardworking attitude of Bill Gates. He understands that in business you will have fluctuations and changes that you must adapt to in order to succeed. With this business attitude, Gates has created a company that has been able to withstand the storm and still come out on top as a shining star. Through the process of delegation of tasks, Gates was able to develop a company—Microsoft that utilizes the skills of his team members to the fullest.

Bill Gates had a unique skill set. He was able to visualize his goal and dreams and move forward with his process to make them come true. His envision for the world to have a computer in every household has gained significant traction and success since his early years.

Conclusion

When comparing the two leadership styles between Bill Gates and Steve Jobs, they are on a completely different spectrum entirely. From the leader and follower relationship style of Bill Gates to the leader style of Steve Jobs, both offered some of the most successful products ever to the world. Each leadership style may have been comparably different but they had one major thing in common to execute their ideas/dream in order to become more productive and successful.

Two of the biggest entrepreneurial names in the business world, Steve Jobs and Bill Gates offer a unique but different set of leadership skills. Both are successful business owners that have named in Fortune 500 companies through their dedication and hardworking personality.

CASE STUDY II

Excel Engineering Company was a multi-products company producing geyser, electric fan and accessories. The organization structure of the company of first two layers is as depicted below:

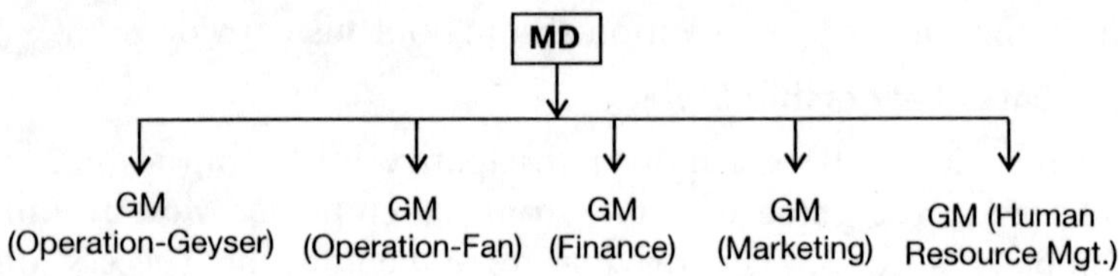

The operation of two products—geyser and fan—is under the control of GM (Operation-Geyser I) and GM (Operation-Fan II) respectively. The target for GM (Oprn.-I) is 800 geysers whereas 750 fans for GM (Oprn.-II) in the current year. The sufficient resources in terms of man, material and finance are provided to earn a 15% ROI in current year. Every month, a review of production is done at GM level. While reviewing the production, GM (Oprn.-I) makes decisions and order for implementation. He is concerned for production which includes quality in all activities relating to production, creativity, work efficiency, and volume of output. Efficiency results from arranging work in such a way that subordinates' ingenuity has little effect. By and large, he operates on the assumptions that "an average human being has an inherent dislike of work and will avoid it if he can." He assumes that if his subordinates were intelligent enough, they would not be in that subordinate position. Hence, he must be constantly watched and supervised in course of his work. Here, the manager's goal is likely to be very high; but the goals of the subordinates are more or less ignored. He practices only one-way communication from top to bottom. In his leadership style of management, morale is low and creativeness is absent among subordinates. He is workaholic and chances that very soon he would be burnt out. At the same time his subordinates have a little opportunity to exert and learn—this situation is not appropriate for the organization. However, GM (Oprn.-I) is able to give results. At times, recognized union raises its reservation for certain issues with him.

GM (Oprn.-II) is more participative in his approach to issues and problems. He believes in the value of input from his employee for achieving the target of the division. He defines problems/issues and suggestions are invited from the team to make decision. His attitude is practical. Equal weight is given to concern for production and concern for employees, and extreme positions are avoided. He gives adequate performance through balance of work requirements and maintaining satisfactory morale. In this style, he achieves organizational goals with minimum effort in the shortest time, and ensure the utmost employee satisfaction. Here is a suitable two-way communication thereby eliciting suggestions from the employees. This style aims to the manager's prime responsibility is to see to it that each and every activity leads to the attainment of organizational goals. For this purpose, the manager delegates adequate authority to subordinates and makes them accountable for the work allocated to them.

Questions

1. Describe the nature of leadership of two GMs in terms of established theories.
2. The styles of working of GMs give the reflection of traits towards more as a manager rather than a leader, elucidate and comment.
3. Under present situation, whether intervention of MD is necessary in term of job rotation and training and development? If so, suggest the mechanism.

Chapter 16
Communication

16.1 INTRODUCTION

Coordination and integration of various human activities is possible only if there is an effective communication in the organization which provides for exchange of information and sharing of various ideas. That is a dynamic transactional process in the managerial work life in motivating people and getting things done, is proved by the observation and actions of many a corporate leader. According to research findings on leadership, the ability to speak and write inspiringly is a significant attribute of effective leadership. It is the dynamic leadership with a strong orientation to focused and well-aimed communication that has played a crucial role.

16.2 DEFINITIONS

Communication involves an exchange of facts, feelings and information by two or more persons and provides the means of putting people into action in an organization. Common forms of information include speaking, writing, gesturing, and broadcasting. The word "communication" takes its origin from the Latin 'Communicate', meaning to impart, to participate to share. It has been said that 'communication is the art of being understood'. Essentially, it is ability of one person to relate with another and to make himself understood while, at the same time, to understand others. Communication depends on the interpretation of a message by the listener. Shared understanding evolves through detection and correction of misunderstandings (as opposed to a one-way communication). The understanding created, though one cycle can never be complete or absolute.

It is an interactive and ongoing process in which common ground, i.e., assumed mutual beliefs and mutual knowledge, is accumulated and updated.

Importance of Communication—In the organization settings, sharing, understanding interchanging ideas has become a conscious process of empowering employees. The basic purpose of communication within the organization is not mere transfer of cognitive knowledge of data or information, but to give employees a sense of involvement in the organizational processes and promote congruence of goals between individuals and the organization. Effective communication helps augment motivation and morale of employees. Trust, openness and transparency as values are basic to the process. Besides clarity of purpose, the manner and style of communication are equally important. Clarity, method and style together give rise to quality communication which, in turn, contributes towards improving the quality of work life in the organization.

Professor Albert Mehrabian is a pioneer in the field of understanding communications. Mehrabian established the following statistics, which have now become a classic, for the effectiveness of spoken communication:

- 7% of meaning is in the words that are spoken.
- 38% of meaning is paralinguistic (the manner in which the words are said).
- 55% of meaning is conveyed through facial expression.

Benefits of Effective Communication: A manager needs certain skills to perform the duties and activities associated with his jobs. Depending upon the level of manager he has to perform technical, human, and conceptual activities accordingly senior-level managers spend about 80% time giving instructions, appointments, listening to employees' grievances, preparing proposals, giving press interviews, etc. This skill is essential, and is as important at top levels of management as it is at the lower levels, since managers deal directly with people. Managers with good human skills—skills to communicate, motivate, lead, and inspire—can get the out of their people. Prof. Peter Drucker, in his book, *Effective Executive* has indicated the four basic requirements of effective human relations:

- Communication,
- Teamwork,
- Self-development, and
- Development of others.

16.3 FUNCTIONS OF COMMUNICATION

Communication must include both transference and understanding of meaning. Perfect communication is never achieved in practice. Communication serves the following four functions within a group or organization.

(i) **Information:** Managers collect and disseminate information for decision making and problem solving. For instance, in case of a strike in an organization, the manager interact with workers to handle the problem of strike.

(ii) **Control:** Control refers to the power to influence workers' behaviour so that they comply with company policies and procedures. But informal communication also control behaviour. The Hawthorne experiments showed how the group maintained control by communicating—sometimes very explicitly—the norms that were to be followed.

(iii) **Motivation:** Communication fosters motivation by clarifying to employees what is to be done; how well they are doing and what can be done to improve performance. The performance of specific goals, feedback on progress towards goals and reinforcement of desired behaviour—all stimulate motivation and require communication.

(iv) **Emotional Expression:** All the four functions of communication mentioned above are of equal importance in an organization.

16.4 PROCESS OF COMMUNICATION

The communication process takes place when an individual (sender) transmits message with meaning to another person (receiver) who receives it and sends back response to sender as shown below:

Step 1—Sender (Source) conceives an idea depending on the purpose of communication. This is called Ideation.

Step 2—Sender chooses appropriate words, signs, symbols in order to formulate the message. This is called Encoding.

Step 3—Sender sends the message through a suitable channel (oral or written).

Step 4—Receiver receives the message.

Step 5—Receiver decodes the message by interpreting the same.

Step 6—Receiver gives feedback to the sender and acts as a check on whether it has been understood as intended. If the message has not been properly understood, the sender may again transmit the information by changing the symbol if needed.

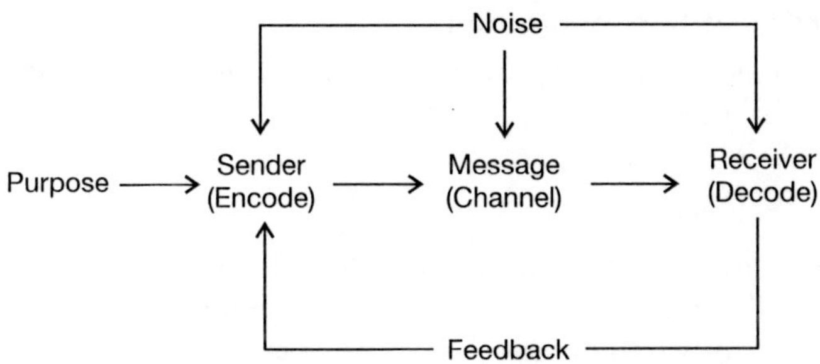

Fig. 16.1: The communication process

The communication will be effective if sender and the receiver are familiar with the context. Noise while transmitting the message creates barriers to effective communication.

One-Way versus Two-Way Communication

All communications are of two categories—one way and two way. In one-way communication, the sender sends message to receiver and he accepts it without giving responses. For example, an office order is issued for implementation and no response is required. Similarly, advertisement always represents a typically one-way communication.

One-way communication has its own advantages and disadvantages. It is fast, it saves time and money. The sender is satisfied because receiver does not question the message and thus probably protects his oversights and mistakes. However, it is very dissatisfying to the receiver who has no opportunity to seek any clarification of the message. The receiver accepts the message as it comes.

Two-way communication has a built-in system of feedback. It ensures that further information clarifications, etc. are provided whenever available. For example, interactive session like seminars and workshops, participative groups, etc.

Two-way communication is slow, time consuming, and probably less efficient, though it may be extremely satisfying to the receiver who has full opportunity to understand the message. In a situation where a decision has to be implemented, two-way communication is definitely better.

Direction of Communication

Communication flows in various directions. Generally, however, it flows:

- Vertically—Downward and Upward
- Laterally

Downward communication: It flows from top to bottom. It goes easily with great force. It goes through the line of authority including private contacts between superior and subordinate. Instructions, orders, policies, rules and regulations, orders for transfers and promotions, leave, etc. have to flow downwards from those at the top to the lowest echelon of workers; and this flow may be in the form of an oral or written communication.

Written communications traveling along downward channels range from handwritten messages notice board, to office memos, circulars, manuals, house organs, etc. Downward oral communications can occur in face-to-face conversations, in group meetings, or conferences, by telephone, tape recordings, and telecasts or by slides and movies. Any confidential information is best handled in personal contact rather than in writing.

Upward communication: Such communication flows upward from the workers to the immediate superior and from latter to the higher management levels. The top management who want to know reactions and suggestions of employees, they encourage them to offer the same by upward communication to the top management through their supervisors. Decision making through participative management is a good example of upward communication. It is seen that upward communication is not as adequate as downward communication. Some organizational examples of upward communication include performance reports prepared by lower management for review by middle and top management, suggestion boxes, employee attitude surveys, exit interviews, grievance procedures, superior-subordinate discussions, and informal 'gripe' sessions where employees have the opportunity to identify and discuss problems with their boss or representatives of higher management. Meetings with union representatives also provide enough clues for improvement of working of organization.

Lateral communication: This is communication taking place among members of the same work group, among members of work groups at the same level, among managers at the same level, or among any horizontally equivalent personnel in an organization. It is particularly frequent between the line and staff units. It provides a means by which managers at the same level of an organization co-ordinate their activities without referring all the matters to their superiors. For example, multiple copies of memoranda that flow downward and horizontal levels improving co-ordination of effort. Dimock observes: The influence an executive has with other executives is partly a matter of his position in the hierarchy, partly a question of his competence and partly dependent upon a complete and sensitised communication system. They occur with the knowledge and support of superiors. But they can create dysfunctional conflicts when the formal vertical channels are breached, when members go above or around their superiors to get things done, or when bosses find out that actions have been taken or decisions made without their knowledge.

16.5 COMMUNICATION NETWORK

In an organization, there are a number of channels or paths connecting various positions for purposes of communications. These channels are called communication network. These channels can be formal or informal. Formal networks are typically hierarchical follows the chain of command and are usually task related. Communication networks also indicate the culture of the organization, superior-subordinate relationship, and, to some extent, the satisfaction of employees. As suggested by studies, there is an effect of communication networks on the satisfaction and productivity of employees. There are following five types of communication network common in organizations.

Formal networks: Figure 16.2 shows three formal networks as shown below.

The **chain** represents a typical bureaucratic system that follows a proper channel of communication—following strictly the hierarchical system. Thus, if A has to communicate with E it will pass through B, C and D in that order. Similarly, E's reply to A will be through D, C and B in that order. A cannot go directly to E. It would represent a five levels hierarchy where communications cannot move laterally, only downward and upward.

If we turn the "Y" network upside down, we can see two subordinates reporting to a supervisor, with two levels of hierarchy still above the supervisor.

The **wheel** represents a supervisor with four subordinates. However, there is no interaction between the subordinates. All communications are channellised the supervisor.

The **circle** network allows members to interact with adjoining members, but no further. It would represent a three-level hierarchy in which there is communication between superiors and subordinates and lateral communication at the lowest level.

Finally, the all-channel network allows each of the subject to communicate freely with the other four. While it is like the circle, in some respects, the all channel has central position. However, there are no restrictions; all members are equal. This network is best illustrated by a committee. Relative effectiveness of each formal networks are as under:

Criteria Chain Wheel Circle/All Chain

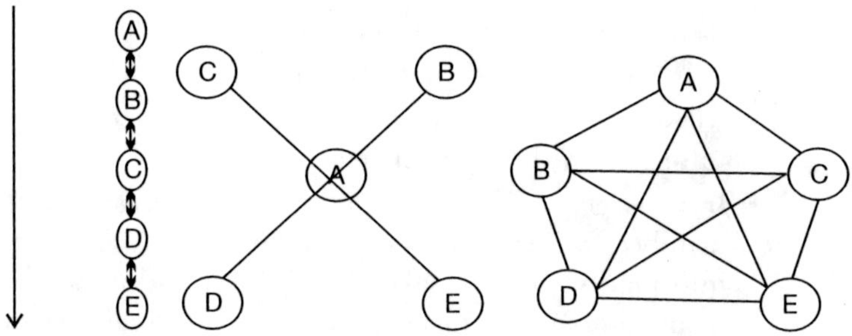

Speed Chain Type Wheel Circle

Speed	Moderate	Fast	Fast
Accuracy	High	High	Moderate
Efficiency of leader	Moderate	High	None
Employees' satisfaction	Moderate	Low	High
Quality of output	Moderate	Inferior	Superior
Resistance to change	Low	Low	More
Overload	Moderate	Very high	Moderate

Fig. 16.2: Formal networks

Each kind of network has been found to show varying influences on task-related activities, as such it is prudent for managers to choose appropriate communication channel depending on such situational factors as speed, accuracy, cost, and time limitation. The choice of a specific communication network depends upon the task, level, technology, and general culture of the organization. Research and development organization usually follows the circle network because ideas have to be generated by a group of employees whereas in an industrial setup chain type communication is more useful because the task is defined. However, it is seen that employees develop their own system of communication which usually are a combination of them.

Here as in a industrial setup chain type communication is more useful because the task is defined. However, it is seen that employees develop their own system of communication which usually are a combination of them.

Informal Network

The informal network has three main characteristics, viz.:

- It is not controlled by management.
- Most employees perceive that they get reliable information through this technique.
- It is largely used to serve the self-interests of the members. There are no clear patterns of flow of information in informal network. Information can flow in any direction in this network. The informal network commonly referred to as the grapevine. It is more likely to satisfy social needs of group members rather than facilitate task needs. Grapevine—rumors are often spread via informal network. Grapevine disrupts morale and employee confidence in management. People will talk, socialize, converse, gossip, make stories rumour. To reduce the rumours is to do a good job of supplying immediate and accurate information to employees at all time on subject of their importance. Rumours are not necessarily counterproductive to the operation of an organization. First, it would appear that rumours occur quite infrequently in organizations. Second, most of the information carried in the grapevine is accurate. Davis reports an accuracy index of 80 to 90 percent for non-controversial information in form of rumour in a particular industry.

16.6 BARRIERS TO COMMUNICATION

Impediments in effective communication are known as barriers. These are kept into three categories:

(1) External Barriers—Again it is of two types—(i) Semantic Barriers—They are obstructions caused in the process of receiving or understanding of the message during the process of encoding and decoding ideas and words. Noise while transmitting the message creates barriers to effective communication.

These barriers arise also from the linguistic capacity of the parties involved. The main semantic barriers are (a) Badly expressed message, (b) Faulty translations, (c) Unclarified assumptions, and (d) Specialist's language.

(ii) Emotional or Psychological Barriers—These are (a) Premature evaluation is the tendency of prematurely evaluating communications rather than to keep an uncompromised position during the interchange, (b) Inattention, (c) Loss by transmission and poor retention, (d) Undue reliance on the written words, (e) Distrust of communicator, and (f) Failure to communicate.

(2) Organizational Barriers—These are—(i) Organizational policies, (ii) Organizational rules and regulations, (iii) Status relationships, (iv) Complexity in organization structure, and (v) Organizational facilities.

(3) Personal Barriers—(i) Barriers in superiors—Role of superiors is very vital such as attitude of superior, fear of challenge to authority, insistence on proper channel, lack of confidence in subordinates, ignoring communication, lack of time and lack of awareness, etc. (ii) Barriers in subordinates are unwillingness to communicate and lack of proper incentive.

The following guidelines will remove communication barriers:

(i) Identify and analyze the barriers.
(ii) Top management must be convinced of the need of communication.
(iii) Emphasis upon the written statement of policies.
(iv) Recognize that communication is a two-way process.
(v) Consistency and Coherence are essential for successful communication.
(vi) Overcome disadvantage of the distance barriers.
(vii) Emphatic speaking and listening are essential.
(viii) Optimum timing is important in communication.
(ix) The use of feedback improves the communication process.
(x) Repetition of message may be helpful in conveying the intended thoughts.

(xi) Messages should be timed, so that they are received when they are needed.

16.7 FEEDBACK

Feedback means that the sender gets normally some sort of acknowledgement/response from the intended receiver. It provides a learning situation to the sender and the receiver because it opens avenues to make corrections in action whenever necessary. Feedback can help improve the quality of communication. Feedback however should be prompt, both positive and negative, focus an action and behaviour instead of individual. All organizations need some feedback from communications on their policies and rules and regulations in order to make improvements wherever necessary. Organizations are always in search of mechanisms to seek and receive feedbacks from employees, so that they feel part of them. The manager needs to be aware of potential resistance and learn to use negative feedback in situations in which it is most likely to be accepted. The negative feedback must be supported by data—it is more likely to be accepted. Subjective negative feedback from experienced managers may be more meaningful and is more likely to be accepted.

There are six specific guidelines of making feedback effective:

(i) *Focus on specific behaviours*: Feedback should be specific rather than general. Vague statement does not focus on positive behaviour of receiver.

(ii) *Keep feedback impersonal*: While giving feedback, be impersonal not to make personal remarks like, "you are lazy" or "highly irresponsible". Feedback should be job related and not evaluative or judgmental.

(iii) *Keep feedback goal oriented*: Never give negative feedback to "get rid of your stress". Wait for the moment before giving feedback which is goal oriented.

(iv) *Feedback should be well timed*: Feedback is effective if it is immediate, so that corrective action can be taken then and there. Immediate feedback does not mean that it should be impulsive.

(v) *Ensure understanding*: It is important that the receiver understands the feedback. It is a good idea to ask the receiver to replace the content of the feedback to ensure whether the recipient has fully understood the message the way it was intended.

(vi) *Direct negative feedback towards behaviour which the receiver can control*: To criticise an employee for coming late when there was a power breakdown and the local train held up for an hour unjustified.

16.8 TECHNOLOGY-BASED COMMUNICATION

There are various technology-based communication tools used in organizations for acquiring, transmitting, and processing. Specific tools that can be used for communication include telephones, mobile phones, facsimile machines, and computer.

The Internet has become a very important business tool. It can be used at a basic level for e-mail and for research as well as activities relating to sales, and transfer of funds to their suppliers and even to individuals.

Web conferencing/computer conferencing are systems that allow numerous users to connect via a network, send e-mail messages to the conference address, and receive the postings of others.

16.9 LISTENING—KEY TO EFFECTIVE COMMUNICATION

Listening is an important aid to communication. Undoubtedly, if people are bad listeners, they will also make bad communicators. Lee Iacocca said, "I only wish I could find an institution that teaches people how to listen. After all, a good manager need to listen at least as much as he needs to talk...real communication goes in both direction." Since communication involves both a source and a receiver, listening consists of the roles receivers play in the communication process. It is a process that includes attending, perceiving, interpreting, assessing, and responding. Listening might be defined as the art of hearing and understanding where each letter of the word listen will guide you towards becoming a better listener. Remember—the brain works approximately four times faster than you can talk, so there is time for the mind to roam if you do not have a plan. Knowing how the speaker stresses important content will help to keep you tuned in. We listen to: (i) obtain information, (ii) solve problems, (iii) share experiences, and (iv) persuade or dissuade. However, it is hard to listen because of certain barriers that we either encounter or erect. If people are poor listeners: (i) only inaccurate and incomplete information is exchanged, (ii) problems are not clearly understood and remain unsolved, (iii) people are unable to share experiences, and (iv) being unable to understand each other due to in attentiveness, they are unable to persuade or dissuade others.

Active listening is as important in conversation as effective speaking. Active listening refers to taking personal responsibility to find out and be sure that what we consciously communicated was received and what we received was what was intended to be sent and any distortions were clarified before proceeding with the conversation. It would be more rewarding if the message is well interpreted, understood, paraphrased, and acknowledged.

Types of Listening: While certain skills are basic and necessary for all types of listening (receiving, attending, and understanding), each type requires some special skills. The following are guidelines to improve listening behaviour in all situations.

Informative Listening: It refers to the situation where the listener's primary concern is to understand the message. Much of our learning comes from informative listening. For example, we listen to lectures or instructions from teachers—and what we learn depends on how well we listen. In the workplace, we listen to understand new practices or procedures—and how well we perform depends on how well we listen. Informative listening depends upon vocabulary, concentration and memory.

Attentive Listening: When people listen attentively, their goal is to understand and remember what they are hearing. In addition, attentive listeners have rational goals like giving a positive impression, advancing the relationship, or demonstrating care.

Relationship Listening: The purpose of relationship listening is either to help an individual or to improve the relationship between people. Therapeutical listening is a special type of relationship listening which brings to mind situations where counselors, medical practitioners, or other professionals allow a troubled person to talk through a problem. It can also be used when you listen to a friend and allow him to converse intimately where attending, supporting, and empathizing behaviour indicates that the listener is focusing on the speaker.

Appreciative Listening: It includes listening to music for enjoyment, to speakers because you like their style, to your choices in theatre, television, radio, or film. The quality of appreciative listening depends upon presentation, perception, and previous experience.

Critical Listening is important while listening to politicians, the media, salesmen, advocates, and one's own financial, emotional, intellectual, physical, and spiritual needs. However, there are three things to keep in mind. Ethos, or speaker credibility—While listening one can judge whether the speaker is both an expert on the subject and he can be trusted to be honest, unbiased, and straightforward. Logos, or speaker logical arguments—The speaker may make errors in logic, not by intention, but by accident, carelessness, inattention to detail, or lack of analysis. Pathos, or psychological appeals—The speaker may use psychological appeals such as adventure, thrift, curiosity, fear, pride, sympathy, etc. to gain an emotional response from listeners.

Discriminative Listening being sensitive to the changes in speaker's rate, volume force, pitch, and emphasis, the listener can detect even the slightest shift in nuances there are three things to consider about this type of listening. These are hearing ability, awareness of sound structure and, integration of non-verbal cues.

16.10 BARRIERS TO LISTENING

1. Physical Environment: Anything which hinders, the process of attentive listening like distracting sound, noise, phone rings, poor acoustics, unstructured sitting obstacles, etc.

2. Physical Distraction: Something which diverts attention and makes it difficult to stay focused on the message like unusual grooming, clothing, gestures, body language, and mannerisms either of one's own or of the speakers.

3. Casual Approach: Many a time though one is in the mist of presentation pretending to be very attentive, yet he is mentally many miles away from the conference room bothering about some other problems. This happens when one is not in the right frame of mind to listen yet giving fake attention or giving an impression of listening. In such a situation, speaker gets only partial attention.

4. Preoccupation: Here one listens facts only as mind is puzzled and preoccupied with other jobs. In this situation, one can be here and yet not listen.

5. Speaking-thinking Rate: It is well known that normally human mind is capable of thinking from 400 to 600 words per minute whereas we speak on an average of 100 to 125 words per minute. The difference between speaking and thinking rates provides listener's brain quite a bit idle time. During this idle time, listener's mind wanders and becomes prone to distractions and loss of concentration.

6. Jumping Ahead: Some people have the habit of jumping into conclusion or drawing inference without even listening to the entire message. The temptation to judge, evaluate or ready to reply rather than listening to the speaker is difficult to control as it is natural tendency of human being.

7. Impatience: Impatience creeps in while listening and people tend to become less receptive to any form of communication. This is basically a poor listening habit and it renders communication less effective.

8. Semantic Difficulties: Many a time people draw different meanings of same word and expression at different times and contexts. Hence, words do not always mean the same thing to all members of group thus creating misunderstanding, though not intentionally. In listening, words are generally symbols to express ideas which creates mental images in the mind of listeners. If a particular word draws different image in the mind of listener than what it was intended by the speaker, misunderstanding is bound to take place.

9. Hierarchy: Sometimes we get influenced while listening by the hierarchy of the of the speaker in organization, society and family. Generally, we listen attentively to our superiors but become impatient in giving patient hearing to our subordinates.

10. Emotions: When someone is stressful, depressed, or in the negative frame of mind he will be over influenced by the negative aspects of message in the process of listening ignoring the positives ones. Similarly, if one is in positive frame of mind, he may get carried away by positive aspects of message only by downplaying the importance of negative ones. Emotion—positive or negative, does play a vital role in listening and restricts accurate message to get across.

Techniques to Overcome these Barriers

1. Do one job at a time.
2. Make speaker at ease-giving the impression of aptly listening.
3. Listen with empathy. Empathy is the ability to understand what the speaker is feeling and acknowledge his right to experience that emotion.
4. Show interest in listening.
5. Do not interrupt unnecessarily.
6. Provide reflective feedback specially to avoid semantic difficulties.
7. Listen to remember as a person generally remembers 20% of what he hears. Taking notes help people reinforcing their memory.

REVIEW QUESTIONS

1. Define communication and describe the important steps involved in communication process.
2. Distinguish between "formal" and "informal" communication. Describe the various directions in which the formal communication generally flows.

3. Management is a two-way traffic, it is based upon an effective communication process. Discuss the statement.
4. What do you mean by communication network? Discuss the merits of each type of network.
5. Distinguish between downward and upward communications. Make out a case for upward communication.
6. Listening is half communication as such discuss the barriers of listening in order to remove them.

Short Notes

1. Grapevine communication
2. Formal communication
3. Feedback skills
4. Types of listening
5. Barriers to communication

Chapter 17
Controlling

Control is the final function of management. Planning and controlling are closely related. Without plans, control is not possible, because performance has to be measured against some standards. Once the plans have been formulated and implemented, the planning loop must be closed by means of control. Only a continuous control can achieve the objectives. Both autonomy and accountability are embedded in the concept of control. Control mechanisms are required in almost all the fields of an organization.

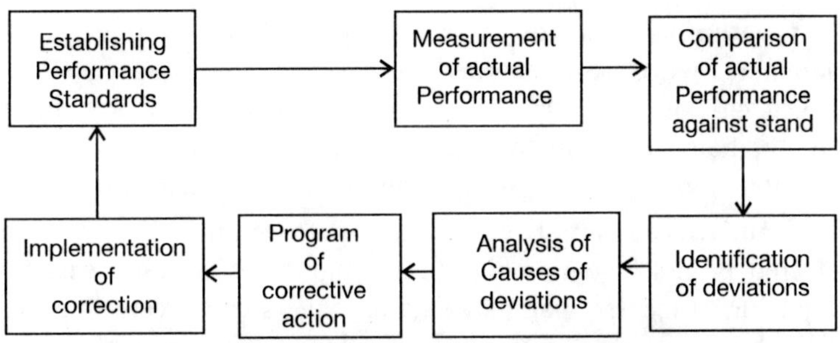

Fig. 17.1: Feedback loop of management control

17.1 THE CONTROL PROCESS

Properly designed control process involves three steps: determining performance standards establishing during the planning process; measuring performance against these standards; and correcting variations from standards and plans. During planning, managers should give thought as to how to measure progress against the plans. Such monitoring of progress is the crux of the control process.

Step 1: Determining Performance Standards

The formation of objectives during planning is the foundation for the development of specific standards. Performance standards are specific statements of expected levels of performance. Just as planning responsibilities differ by managerial level, parallel control responsibilities exist at each level: strategic (top management), tactical (middle management), and operational (first-level management) levels of control increase the probabilities of realizing plans at respective managerial levels.

Strategic control involves monitoring critical environment factors that could affect the viability of strategic plans. Control at the strategic level is mainly the responsibility of top-level managers who often concentrate on long time frame.

Tactical control focuses on monitoring periodic results of tactical plan and taking corrective action as necessary. Control at the tactical level mainly involves middle managers, who are concerned with department-level objectives, programs, and budgets. They concentrate on periodic or middle-term time frames.

Operational control is the responsibilities of lower-level managers, who are concerned with schedules, budgets, rules, and specific outputs. Operating control provides feedback about what is being done in the very near term to achieve both the short-term and the long-term goals of the organization.

Standards are simply yardstick of performance. They are the selected points in entire planning program at which measures of performance are made so that managers can receive signals about how things are going and thus do not have to watch every step in the execution of plans.

There are many kinds of standards. In practice, standards tend to be of following types: physical standards, cost standards, capital standards, revenue standards, program standards, goals as standards, and strategic plans as control points for strategic control.

Physical Standards: They are generally related to production indices such as labour-hours per unit of output, unit of production per machine-hour, etc. Physical standards may also reflect quality of output such as quality of tensile strength of steel, etc.

Cost Standards: They attach monetary values such as direct and indirect cost per unit produced, labour cost per unit or per hour, material cost per unit, machine-hour costs, and selling costs per unit of sales.

Capital Standards: They indicate capital invested in the firm. They reflect other capital standards, such as the ratios of current assets to current liabilities, debt to net worth, return on investment as well as the size and turnover of inventories.

Revenue Standards: They are monetary values to sales, profits and other revenue matters.

Program Standards: They are assigned to install a variable budget program for development of new products or a program for improving the quality of sales personnel.

Goals as Standards: It is possible to define goals that can be used as performance standards. While the quantitative goals are standards mentioned above, qualitative goal represents another area of standards relating to employee behaviour. For example, if the training program of an area sales manager included in the plan with specific characteristics—quantity of sale of product per half-yearly, this itself indicates standards that tend to become objective and therefore, "tangible". Standards help reduce the potential negative effects of goal incongruence. Goal incongruence is a condition in which there are major incompatibilities between the goals of an organization member and those of the organization. Such incompatibilities can occur due to lack of support for organizational objectives and often result in behaviours that are incompatible with reaching organizational goals.

The final stage is to develop performance standards for each job in department. These are standards for individuals performing those jobs. It is manager's responsibility to ensure that performance standards have been established for all relevant performance areas.

Step 2: Measurement of Performance

If standards are set clearly, the measurement of performance becomes simple. Financial performance largely quantitative such as profits, return on investment, sales, productivity have been measured vis-à-vis their standards which are easy to measure. On the other hand, many important qualitative aspects of performance such as employees behaviour which have bearing on performance can be difficult to measure in exact terms. Similarly, areas such as research and development can be difficult to measure quantitively. Most organizations use combinations of both quantitative and qualitative performance measures in carrying out the control process.

Further, periodicity of measurement as well as levels of management generally depend on how important the goal is to the organization, how quickly the situation is likely to change, and how difficult and expensive it would be to rectify a problem if one were to occur. Power plants, for example, have elaborate systems of controls that continuously provide data on all major aspects of the operation.

Step 3: Comparing Actual Performance and Desires Performance/Standards

It is the responsibility of managers to compare actual performance against established standards for all areas of operations. The reasons for any deviation must be examined. *Management by exception,* a control principle which suggests that managers should be informed of a situation only if control data show a significant deviation from standards. Use of the management by exception principle, with or without computers, helps save managers time and easy to understand deviations for further managerial action. The deviations that managers need to control are the negative deviations. Negative deviations are deviations which occur when actual performance is below expected performance. However, positive performance, i.e., over performance is also deviation as well zero deviation but does need to be corrected.

Step 4: Corrective Action

When standards are not met, managers must carefully assess the reasons and take corrective action. During evaluation, sometimes, managers may conclude that the standards are, in fact, inappropriate—usually because of changing conditions—and that corrective action to meet standards is therefore not desirable. More often, though, corrective actions are needed to reach standards.

17.2 TYPES OF CONTROLS

After deciding the area of control, managers decide the types of controls that they wish to use. Using system perspective, the organization which is an open system does not have self-control. It requires constant monitoring and control to manage deviations from standards. Accordingly, the three types of controls based on timing are feedforward, concurrent, and feedback (Fig. 17.2).

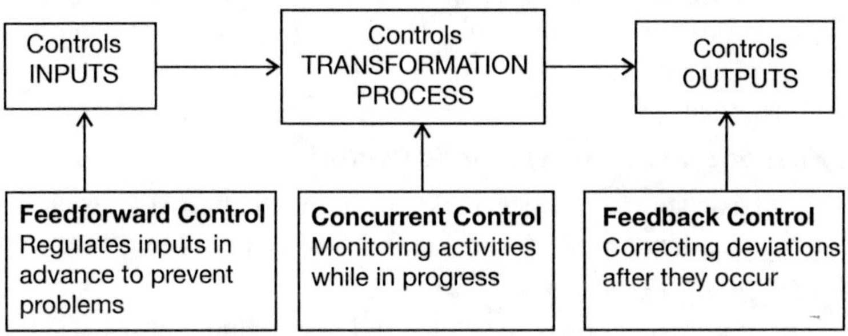

Fig. 17.2: Types of control by timing

Feedforward control focuses on the regulation of inputs in advance to ensure that they meet the standards necessary for the transformation process. Inputs include materials, people, finances, time, and other resources used by the organization. For example, if the firm hires competent personnel, it can prevent difficulties in the production process in later date thereby helping to meet the standards. Feedforward control is also called *preventive control*. Preventive maintenance of aircraft is another example of feedforward control. This type of control is possible and effective only when timely and accurate information is available.

Concurrent control or real-time control takes place while an activity is in progress. It involves monitoring and adjusting ongoing activities then and there. It is controlling the process of production before the goods and services are produced. Modern production unit is so programmed that it provides the operator the immediate signal if an error is detected in the process.

Feedback control occurs after an activity has occurred. Manager gathers information about a completed activity, evaluate that information to know the deviation, and takes steps to improve similar activities in the future. It is often used when feedforward and concurrent controls are not feasible or are too costly. For example, a sales manager found feasible to use feedback control by periodically comparing sales quotas (standards) with actual sales.

Another function of feedback control is providing information that will facilitate the planning process. The data can be used in revising existing plans and formulating new ones. Finally, feedback control provides output information that is particularly useful in the process of rewarding employee performance.

Cybernetic and Non-cybernetic Control

A basic control process can be either cybernetic or non-cybernetic, depending on the degree to which human discretion is part of the system.

A cybernetic control system is self-regulating control system that once put into the operational system can automatically monitor the situation and take corrective action when necessary. A heating system controlled by a thermostat is a cybernetic control system.

Although the growing use of computers is increasing the possibilities for cybernetic control, most control systems used by organizations are the non-cybernetic type. A non-cybernetic control system is one that relies on human discretion as a basic part of its process. They have built-in monitoring systems designed to alert members if things are not progressing as intended. Accordingly, systems generate reports for members perusal to determine what corrective action is needed.

Managerial Approaches to Control

According to Ouchi (1980), there are three approaches to designing the control systems: Market, Bureaucratic, and Clan.

Market Control

It is an approach to control the use of market mechanisms to control prices as standards for certain clearly specified goods and services needed by an organization, thus relieving managers of the need to establish more elaborate control over costs. In order to use market control, a reasonable level of competition must exist in the relevant goods and services and requirements must be specified clearly. For example, purchasing department develops detailed standards or specifications for goods purchased. While purchasing, managers have to determine whether particular price quotes are reasonable thereby attempting costs in this way.

It is sometimes used to set up profit centers, such as computer services, which charge other departments for services offered to them.

Bureaucratic Control

Bureaucratic control is characterized by a wide use of rules, regulations, policies, procedures, reward systems, and formal authority reflected in hierarchy. This kind of control requires clear job descriptions, budgets, and often standardized tasks aimed at ensuring that employees exhibit appropriate behaviours and meet performance standards. This limits opportunities for participation which is not conducive to innovation.

Clan Control

Employee behaviours are regulated by share values, norms, beliefs, traditions, corporate culture, and informal relationships. Clan control places greater emphasis on internal motivation, flexible duties and broad tasks and influence based on relevant information and expertise rather than position in the hierarchy.

With clan control, as the name implies, there is greater emphasis on use of teams and organizations that often operate in a very dynamic environment that requires quick adaption to changes in that environment. Partially for these reasons, a number of organizations with relatively routine types of jobs are substituting clan control over bureaucratic control.

However, most of the organizations try to blend strong clan control with advantageous use of bureaucratic control.

17.3 CONTROL TECHNIQUES

Managers use a variety of tools and techniques to measure and monitor performance. Some of the important techniques are mentioned below:

Financial Control: Corporate managers in most major companies make strong use of financial controls. The return on investment (ROI) is a useful technique of controlling overall performance. ROI measures the overall effectiveness of management in generating profits from its total investment in assets. Rate of return is calculated by dividing net profits with the total investment. In order to avoid the distorting effect of fluctuations in operating assets and liabilities, gross assets are taken as investment. These are, therefore, primarily related to balance sheet rather than to the income statement. It is expressed by the following formula:

$$\text{ROI} = \frac{\text{Sales}}{\text{Investment (fixed and working capital)}} \times \frac{\text{Profit}}{\text{Sales}}$$

Capital turnover = sales/investment whereas Earning = profit/ sales. Thus, ROI is calculated on the basis of capital turnover (sales/investment) multiplied by earnings as proportion of sales (profit/sales). This ratio (ROI) recognizes that one division, with a high capital turnover and a lower percentage of earnings to sales, may be more profitable in terms of return on investment than another with a high percentage of profits to sales but with low capital turnover. Managers may want to consider either increasing sales relative to costs or reducing costs relative to sales.

Break-even Analysis: This control device involves the use of a chart to depict the overall volume of sales necessary to cover costs. It is that point at which the cost and revenue of the organization are exactly equal. It is that point where the organization neither earns a profit nor incurs a loss. The organization attempt to go above that point from there it started getting profit.

Figure 17.3 depicts a break-even chart for a product of a company. The horizontal axis shows unit of sales. The vertical axis identifies both costs and revenues. Break-even point lies at a sales volume of 3000 units with ₹ 2400 both costs and revenue. At this point revenue exactly covers the cost.

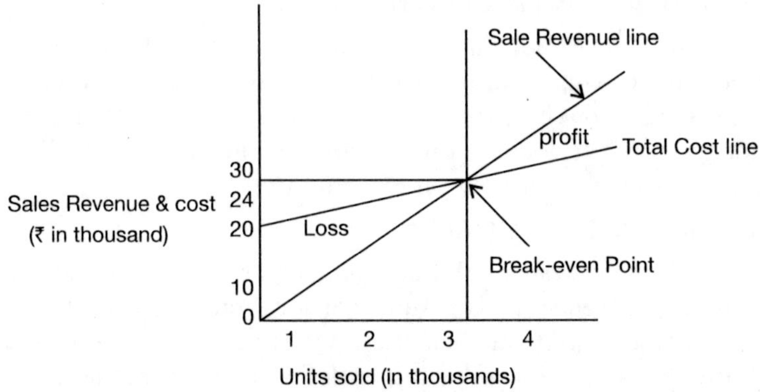

Fig. 17.3

Most organizations conduct yearly financial audits to ensure that accounting systems follow generally accepted procedures, policies, legal and ethical guidelines.

17.4 BUDGET CONTROLS

Budget is a financial and/or a quantitative statement prepared in advance normally for a year to compare it with performance of the organization. This information enables managers to take corrective action on day-to-day basis for bringing actual performance in conformity with desired performance as indicated in the plans. A budget is, therefore, viewed as both a plan and a device for control.

There are various types of budgets such as **sales budget, production budget, material budget** and **labour budget** and so on.

Flexible budgets as against fixed budgets are prepared to cope with future changes. A flexible budget is a budget designed to change in accordance with the level of activity actually attained. A flexible budget is of great help when it is not possible to predict accurately the level of sales or production within a practical range of variation.

Performance budget is an input/output or costs/results budget. It shows expenses according to specified heads of performance against developed yardstick or unit of performance which serves as a measure of performance (standards). For objective performance budgeting, care should be taken on the criteria of measurement of performance.

Performance budgeting is being increasingly used in business, government, banks and other organizations. It reveals whether the organization is getting adequate results (output) for the money spent. It focuses on decision-making and control on results rather than merely on expenditure.

Zero-base Budgeting (ZBB)

Traditional system of budgeting tends to rely too much on past experience. As a result, it incorporates past mistakes, extravagances and inefficiencies. It stifles innovation and creativity. Zero-base budgeting is designed to overcome these problems. It is based on the premise that the past is not sacrosanct so as to incorporate in future budgeting. Therefore, comprehensive analysis and review of criteria of proposals is made every time afresh. While preparing the budget for the next financial year the budget is constructed from a zero-base. This is contrary to conventional budgeting where basis of preparing the new budget is the current year's budget. Here, all budget proposals are considered from scratch as if it were the first ever budget of the enterprise.

Zero-base budgeting process involves three major steps: (1) activities are divided into parts known as 'decisions packages', each package sharing the purpose, cost and expected benefit of activity; (2) all activities are evaluated and ranked on the basis of benefits to the organization; and (3) resources are allocated according to these priorities. Thus, managers are encouraged to plan each programme afresh and to review each expense again. It helps to avoid mistakes and inefficiencies of the past.

Inventory Control: Inventory is a stock of materials that are used to for production or to satisfy customer demand. There are three major types of inventory: raw materials, work-process, and finished goods. Raw materials inventory is the stock of ingredients and other basic inputs to a production or service process. Work-in-progress inventory is the stock of items currently being transformed into a final product or service. Finished-goods inventory is the stock of items that have been produced and are awaiting sale to customers. In order to minimize the cost of inventory is the use of an inventory method called the Economic Order Quantity. The method involves an equation that includes annual demand (D), ordering costs (O), the expenses involved in placing an order and holding costs (H), the expenses associated with carrying/holding the inventory in the warehouse. Assume that a restaurant estimates a total of quarterly demand of 1470 quintal of potatoes for use in manufacturing process, ordering costs of ₹ 10 per order, and holding costs of ₹ 6 per quintal per quarter. Thus, economic order quantity is

$$\text{EOQ} = \frac{\text{2DO (square root)}}{\text{H}} = \frac{2(1417)(10)}{6} = 70$$

The EOQ equation helps managers decide how much to order but they also need to know the reorder point (ROP), inventory level at which a new order should be placed. To determine the reorder point, managers estimate Lead Time (L), the time between placing an order and receiving it. Assume lead time is four days, then

$$\text{ROP} = \text{(L) D/91} = \text{(4) 1470/91} = \text{65(rounded)}$$

After 65 days, order is to be placed. In using the EOQ, an organization will often add some safety stock for unforeseen additional requirement.

17.5 CHARACTERISTICS OF AN EFFECTIVE CONTROL SYSTEM

Effective control systems have certain characteristics in common. As such, managers should design the control systems incorporating the following characteristics as a checklist and use in operation.

1. Future-oriented: Control systems should be such so that to uncover unforeseen opportunities that might be developed in future. It is a future-oriented process that focuses on future plans.

2. Multiple criteria: Controls should not be based on single system of control. Depending upon the feasibilities, the control system is to be used even at time multiple control systems are used to evaluate the all aspect of performance. For example, bureaucratic control and clan control are used side by side.

3. Timeliness: Control systems are such that they must provide relevant information soon enough to allow corrective action in time before there are serious repercussions.

4. Cost-effective: It is costly to operate a control system. In majority of cases, it is such that benefits should be more than cost of control system. This is possible by applying an elaborate control system where deviations are significant.

5. Accurate: Since controls provide the basis for future actions, accuracy is vital. Inaccurate control data may make poor decisions meaning no control.

6. Flexible: Control systems need to be flexible enough to meet new or revised requirements. Accordingly, control systems are such that they can be changed quickly to measure and report deviations as quickly as possible.

7. Acceptable to organization members: Control systems operate best when they are accepted by the organization members who are affected by them. Otherwise members may avoid the controls. Employees accept control systems when the systems focus on important issues that are compatible with organizational goals and provide a fair and accurate picture of employee performance.

8. Strategic control: Everything within the organization cannot be controlled. Managers should therefore exercise control on those critical points that are strategic to the organization's performance only by exceptions.

9. Coordination: Organizational performance is sum total of performances of all the departments in the organization. Also, their tasks are interdependent as such strong coordination among departments are needed for the success of control systems.

10. Corrective action: Effective controls not only indicate a deviation, but also suggest a corrective method to improve performance.

17.6 TOTAL QUALITY MANAGEMENT (TQM)

TQM is perhaps one answer to attempting change. Considering the formidable challenges of bringing about changes in organizations. Management will do well to adopt TQM in their organizations.

TQM has been seen as 'technical' in nature and perceived more as a tool, a technique or an aid in the manufacturing process. This relegates TQM to its most narrow sense. TQM, in its most comprehensive sense is a Goal, Strategy, and a Process, all rolled into one. In its true sense, it is perhaps one of the most potent OD interventions that, once begun, never ceases. TQM operates on six basic principles:

1. A customer defines our business and therefore, our existence. The customer, therefore, comes first.
2. The success of a business depends on the involvement and empowerment of trained and highly motivated employees.
3. The role of the management is to develop, articulate and deploy a vision, a direction and a commitment.
4. The team comes before the individual, the organization comes before the team, the customer comes before the organization.
5. Things must be done right the first time.
6. Employee satisfaction is a pre-requisite to ensure customer satisfaction.

The total quality management approach is aimed at achieving **zero defects,** a quality concept in which the employees strive to make a product conform exactly to desired standards.

American quality management expert W. Edwards Deming developed ideas on statistical methods for improving quality. He took his concepts to Japan in the late 1940s. He set forth 14 improvement points that portray his overall philosophy which was appreciated by Japanese companies. These are:

1. Create and publish to all employees a statement of the aims and purposes of the company. The management must demonstrate constantly their commitment to this statement.
2. Learn the new philosophy, top management and everybody.
3. Understand the purpose of inspection, for improvement of processes and reduction of cost.
4. End of practice of awarding business on the basis of price tag alone.
5. Improve constantly and forever the system of production and service.
6. Institute training.
7. Teach and institute leadership.
8. Drive out fear. Create trust. Create a climate for innovation.
9. Optimize toward the aims and purposes of the company the effort of teams, group, staff areas.
10. Eliminate exhortations for the workforce.
11. (a) Eliminate numerical quotas for production. Instead, learn and institute methods of improvement.

    (b) Eliminate M.B.O. Instead, learn the capabilities of processes, and how to improve them.
12. Remove barriers that rob people of pride of workmanship.
13. Encourage education and self-improvement for everyone.
14. Take action to accomplish the transformation.

In the 1950s, another American quality expert, J.M. Juran, also helped Japanese companies develop their total quality management efforts.

An important aspect of TQM is its emphasis on the cost of quality, the cost of not doing thing right the first time. Quality efforts make use of several important tools such as Quality Improvement Teams, Benchmarking, and Statistical Quality Control.

Quality improvement teams are small groups of employees who work on solving specific problems related to quality and productivity, often with stated targets for improvement. Members of this team is mandatory of their own department, however, other individuals are qualified to work on problem, team membership may be voluntary. Quality circle is another quality team effort used substantially in Japan, India other countries. Details of QC is described in earlier chapter.

Many companies transform themselves after applying TQM. Fuji Xerox, Japan is one such company. The new Xerox movement was charged with four basic responsibilities: (a) harnessing the power of each employee through clear management objectives, (b) establishing and communicating companywide philosophy rooted in an absolute dedication to continuous improvement, (c) promoting the use of scientific and statistical tools and techniques, and (d) seeking the coveted Deming Prize. This led to company's success in terms of revenues and profits, quality of products and ensuring long-term improvement through employee and customer satisfaction.

Benchmarking is the process of comparing the practices especially productivity and quality in specific areas of one's own company with those of the best practices of other organizations. For example, a car company need three days to paint the body of car and the competitor of the similar car industry needs only two and half days, then two and half days does not become the standard if a company in an unrelated industry like two-wheeler can paint proportionate sq. feet area in two days. The two-day criterion becomes the benchmark even when at the face of it, this seems to be an unachievable standard. The stages involved in painting in all the three cases needs to be thoroughly analyzed to achieve the benchmark.

There are three types of benchmarking, first, *strategic benchmarking* compares various strategies and identifies the key strategic elements of success. Second, *operational benchmarking* compares relative costs or possibilities for product differentiation. Third, *management benchmarking* focuses on support functions such as market planning and information systems, logistics, human resource management, and so on.

Statistical process control is a statistical quality control technique that uses periodic random samples taken during actual production to determine whether acceptable quality levels of production are being met or production should be stopped for remedial action. Since the emphasis is on prevention of poor-quality output during the actual process, this approach represents concurrent control. This technique uses statistical tests to determine when variations fall outside a narrow range around the acceptable quality level.

17.7 QUALITY CIRCLE

The concept of quality circle (QC) is an outcome of the Japanese's concern for the quality control of products. They are of the view that if employees are treated with dignity and train them to accept responsibility and contribution to their job, they can do exceptionally good work including improvement of quality of product, facilities and well-being. Thus, if motivated, they would be capable of making their valuable suggestions through the use of their initiative, experience and innovative ideas without just putting in physical efforts. QC is constituted with 5-10 workers chosen from different sections with a topic/problem to do the brainstorming session with a view to offer interesting innovating suggestions/solutions to the problem including quality of product. Once solution is achieved, the members of QC may be changed and new issue may be taken for improvement of either quality or cost cutting solutions.

Organizational Structure of QC consists of four levels, viz.: (1) Steering Committee, (2) Facilitator, (3) QC leader, and (4) QC members.

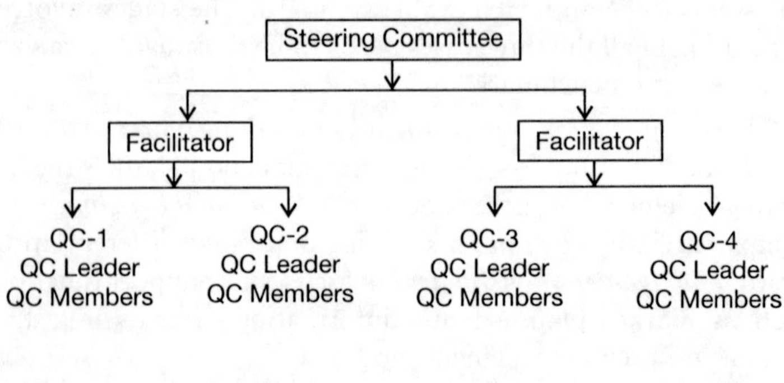

Steering Committee consists of representatives of management and unions at apex level of QC. It defines objectives and operating procedures of QC. It sets up guidelines for training to leaders and members of QCs.

Facilitator acts as an internal consultant and guide to the QC leaders, initiates the setting up of QCs by persuading the supervisor by teaching and training the QC leaders and members; provide feedback to the steering committee about the proceedings and results of the QCs and acts as evaluator and reviewer of QC operation and programmes.

The facilitator maintains sound inter-personal relations in order to function as a social leader. He should act as a promoter, teacher and innovator. He should be an excellent resource person for training managers at higher level.

QC leader co-ordinates and streamlines the activities of the QC who is an elected member of the circle generally a manager/supervisor of the department/section in which the QC is set up. The leader must have skills in discussion, initiation and promotion of active participation. He should be a trained one in group dynamics, human behaviour and participative leadership style. QC leader activities include conducting meetings initiating the discussion and motivate the members to participate actively. The leader acts as a link between the members and facilitator and train the members in problem identification, discussion and problem-solving techniques.

QC Members of a single QC join voluntarily or on invitation. Their activities include: attending meetings, participating actively in problem-identification, contributing ideas in developing solutions to the problems and the like.

REVIEW QUESTIONS

1. Outline general process that can be applied to most control situations. Using this process, design a system to control the home delivery staff of local pizza mart.
2. Discuss the concept of managerial control and give the steps of the control process.

3. What are the main types of control? Which is more important and why?
4. How does zero-base budgeting differ from traditional budgeting? Could budgeting be better compared to financial control?
5. What is performance budgeting? What is zero-based budgeting? What is the difference between these two?
6. Describe the characteristics of effective control systems. Use these characteristics to evaluate the clan controls approach applied to a medium type of manufacturing unit.
7. Explain the concept of Total Quality Management. How do TQM enrich the quality of products thereby productivity of an organization.
8. Describe the various steps Edwards Deming, pioneer of TQM suggest to achieve zero defects—a quality concept in which the employees strive to make a product conform exactly to desired standards.

Short Notes

1. Quality improvement teams
2. Benchmarking
3. ROI
4. Clan control
5. Flexible budgeting
6. Quality circle

CASE STUDY

Victor Mathew after graduated from I.I. Hotel Management, New Delhi joined Welcome Group of Hotels in Jaipur. He served there for five years and got experience in all the fields of hotel industry. Got the confidence in this, he resigned from the service with a view to start his own Fast Food Restaurant at Nashik, Maharashtra named VIMIK. For this, he has persuaded his fellow classmate Pradeep Mittal to join the venture. Victor's father has offered seed money for opening of the restaurant. Both have gone with the following aspects of restaurant management: planning, organizing, leading and controlling. The ultimate goal is to provide customers reliable food, quick services and clean premises with a view to have a viable organization. Besides all aspects of management, greater emphasis is given on planning and controlling of every fields of restaurant. While Mittal is overviewing production, quality, services and cleanliness, Victor is mainly associated with financial and marketing aspects of the organization. In first year of operation, the restaurant has achieved a breakeven stage without making profit. They have pondered the situation and decided to install afresh control aspect of management. The present situation has been examined and found the following:

There are many indicators that the restaurant was not operating as it should need to be seen.

1. Waste in some of products as high as 20 to 30 percent.
2. Quality problem in four input.
3. Inventory of three input as it is shown as high as 30% above the requirement in second quarter.
4. Delivery service shows slackness.
5. Productivity of pizza unit needs improvement.

The entire team of executives examine the operation, quality management, and financial aspects of restaurant with the following outcomes:

In the control process, standards are essential because they spell out specific criteria for evaluating performance and related employee skills. Often such standards are established at the planning stage itself. At the start of the control process, managers must decide which major areas will be controlled tailored to specific situations.

Among the major control system used in organizations are financial control, budgetary control, quality control, and inventory control.

1. Regulation of input especially potato, tomato and non-vegetarian items to ensure that they meet the standards necessary for value-added food. It emphasizes on prevention to arrest wastage later in output.

2. Victor identifies difficulties in production process that could result in faulty output. Quality standards of output must be ensured for which standard quality manual be developed so that wastage is to the minimum. Quality standards involve performance, features, reliability, conformance, durability, serviceability, aesthetics, and perceived quality.
3. Inventory control aims to minimize the costs of inventory. They have to apply the economic order quantity to minimize inventory cost.
4. To improve the performance of salespeople, extensive training program, standard operative procedure (SOP), reward to people to perform high level of performance.
5. To improve productivity, automated machines are to be installed. For taking corrective action on just in time computerize management information system is to be installed.

Questions for Case

1. What type of controls would you have established to achieve major returns?
2. How would you have controlled the input inventory to avoid its growing to twice the size that it was in the previous year?
3. What role did financial controls play in helping VIMIK? What action would you have taken to improve ROI by 10%?
4. To what extent does VIMIK appear to have initiated total quality management?

Subject Index